W9-CKS-260

PRINCIPLES
OF LANGUAGE LEARNING
AND TEACHING

H. DOUGLAS BROWN
University of Illinois

Prentice-Hall, Inc., Englewood Cliffs, New Jersey 07632

Library of Congress Cataloging in Publication Data

Brown, H   Douglas.
    Principles of language learning and teaching.

    Includes bibliographies and index.
    1. Language and languages—Study and teaching.
2. Language acquisition.   I. Title.
P51.B775   405   79-19874
ISBN   0-13-709295-4

To Mary

Printed in the United States of America

10   9   8   7   6   5   4   3   2   1

Editorial/production supervision and interior design: Robert Hunter
Cover design: Wanda Lubelska
Manufacturing buyer: Harry P. Baisley

PRENTICE-HALL INTERNATIONAL, INC., *London*
PRENTICE-HALL OF AUSTRALIA PTY. LIMITED, *Sydney*
PRENTICE-HALL OF CANADA, LTD., *Toronto*
PRENTICE-HALL OF INDIA PRIVATE LIMITED, *New Delhi*
PRENTICE-HALL OF JAPAN, INC., *Tokyo*
PRENTICE-HALL OF SOUTHEAST ASIA PTE. LTD., *Singapore*
WHITEHALL BOOKS LIMITED, *Wellington, New Zealand*

Contents

12
FROM THEORY TO PRACTICE   229

Preface

For several decades now foreign language teachers have been engaged in scientific approaches to the methodology of foreign language teaching—principled approaches based, in varying degrees, on experimentation and research on linguistic, psychological, and pedagogical foundations. But recent years have brought about a mushrooming of research on second language acquisition. The resulting increase in our knowledge of principles of language learning and teaching has led to a situation in which teacher training programs can no longer present one or two methods and a number of techniques, in "cookbook" fashion, and thereby expect trainees to be adequately prepared to teach a foreign language. The complexity of the process of second language acquisition in all its contexts is becoming apparent as teachers and researchers discover a multiplicity of variables at play.

Teacher trainees must therefore be carefully schooled in an integrated understanding of these many variables so that, when faced with practical teaching contexts, they will be able to make intelligent, informed choices of a particular method or a particular technique for a given set of learners and learning goals in a given context.

Principles of Language Learning and Teaching is designed to provide teachers and teacher trainees with a comprehensive and up-to-date grasp of the theoretical foundations of foreign language teaching. No particular foreign language is highlighted since general principles of language learning are applicable to all languages. Many of the illustrative examples here are in English since that is the language common to all readers of the volume; occasional references are also made to French and Spanish. Techniques and procedures are not within the scope of the book. General approaches and methods are described in Chapter 12, but specific classroom applications are the province of concurrent or subsequent practical training in the teaching of a particular language. The assumption here is that a teacher trainee needs to gain broad but systematic knowledge of the process of second language acquisition in order to effectively understand and adapt teaching techniques.

The text covers a variety of topics as indicated in the Table of Contents. The subject matter is examined from the interdisciplinary perspectives of linguistics, psychology, and education, the three major disciplines which have contributed to language teaching methodology over the past four decades. The plan of the text is, through the chapters, to build toward a comprehensive, integrated understanding of the teaching-learning process, such that one will be able to construct a pesonalized rationale, or theory, of second language acquisition. This theory-building is the substance of the final chapter.

A spiraling approach is used for presenting material. A concept may be introduced in one chapter but not dealt with substantially until a later chapter. Or a concept may be defined at one point but its significance and implications discussed at a later point. For example, behaviorism is defined in Chapter 1, related to first language learning in Chapter 2, then treated technically in Chapter 4 in reference to learning theories and used as a reference point throughout the rest of the book. The importance of the distinction between rote and meaningful learning is noted in the discussion of first language acquisition in Chapter 2, but is not substantively defined until Chapter 4. Learning theories are summarized in Chapter 4 but the implications of learning theories are evident throughout the volume in almost every chapter. The interrelated nature of aspects of second language acquisition make such spiraling a necessity.

The substance of *Principles of Language Learning and Teaching* is clearly not exhausitve. The complexity of second language acquisition makes it necessary here to capture essentials and to weed out a number of considerations which are peripheral. The systematic elimination of certain factors is the product of a particular theoretical stance on the part of the author. Such omissions are ultimately essential for the construction of a theory of second language acquisition: no theory can be comprehensive enough to encompass every possible variable within the system. The content of this book thus serves not as an encyclopedia but rather as an integrated framework within which a foreign language teacher can operate to formulate an understanding of how people learn foreign languages—and why people sometimes do *not* learn a language.

The text is designed for graduate students or advanced undergraduates who have a general background in the liberal arts. Prior technical knowledge of linguistics or psychology is not necessary. An attempt has been made to build, from the beginning, on what an educated person knows about the world, life, people, and communication. By the last chapter the reader will have been led to an understanding of reasonably sophisticated concepts in linguistics and psychology.

Each chapter is supplemented by *suggested readings* and *topics and questions for study and discussion.* The suggested readings offer brief annotations on possible further reading which could enhance one's understanding of the material in the chapter. The readings consist of a number of key articles and books in relevant subfields of second language acquisition, providing a means of fruitful exploration beyond and beneath the words of this volume. The topics and questions serve two purposes. One is to capsulize and review some of the important topics and issues presented in the chapter. The other purpose is to lead one into a consideration of further issues related to those presented in the chapter and into a refining of concepts whose groundwork has been laid in the chapter. This exploring and refining sometimes takes the form of making practical applications of some of the more abstract or theoretical material presented in the chapter.

To that end it is strongly recommended that the user of this book maintain regular contact with a group—however small—of second language learners. That group may be a class in a foreign language or it may be a conversation or tutorial group that meets, say, once a week. That regular contact with second language learners will provide the opportunity to observe persons engaged in the process of second language learning in a real situation and to put certain principles into practice. Without this regular exposure to second language learners one runs the risk of placing the material in this book into abstract compartments which may not square with reality. The feedback of the real world is an important if not essential facet of building a viable understanding of the second language acquisition process.

Principles of Language Learning and Teaching is designed for use in programs for training teachers of any modern language. It can be used as the single textbook for a course on theoretical foundations of language teaching, especially if the suggested readings and discussion questions are fully utilized. It is also approriate as a basic text to accompany a second text on methods, techniques, and procedures for the particular language in question. In fact, it is assumed that at some point the teacher trainee will gain instruction in those specific classroom techniques and procedures—an obviously essential component of a teacher training program. What this book does is to undergird those practices. It provides necessary and sufficient foundation stones for building the capacity to understand, evaluate, and perfect language teaching practices.

The book has grown out of graduate courses in the theoretical foundations of language teaching which I have taught at the University of Michigan and the University of Illinois. My first debt of gratitude is therefore to my students—for their insights and experiences, for their questions, and for their enthusiastic search for ultimate answers to the deepest mysteries of language acquisition. I also want to thank those who have read and offered comments on portions of this book in draft versions: Bill Acton, Larry Bouton, Cathy Day, Nina Garrett, Adelaide Heyde, Joan Morley, Kyle Perkins, Greg Strick, and Barry Taylor. Special thanks are given my father, Harry D. Brown, for painstaking scrutiny of the style of the manuscript. For meticulous clerical work I am grateful to Sheila Barnes, Judie Birdsall, Carol Myer, and Deborah Snapp. Finally, thank you, Mary, Stefanie, and Jeff, for putting up with an author in your home for these many months.

H. Douglas Brown
Urbana, Illinois

ACKNOWLEDGMENTS

Grateful acknowledgment is made to the following publishers for permission to reprint copyrighted material:

C-L/CLL Institutes, for material from Charles A. Curran, *Counseling-Learning in Second Languages*, p. 53. Copyright 1976 by the Apple River Press. Available from C-L/CLL Institutes, Box 383, E. Dubuque, Ill. 61025.

English Language Teaching Journal, for material from H. Douglas Brown, "The English teacher as researcher," Vol. 31, No. 4 (July 1977), and from Jack C. Richards, "A noncontrastive approach to error analysis," Vol. 25, No. 3 (June 1971).

Holt, Rinehart & Winston, for material from H. A. Gleason, Jr., *An Introduction to Descriptive Linguistics*, rev. ed. Copyright 1955, © 1961 by Holt, Rinehart & Winston. Reprinted by permission of Holt, Rinehart & Winston.

International Review of Applied Linguistics, for material from S. Pit Corder, "Idiosyncratic dialects and error analysis," Vol. IX, No. 2, copyright 1971.

Language Learning: A Journal of Applied Linguistics, for the following material: H. Douglas Brown, "Affective variables in second language acquisition," Vol. 23, No. 2, pp. 231-244; Barry P. Taylor, "The use of overgeneralization and transfer learning strategies by elementary and intermediate students in ESL," Vol. 25, No. 1, pp. 95-98; John H. Schumann, "Second language acquisition research: Getting a more global look at the learner," Special Issue No. 4, p. 15; Carlos A. Yorio, "Discussion of explaining sequence and variation in second language acqusition," Special Issue No. 4, p. 61; Ellen Bialystok, "A theoretical model of second language learning," Vol. 28, No. 1, p. 71; John Oller, "A program of language testing research," in Special Issue No. 4 (1976), p. 150; Editorial, Vol. 21, No. 1 (1971), p. v.

The Modern Language Journal, for material from H. Douglas Brown, "Cognitive pruning and second language acquisition," Vol. 56, No. 4 (April 1972), pp. 218-222.

Prentice-Hall, Inc., for material from John Carroll, *Language and Thought* (Foundations of Modern Psychology Series) p. 96. Copyright 1964 by Prentice-Hall, Inc.

Teachers of English to Speakers of Other Languages, for material from: H. Douglas Brown, "The psychological reality of 'grammar' in the ESL classroom," *TESOL Quarterly*, Vol. 6, No. 2 (1976), pp. 263-269; Peter Strevens, "Causes of failure and conditions for success in the learning and teaching of foreign languages," in H. Douglas Brown, Carlos Alfredo Yorio, and Ruth H. Crymes (editors), *On TESOL 77: Teaching and Learning English as a Second Language—Trends in Research and Practice*. Copyright 1977 by TESOL.

University of Chicago Press, for material from Robert Stockwell, J. Donald Bowen, and John W. Martin, *The Grammatical Structures of English and Spanish*, pp. 12-13. Copyright 1965 by University of Chicago Press.

University of Michigan Press, for material from H. Douglas Brown, "What is applied linguistics?" in *A Survey of Applied Linguistics*, eds. R. Wardhaugh and H. D. Brown. Copyright 1976 by the University of Michigan.

Grateful acknowledgment is made to the following author for permission to reprint uncopyrighted material:

Merrill Swain, "Future directions in second language research," Figure 2, in Carole Henning (editor), *Proceedings of the Los Angeles Second Language Research Forum*, 1977.

1

Language, Learning, and Teaching

Becoming bilingual is a way of life. Every bone and fiber of your being is affected in some way as you struggle to reach beyond the confines of your first language and into a new language, a new culture, a new way of thinking, feeling, and acting. Total commitment, total involvement, a total physical, intellectual, and emotional response is necessary to successfully send and receive messages in a second language. Second language learning is not a set of easy steps that can be programmed in a quick do-it-yourself kit. No one can tell you "how to learn a foreign language without really trying." The learning of a second language is a complex process, involving a seemingly infinite number of variables. So much is at stake that academic courses in foreign languages are usually pitifully inadequate training grounds, in and of themselves, for the mastery of a second language. Few if any people learn a foreign language fluently within the confines of the foreign language classroom. In fact, it may be that very few aspects of a foreign language can actually be taught!

It may appear contradictory, then, that this book is about both learning and teaching. But some of the contradiction is removed if you look at the teaching process as the facilitation of learning, in which you can "teach" a foreign language successfully if, among other things, you know something about that intricate web of variables that are spun together to affect how and why you learn or fail to learn a second language. Where does a teacher begin the quest for an understanding of the principles of foreign language learning and teaching? By first asking some questions.

Who? Who does the learning and teaching? Obviously, the learner and the teacher. But who is this learner? Where does he* come from? What is his native language? level of education? socioeconomic level? Who are his parents? What is his intellectual capacity? What sort of personality does he have? There are hundreds of other questions that could be asked, but these will do for starters. These questions, if addressed carefully, focus attention on some of the crucial variables affecting both the learner's success in mastering a foreign language and the teacher's capacity to enable the learner to achieve that mastery. The chapters that follow will help to tease out those variables.

In the case of the teacher, another set of questions emerges. What is the teacher's native language? experience and/or training? knowledge of the second language and its culture? philosophy of education? personality characteristics? Most importantly, how do the teacher and the student interact with each other as human beings engaged in linguistic communion?

What? No simpler a question is one that probes the nature of the subject matter itself. What is it that the learner must learn and the teacher teach? What is language? How can the second language be described adequately? What are the linguistic differences between the first and the second language? These profound questions are of course central to the discipline of linguistics. The language teacher needs to understand the system and functioning of the second language and differences between the first and second language of the learner. It is one thing for a teacher to speak and understand a language and yet another matter to consciously understand and explain the system of that language—its phonemes and morphemes and words and sentences and discourse structures.

How? How does learning take place? How can a person insure success in language learning? What cognitive processes are utilized in second language learning? What kinds of strategies and styles does the learner use? What is the optimal interrelationship of cognitive, affective, and physical domains for successful language learning?

When? When does second language learning take place? One of the key issues in second language research and teaching is the differential success of children and adults in learning a second language. Common observation tells us that children are "better" language learners than adults. Is this true? If so, why does the age of learning

---

*In cases in which the use of both third-person pronouns (he/she, her/his) is cumbersome, I have used the masculine form; but where possible, I have tried to avoid any sexist stereotyping.

make a difference? How is a second language learned by a preschool child, still very much involved in the acquisition of his first language? Or by a preadolescent who has virtually mastered his first language and is now embarking on the second? Or by a teenager with the insecurities and ego identification dynamics involved in that period of life? Or an adult who is affectively and cognitively mature? Other *when* questions center around the amount of time spent in the activity of learning the second language. Is the learner exposed to three or five or ten hours a week in the classroom? Or a seven-hour day in an immersion program? Or twenty-four hours a day totally submerged in the culture?

Where? Is the learner attempting to acquire the second language within the cultural and linguistic milieu of the second language—that is, in a "second" language situation in the technical sense of the term? Or is he focusing on a "foreign" language context in which the second language is heard and spoken only in an artificial environment, such as the modern language classroom in an American university or high school? How might the sociopolitical conditions of a particular country affect the outcome of the learner's mastery of the language? How do general intercultural contrasts and similarities affect the learning process?

Why? Finally, the most encompassing of all questions: Why is the learner attempting to acquire the second language? What are the learner's purposes? Is he instrumentally motivated, seeking a successful career or fulfilling a foreign language requirement? Or is the learner integratively motivated, wishing personally to identify closely with the culture and people of the target language? Beyond these two categories, what other affective, emotional, personal, or intellectual reasons does the learner have for pursuing this gigantic task of learning another language?

These questions have been asked, in very global terms, to give you an inkling of the diversity of problems that can be posed in the quest for understanding the principles of language learning and teaching. And while you cannot hope to find final answers to all the questions, or even some of the questions, you can begin to achieve some tentative answers as you move through the chapters of this book. Or you can hone the global questions into finer, subtler questions, which in itself is an important task, for often being able to ask the right questions is more valuable than possessing storehouses of knowledge.

Thomas Kuhn (1970) referred to "normal science" as a process of puzzle solving in which part of the task of the scientist, in this case the teacher, is to discover the pieces, and then to fit the pieces together. Many of the pieces of the language-learning puzzle are not yet discovered, and the careful defining of questions will lead to finding those pieces. We can then undertake the task of fitting the pieces together into a "paradigm"—an interlocking design, a theory of second language acquisition.

That theory, like a jigsaw puzzle, needs to be coherent and unified. If only one point of view is taken, if you look at only one facet of second language learning and teaching, you will derive an incomplete, jaundiced theory. The second language teacher, with eyes wide open to the total picture, needs to form an integrated understanding of the many aspects of the process of second language learning.

In order to begin to define further questions and to find answers to some of those questions, this first chapter addresses some fundamental issues which form essential foundations of an integrated understanding of second language acquisition. These issues are: what is *language*, and how do persons *learn* and *teach* language?

LANGUAGE

To presume to define *language* simply would be sheer folly. Linguists and philologists have been trying for centuries to define the term. A definition is really a condensed version of a theory, and a theory is simply—or not so simply—an extended definition. Yet second language teachers clearly need to know generally what sort of entity they are dealing with and how the particular language they are teaching fits into that entity.

Suppose you were stopped by a reporter on the street and in the course of an interview about your vocational choice you were asked: "Well, since you are a foreign *language* teacher, would you define *language* in a sentence or two?" Nonplused, you would no doubt dig deep into your memory for a typical dictionary-type definition of language. Such definitions, if pursued seriously, could lead to a lexicographer's wild-goose chase, but they also can reflect a reasonably coherent synopsis of current understanding of just what it is that linguists are trying to study. Consider the following definitions of *language* found in dictionaries and introductory textbooks:

> Language is a system of arbitrary, vocal symbols which permit all people in a given culture, or other people who have learned the system of that culture, to communicate or to interact (Finocchiaro 1964:8).

> Language is a system of communication by sound, operating through the organs of speech and hearing, among members of a given community, and using vocal symbols possessing arbitrary conventional meanings (Pei 1966:141).

> Language is any set or system of linguistic symbols as used in a more or less uniform fashion by a number of people who are thus enabled to communicate intelligibly with one another (*Random House Dictionary of the English Language* 1966:806).
>
> Language is a system of arbitrary vocal symbols used for human communication (Wardhaugh 1972:3).
>
> [Language is] any means, vocal or other, of expressing or communicating feeling or thought ... a system of conventionalized signs, especially words, or gestures having fixed meanings (*Webster's New International Dictionary of the English Language* 1934:1390).
>
> [Language is] a systematic means of communicating ideas or feelings by the use of conventionalized signs, sounds, gestures, or marks having understood meanings (*Webster's Third New International Dictionary of the English Language* 1961:1270).

Still other common definitions found in introductory textbooks on linguistics include the concepts of (1) the generativity or creativity of language, (b) the presumed primacy of speech over writing, and (3) the universality of language among human beings.

Many of the significant characteristics of language are capsulized in these definitions. Some of the controversies about the nature of language are also illustrated through the restrictions that are implied in certain definitions. Finocchiaro, Pei, and Wardhaugh, for example, restrict themselves to the notion of vocal symbols, while both of the *Webster's* definitions include more than merely vocal symbols as the proper domain of language. Finocchiaro, *Random House*, and Wardhaugh restrict their definitions to human language, thereby implying that animal communication and language are essentially different.

A consolidation of the definitions of language yields the following composite definition:

1. Language is systematic—possibly a generative—system.
2. Language is a set of arbitrary symbols.
3. Those symbols are primarily vocal, but may also be visual.
4. The symbols have conventionalized meanings to which they refer.
5. Language is used for communication.
6. Language operates in a speech community or culture.
7. Language is essentially human, although possibly not limited to humans.
8. Language is acquired by all people in much the same way—language and language learning both have universal characteristics.

These eight statements provide a reasonably concise "twenty-five-words-or-less" definition of language. But the simplicity of the eightfold definition should not be allowed to mask the sophistication of linguistic endeavor underlying each concept. Enormous fields and subfields, year-long university courses, are suggested in each of the eight categories. Consider some of these possible areas:

1. Explicit and formal accounts of the system of language on several possible levels (most commonly syntactic, semantic, and phonological).
2. The symbolic nature of language; the relationship between language and reality; the philosophy of language; the history of language.
3. Phonetics; phonology; writing systems; kinesics, proxemics, and other "paralinguistic" features of language.
4. Semantics; language and cognition; psycholinguistics.
5. Communication systems; speaker-hearer interaction; sentence processing.
6. Dialectology; sociolinguistics; language and culture; bilingualism and second language acquisition.
7. Human language and nonhuman communication; the physiology of language.
8. Language universals; first language acquisition.

Serious and extensive thinking about these eight topics involves a mind-boggling journey through a labyrinth of linguistic science—a maze that has yet to be mastered. Yet the language teacher needs to know something about this system of communication which we call language. Can the foreign language teacher effectively teach a language if he does not know, even generally, something about the relationship between language and cognition, writing systems, nonverbal communication, sociolinguistics, and first language acquisition, just to name a few items at random? The teacher need not be a master linguist, but he cannot hope to teach a part (the particular language) of reality without knowing how that part fits into the whole (language in general).

The TESOL (Teachers of English to Speakers of Other Languages) organization, in its *Guidelines for the Certification and Preparation of Teachers of English to Speakers of Other Languages in the United States* (1975), cited the necessity for the teacher to "understand the nature of language, the fact of language varieties— social, regional, and functional, the structure and development of the English language systems. ... " Surely if the second language learner is being asked to be successful in acquiring a system of communication of such vast complexity, it is only reasonable that the teacher have awareness of what the components of that system are.

Your understanding of the components of language will determine to a large extent how you teach a language. If, for example, you believe that nonverbal communication is a key to successful second language learning, you will center attention on nonverbal systems and cues. If you perceive language as a phenomenon that can be dismantled into thousands of discrete pieces and those pieces programmatically taught one by one, you will attend carefully to an understanding of the separability of the forms of language. There are few right and wrong answers to questions about language. Truth is multifaceted and usually lies in an undecipherable gray area.

This book touches on some of the general aspects of language as defined above. Many other—more particular—aspects will have to be understood in the context of the teacher's training program in a particular language, in which specialized training in linguistics is obviously recommended along with a careful analysis of the foreign language itself.

LEARNING AND TEACHING

What is *learning* and what is *teaching* and how do they interact? Consider again some traditional definitions. A search in contemporary dictionaries reveals that learning is "acquiring or getting of knowledge of a subject or a skill by study, experience, or instruction." A more specialized definition might read as follows: "Learning is a relatively permanent change in a behavioral tendency and is the result of reinforced practice" (Kimble and Garmezy 1963:133). Similarly, teaching, which is implied in the first definition of learning, may be defined as "showing or helping someone to learn how to do something, giving instructions, guiding in the study of something, providing with knowledge, causing to know or understand." How awkward these definitions are! Isn't it rather curious that learned lexicographers cannot devise more precise scientific definitions? More than perhaps anything else, such definitions reflect the difficulty of defining complex concepts like learning and teaching.

Breaking down the components of the definition of learning, one can extract, as we did with language, domains of research and inquiry:

1. Learning is acquisition or "getting."
2. Learning is retention of information or skill.
3. Retention implies storage systems, memory, cognitive organization.
4. Learning involves active, conscious focus on and acting upon events outside or inside the organism.
5. Learning is relatively permanent, but subject to forgetting.
6. Learning involves some form of practice, perhaps reinforced practice.
7. Learning is a change in behavior.

These concepts can also give way to a number of subfields within the discipline of psychology: acquisition processes, perception,

memory (storage) systems, recall, conscious and subconscious learning, learning styles and strategies, theories of forgetting, reinforcement, the role of practice. Very quickly the concept of learning
becomes every bit as complex as the concept of language. Yet the
second language learner brings all these and more variables into
play in the learning of a second language.

Teaching cannot be defined apart from learning. Nathan Gage
(1964:269) noted that "to satisfy the practical demands of education, theories of learning must be 'stood on their head' so as to yield
theories of teaching." Teaching is guiding and facilitating learning,
enabling the learner to learn, setting the conditions for learning.
Your understanding of how the learner learns will determine your
philosophy of education, your teaching style, your approach, methods, and classroom techniques. If, like B. F. Skinner, you look at
learning as a process of operant conditioning through a carefully
paced program of reinforcement, you will teach accordingly. If you
view second language learning basically as a deductive rather than an
inductive process, you will probably choose to present copious
rules and paradigms to your students rather than let them "discover"
those rules inductively. An extended definition—or theory—of
teaching will spell out governing principles for choosing certain
methods and techniques. A theory of teaching, in harmony with your
integrated understanding of the learner and of the subject matter to
be learned, will point the way to successful procedures on a given
day for given learners under the various constraints of the particular
context of learning.

The chapters of this book are intended to serve not as a theory
of teaching or instruction, but rather as an essential component
underlying the subsequent formulation of a theory of instruction.
Jerome Bruner (1966:40-41) noted that a theory of instruction
should specify the following features:

1. The experiences which most effectively implant in the individual a predisposition toward learning
2. The ways in which a body of knowledge should be structured so that it
   can be most readily grasped by the learner
3. The most effective sequences in which to present the materials to be
   learned
4. The nature and pacing of rewards and punishments in the process of
   learning and teaching

At least the first three features refer quite pointedly to the subject
matter itself and to the learner, implying that one needs an understanding of the subject matter and a practical theory of learning

before a theory of instruction can be formed. The purpose of this volume is to focus on the general nature of the subject matter, *language*, and upon the process of *learning* as essential foundation stones for building a theory of teaching.

PARALLEL POLARIZATION

While the general definitions of language, learning, and teaching offered here might meet with the approval of most linguists, psychologists, and educators, you can find points of vast disagreement upon a little probing of the components of each definition. For example, is language a "set of habits" or a "system of internalized rules"? Differing viewpoints emerge from equally expert linguists and psychologists.

Yet with all the possible disagreements among linguists and among psychologists, the two disciplines themselves are not that far apart. A historical glance back through the last few decades of linguistic and psychological research reveals some rather striking parallels in the philosophies and approaches of the two disciplines. In linguistics the *structural* school, in its heyday in the 1940s and 50s, gave way to the *generative* school with its beginnings in the early 60s and continuing in various manifestations to the present day. Similarly, psychologists in the 40s and 50s were predominantly committed to a *behavioristic* mode of thinking—or even "neobehavioristic"—while the 60s and 70s brought increasing attention to *cognitive* psychology. The respective revolutions in thinking are important for the second language teacher to understand, because they highlight contrastive ways of thinking within disciplines yet parallel approaches across disciplines. An understanding of the varied philosophies can serve as "cognitive pegs" on which to hang further information specialized to second language learning and teaching. The polarization of thought presented in the following explanations may not so much depict reality as they act as a means of providing a contrastive description. Just as any population is, in statistical terms, normally distributed between two end points, so too each individual's philosophy falls somewhere in between two contrasting poles. You may never find a really "hardnosed" behaviorist in all the possible extremes, or a cognitivist who recognizes absolutely no legitimacy in the constructs of behaviorism. You too will in all likelihood fall somewhere in between the poles described here, but you, and only you, by fitting various pieces of the puzzle together, can fashion your own personal theory of learning or theory of language.

What then, in a nutshell, are these theories whose popularity has fallen and risen in parallel chronology? In the 1940s and 50s the *structural*, or *descriptive* school of linguistics, with its advocates—Leonard Bloomfield, Edward Sapir, Charles Hockett, Charles Fries, and others—prided itself in a rigorous application of the scientific principle of *observation* of human languages. Only the "publicly observable responses" could be subject to investigation. The linguist's task, according to the structuralist, was to describe human languages and to identify the structural characteristics of those languages. This led to the unchecked rush of linguists to the far reaches of the earth to write the grammars of exotic languages. An important axiom of structural linguistics, however, was that "languages can differ from each other without limit," and that no preconceptions must be taken to the field. Freeman Twaddell (1935:57) stated this principle in perhaps its most extreme terms. "Whatever our attitude toward mind, spirit, soul, etc., as realities, we must agree that the scientist proceeds as though there were no such things, as though all his information were acquired through processes of his physiological nervous system. Insofar as he occupies himself with psychical, non-material forces, the scientist is not a scientist. The scientific method is quite simply the convention that mind does not exist. . . . " The structural linguist examined only the overtly observable data with no assumption that another human being might have cognitive processes that resembled his own. Such attitudes prevail in Skinner's thought, particularly in *Verbal Behavior* (1957), in which he says that any notion of "idea" or "meaning" is explanatory fiction, and that the speaker is merely the locus of verbal behavior, not the cause. Charles Osgood reinstated meaning in verbal behavior, explaining it as a "representational mediation process," but still did not depart from a generally nonmentalistic view of language.

Of further importance to the structural or descriptive linguist was the notion that language could be dismantled into small pieces or units and that these units could be described scientifically, contrasted, and added up again to form the whole.

In the 1960s the generative-transformational school of linguistics emerged through the influence of Noam Chomsky. What Chomsky was trying to show is that language (not languages) cannot be scrutinized simply in terms of observable stimuli and responses or the volumes of raw data gathered by field linguists. The generative linguist is interested not only in describing language or achieving the level of *descriptive* adequacy but also in arriving at an *explanatory* level of adequacy in the study of language—that is, a "principled basis, independent of any particular language, for the selection of the descriptively adequate grammar of each language" (Chomsky 1964:63).

Over sixty years ago, Ferdinand de Saussure (1916) said that there was a difference between *parole* (what Skinner "observes," and what Chomsky calls "performance") and *langue* (akin to the "competence" which generative theory seeks to account for), but descriptive linguistics chose largely to ignore *langue* and to study *parole*. The revolution brought about by generative linguistics broke with the descriptivists' penchant for studying performance—the outward manifestation of language—and capitalized on the important distinction between the overtly observable *surface* level of language and the *deep* structure of language, that hidden level of meaning and thought which gives birth to and generates observable surface linguistic performance.

On the psychological side, a similar revolution came about with the scrutiny of the adequacy of behavioral theories to account for human behavior. Like the structural linguistic position, the behavioristic view focused on publicly observable responses—those which can be objectively perceived, recorded, and measured. The "scientific method" was rigorously adhered to, and therefore such concepts as consciousness and intuition were regarded as "mentalistic," illegitimate domains of inquiry. The unreliability of observation of states of consciousness, thinking, concept formation, or the acquisition of knowledge made such topics impossible to examine in a behavioristic framework. Typical behavioristic models were classical and operant conditioning, rote verbal learning, instrumental learning, and discrimination learning. You are familiar with the classical experiments with Pavlov's dog and Skinner's boxes—these too typify the position that organisms can be conditioned to respond in desired ways, given the correct degree and scheduling of reinforcement.

Cognitive psychologists, on the other hand, take a contrasting theoretical stance. Meaning, understanding, and knowing are significant data for psychological study. Instead of focusing rather mechanistically on stimulus-response connections, cognitivists try to discover psychological *principles* of organization and functioning. David Ausubel (1965:4) notes: "From the standpoint of cognitive theorists, the attempt to ignore conscious states or to reduce cognition to mediational processes reflective of implicit behavior not only removes from the field of psychology what is most worth studying but also dangerously oversimplifies highly complex psychological phenomena." By using a *rationalistic* approach instead of a strictly *empirical* approach, cognitive psychologists, like generative linguists, have sought to discover underlying motivations and deeper structures of human behavior; going beyond descriptive to explanatory power has taken on utmost importance.

Both the structural linguist and the behavioral psychologist are interested in description, in answering *what* questions about human behavior: objective measurement of behavior in controlled circumstances. The generative linguist and cognitive psychologist are, to be sure, interested in the *what* question; but they are far more interested in a more ultimate question, *why*: what underlying reasons, thinking, and circumstances caused a particular event? If you were to observe someone walk into your house, pick up a chair and fling it through your window, and then walk out, different kinds of questions could be asked. One set of questions would relate to what happened: the physical description of the person, the time of day, the size of the chair, the impact of the chair, etc. Another set of questions would ask why the person did what he did: what were his motives, what was his psychological state, was he agitated, was he a political enemy of yours, etc. The first set of questions is very rigorous and exacting; it allows no flaw, no mistake in measurement, but does it give you ultimate answers? The second set of questions is richer, but obviously riskier. By risking asking some difficult questions about the unobserved, we may lose some ground, but gain more profound insight about human behavior.

Table 1-1 summarizes concepts and approaches germane to each of the two polarized theories that have been presented here. The table may help to pinpoint certain broad ideas that are associated with the respective positions.

The parallel between the two disciplines is not really surprising when one considers the fact that the disciplines of psychology and linguistics are closely related. Both disciplines focus on human behavior, with linguistics representing a somewhat more specialized aspect of human behavior. A number of psychologists have made a lasting impact on linguistic theories, not the least of them B. F. Skinner, Charles Osgood, and George Miller. And linguists of the caliber of Ferdinand de Saussure, Benjamin Whorf, and Noam Chomsky have influenced psychological thinking. And so, as Kuhn (1970) points out in his treatise on the structure of scientific revolutions, all "normal" sciences go through a revolutionary pattern that begins with a successful paradigm within which to work, followed by a period of anomaly (doubt, uncertainty, questioning of prevailing theory), then crisis (the fall of the existing paradigm) with all the professional insecurity that comes therewith, and then finally a new paradigm, a novel theory, is put together. This cycle is evident in both psychology and linguistics, though the limits and bounds are not always easily perceived—perhaps less easily perceived in psycholo-

Table 1-1   Linguistic-Psychological Parallels

Schools of Psychology	Schools of Linguistics	Characteristics
		Repetition and reinforcement
		Learning, conditioning
Behaviorism		Publicly observable responses
	Structural	Empiricism
Neobehaviorism		Scientific method
	Descriptive	Performance
S-R		Surface structure
		Description—"what"
		Analysis and insight
		Acquisition, innateness
		States of consciousness
Cognitive	Generative	Rationalism
		Mentalism, intuition
Process	Transformational	Competence
		Deep structure
		Explanation—"why"

gy, in which both paradigms currently operate somewhat in tandem. The cyclical nature of theories underscores the fact that no single theory or paradigm is either right or wrong. It is impossible to refute with any finality one theory with another. Some truth can be found in virtually every theory.

PUTTING IT ALL TOGETHER

The language teacher cannot teach effectively without understanding varied theoretical positions—alternative ways of looking at the phenomena of language, learning, and teaching. This understanding forms the principled basis upon which you can choose particular approaches, methods, and techniques for teaching a foreign language. And unless that principled basis is your own carefully and thoughtfully devised theory, you become a slave to one way of thinking, a puppet without self-control. Your task in the formulation of an integrated understanding of the principles of language learning and teaching is to find those points of compromise or tension between two poles of possibilities which will best fit a global theory of second language acquisition. Rather than yielding to the temptation of making a quick, haphazard choice of a stance, it is imperative first to sift through the many variables that come to bear on learning and teaching a second language.

Such a prospect may seem formidable, a situation not unlike that which Charlie Brown faced in a *Peanuts* cartoon: Charlie the baseball pitcher was depicted walking off the baseball diamond, head hung low, dejected, and sighing, "184 to nothing! I can't believe it. Good grief, how can we lose when we're so sincere?"

There may be at least 184 variables to understand in second language learning and teaching, and more than sincerity is needed to master them. There are no instant recipes. No quick and easy method is guaranteed to provide success. Every learner is unique. Every teacher is unique. And every learner-teacher relationship is unique. Your task is to understand the properties of those relationships. Using a cautious, enlightened, eclectic approach, you can build a theory—an understanding of the principles of second language learning and teaching. The chapters that follow are designed to help you formulate that understanding.

SUGGESTED READINGS

Chapter 1 of *Wardhaugh* (1976) is an excellent introduction to the nature of language and issues in the discipline of linguistics. Chapter 11 of a different volume by *Wardhaugh* (1974) provided a clearly written synopsis of the interdisciplinary nature of language teaching, especially the relevance of linguistics, psychology, and pedagogy for an understanding of what language teaching is all about.

Kuhn (1970) will give you a comprehensive understanding of the cyclical nature of theories and models in all disciplines. Language teaching methods and approaches can be more perceptively understood when they are placed within Kuhn's model.

The four components of a theory of instruction as outlined by *Bruner* (1966:40f.) help to put a theory of learning into the perspective of teaching in the classroom. You may wish to specify the particular second language features of each of Bruner's four components.

For a rather concise—if somewhat biased—comparison between behavioral and cognitive psychology, read *Anderson and Ausubel* (1965:3-17). Other accounts of differing psychological perspectives can usually be found in introductory psychology textbooks. Such material may also be appropriate to read in conjunction with the material in Chapter 4. *Chastain* (1970) provided an interesting example of the application of behavioristic and cognitive approaches in actual foreign language instruction—in this case, programmed instruction.

It is difficult to cite one source that expands on the distinction between structural and generative linguistics; however, most introductory textbooks in linguistics summarize both points of view. *Wardhaugh* (1977) or *Langacker* (1973) provided such explanations.

TOPICS AND QUESTIONS FOR STUDY
AND DISCUSSION

1. In the first part of the chapter a number of "who, what . . . " questions were posed. What other possible questions occur to you? Attempt some tentative answers to at least a few of the questions, and write them down for referral as you progress through the chapters of this book.

2. Write your *own* "twenty-five-word-or-less" definitions of *language, learning,* and *teaching.* What would you add to or delete from the definitions given in this chapter? Save your definitions and when you finish the book determine if you would revise those definitions in any way.

3. Show, in other disciplines with which you are familiar, how a theory is an extended definition. How does a definition reveal certain theoretical biases on the part of the definer?

4. What kind of *teaching* emphases would emerge in the second language classroom by keying the *exclusive* importance of any *one* of the eight subfields of linguistics listed on page 6? Take several subfields and discuss the type of approach, methods, and techniques that might emerge.

5. Summarize, in your own words, what is meant by behavioristic psychology and cognitive psychology. Give examples in your own education of subject-matter areas, methods, or materials which have stressed one or the other side of the continuum.

6. What did Twaddell (1935:57) mean when he said, "The scientific method is quite simply the convention that mind does not exist. . . . "? Discuss the advantages and disadvantages of attending only to "publicly observable responses" in studying human behavior. Don't limit yourself just to language teaching in considering the ramifications of behavioristic principles.

7. Explain what Chomsky (1964:63) meant by "explanatory adequacy." You might wish to read the original article.

8. Define *rationalism* and *empiricism.* You should consult an encyclopedia or other reference for some details. Why are generative grammar and cognitive psychology classified as rationalistic approaches?

9. Give examples of polarization in society, government, or some other sphere of activity. Discuss the advantages and disadvantages of polarization. How do you find appropriate middle ground?

10. What is meant by "cautious, enlightened" eclecticism (p. 14)?

2

First Language Acquisition

That marvelous capacity for acquiring competence in one's native language within the first few years of life has been a subject of interest for many centuries. "Modern" research on child language acquisition dates back to the late eighteenth century when the German philosopher Dietrich Tiedemann recorded his observations of the psychological and linguistic development of his young son. For a century and a half, few if any significant advances were made in the study of child language; for the most part research was limited to diary-like recordings of observed speech with some attempts to classify word types. Only in the 60s and 70s did researchers begin to analyze child language systematically and to try to discover the nature of the psycholinguistic process which enables every human being to gain fluent control of an exceedingly complex system of communication. In those two decades some giant strides were taken, especially in the generative and cognitive models of language, in describing the acquisition of particular languages, and in probing universal aspects of acquisition. Today literally hundreds of linguists and psychologists are studying linguistic, psychological, sociological, and physiological aspects of first language acquisition.

This recent wave of research in child language acquisition has led foreign language teachers and teacher trainers to study some of the general findings of such research with a view to drawing analogies between first and second language acquisition, and even to justifying certain teaching methods and techniques on the basis of first language learning principles. On the surface, it is entirely reasonable to make the analogy. After all, every child, given a normal developmental environment, acquires his native language fluently and efficiently; moreover, he acquires it "naturally," without special instruction, though not without notable conscious effort and attention to language. However, the direct comparisons such as those that have been made must be treated with caution. There are dozens of salient differences between first and second language learning; the most obvious difference, in the case of adult second language learning, is the tremendous cognitive and affective contrast between adults and children. A detailed examination of these differences is made in the next chapter.

This chapter is designed to outline issues in first language learning as a foundation on which you can come to an understanding of principles of second language learning. A coherent grasp of the nature of first language learning is an invaluable aid, if not an essential component, in the construction of a theory of second language acquisition. This chapter provides an overview of various theoretical positions—positions that can be related to the paradigms discussed in Chapter One—in first language acquisition, and a discussion of some key issues that are particularly significant for an understanding of second language learning. Information on first language acquisition beyond that which is presented here should be sought in the suggested readings at the end of this chapter.

THEORIES OF FIRST LANGUAGE ACQUISITION

There is no one who has not at some time witnessed the remarkable ability of children to communicate. As small babies, children babble and coo and cry and vocally or nonvocally send an extraordinary number of messages and receive even more messages. As they reach the end of their first year, specific attempts are made to imitate words and speech sounds heard around them, and about this time they utter their first "words." By about 18 months of age these words have multiplied considerably and are beginning to appear in combination with each other to form two-word and three-word "sentences"—commonly referred to as "telegraphic" utterances—such as "allgone milk," "bye-bye Daddy," "gimme toy," and so forth. The production tempo now begins to increase as more and more words are spoken every day and more and more combinations of two- and three-word sentences are uttered. By about age 3, the child can comprehend an incredible quantity of linguistic behavior; his speech capacity mushrooms as he becomes the generator of non-stop chattering and incessant conversation, language thus becoming a mixed blessing for those around him! This fluency continues into school age as the child internalizes increasingly complex structures, expands his vocabulary, and sharpens communicative skills. At school age the child not only learns what to say, but what *not* to say, as he learns the social functions of his language.

How can we explain this fantastic journey from that first anguished cry at birth to adult competence in a language? From the first word to tens of thousands? From telegraphese at 1½ years to the compound-complex, cognitively precise, socioculturally appropriate sentences just a few short years later? It is these sorts of questions that theories of language acquisition attempt to answer.

In principle you can adopt one of two extremist polarized positions in the study of first language acquisition. The extreme behavioristic position would be that the child comes into the world with a *tabula rasa*, a clean slate bearing no preconceived notions about the world or about language, and this child is then shaped by his environment, slowly conditioned through various schedules of reinforcement. At the other extreme, you would find a position that claims that the child comes into this world with very specific innate knowledge, knowledge which includes not only general predispositions and tendencies but also knowledge of the nature of language and of the world. Then, through his own volition, he acts upon his environment by developing these bodies of knowledge.

Clearly both of the extreme positions are too farfetched for respectable credibility, but they do represent opposites on a continuum with many possible positions in between. Three such points are elucidated in this chapter. The first (behavioristic) position is set in contrast to the second (nativist) and third (cognitive) positions, which are more clearly on the generative/cognitive side of the continuum.

Behavioristic Theories

Language is a fundamental part of total human behavior, and behaviorists have examined it as such and sought to formulate consistent theories of first language acquisition. The behavioristic approach focuses on the immediately perceptible aspects of linguistic behavior—the publicly observable responses—and the relationships or associations between those responses and events in the world surrounding them. A behaviorist might consider effective language behavior to be the production of correct responses to stimuli. If a particular response is reinforced, it then becomes habitual, or conditioned. Thus the child produces linguistic responses that are reinforced. This is true of his comprehension as well as production responses, though to consider comprehension is to wander just a bit out of the publicly observable realm. One learns to comprehend an utterance by reacting appropriately to it and by being reinforced for that reaction.

One of the best-known attempts to construct a behavioristic model of linguistic behavior is embodied in B. F. Skinner's (1957) classic, *Verbal Behavior*. Skinner is commonly known for his experiments with animal behavior in "Skinner's boxes," but he has also gained recognition for his contributions to education through teaching machines and programmed learning (Skinner 1968). Skinner's theory of verbal behavior was an extension of his general theory of learning by *operant conditioning*. Operant conditioning refers to conditioning in which the organism (in this case, a human being) emits a response, or *operant* (a sentence or utterance), without necessarily observable stimuli; that operant is maintained (learned) by reinforcement (for example, a positive verbal or nonverbal response for another person). If a child says "want milk" and a parent gives the child some milk, the operant is reinforced and, over repeated instances, is conditioned. According to Skinner, verbal behavior, like other behavior, is controlled by its *consequences*. When consequences are rewarding, behavior is maintained and is increased in strength and perhaps frequency. When consequences are punishing, or when there is lack of reinforcement entirely, the behavior is weakened and eventually extinguished.

Skinner has not been without his critics, not the least among them Noam Chomsky (1959), who penned a highly critical review of *Verbal Behavior*. Some years later, however, Kenneth MacCorquodale (1970) published a reply to Chomsky's review in which he eloquently and quite convincingly defended Skinner's points of view. And so the battle raged on. Today few linguists and psychologists would agree that Skinner's model of verbal behavior adequately accounts for the capacity to acquire language, for language development itself, for the abstract nature of language, and for a theory of meaning. A theory based on conditioning and reinforcement is hardpressed to explain the fact that every sentence you speak or write—with a few trivial exceptions—is novel, never before uttered either by you or by anyone else! These novel utterances are nevertheless created by the speaker and processed by the hearer.

In an attempt to broaden the base of behavioristic theory, some psychologists proposed modified theoretical positions. One of these positions is *mediation* theory, which developed out of Pavlov's *contiguity* theory. Meaning, for example, is accounted for by the claim that the linguistic stimulus (a word or sentences) elicits a *mediating* response that is self-stimulating. Charles Osgood (1953, 1957) called this self-stimulation a "representational mediation process," a process that is really covert and invisible, acting within the learner. Interestingly, mediation theory thus attempted to account for abstraction by a notion that reeks of "mentalism"—a cardinal sin for dyed-in-the-wool behaviorists!

Mediation theories still leave many questions about language unanswered. The abstract nature of language and the integral relationship between meaning and utterance are unresolved. All sentences have deep structures—the level of underlying meaning that is only manifested overtly by surface structures. These deep structures have psychological reality, a reality related to one's systems of meaning and knowledge, all of which are intricately bound up in a person's total cognitive and affective experience. These depths of language have scarcely been plumbed by mediational theory.

Yet another attempt to account for first language acquisition within a behavioristic framework was made by Jenkins and Palermo (1964). While admitting that their conjectures were "speculative" and "premature" (p. 143), the authors attempted to synthesize notions of generative linguistics and mediational approaches to child language. They claimed that the child may acquire frames of a phrase-structure grammar and learn the stimulus-response equivalences that can be substituted within each frame; imitation was an important if not essential aspect of establishing stimulus-response associations. But this theory, too, fails to account for the abstract nature of language, nor does it account satisfactorily for the generalization process that is inferred in the theory. Also, it does not account for the creativity evident in even a young child's ability to comprehend and produce novel utterances. David McNeill (1968:408-409) further pointed out that it is mathematically impossible for a child to acquire all the frames and items implied by Jenkins and Palermo's theory.

> The difficulties with finite-state grammars are simple and arithmetical. In order to acquire grammar through mediation paradigms, a child must learn all the transitions among grammatical classes that are allowable in English. The number of these, however, is astronomical. Take, for example, the sentence, "The people who called and wanted to rent your house when you go away next year are from California" (Miller and Chomsky 1963). There is a dependency between the second word (people) and the seventeenth word (are). If this intuition was learned through mediation,

then each of us has learned a unique set of transitions covering a sequence of 15 grammatical categories. Assuming (conservatively) that an average of four grammatical categories might occur at any point in the development of an English sentence, detection of the dependency between "people" and "are" signifies that we have learned at least $4^{15} = 10^9$ different transitions, which means, as Miller and Chomsky point out, that we learned " ... the value of 10^9 parameters in a childhood lasting only 10^8 seconds" (p. 430). Evidently, mediation paradigms yield the wrong kind of structure. At the very least, we need a theory which avoids assuming that sentences consist of nothing more than simple left-to-right transitions.

It would appear that the rigor of behavioristic psychology, with its emphasis on empirical observation and the scientific method, can only begin to explain the miracle of language acquisition. It leaves untouched a vast domain which can be explored only by an approach that probes deeper.

Generative Theories

On the opposite end of the theoretical continuum we find generative theories of child language, with their typical rationalistic approach—asking deeper questions, looking for clearer explanations of the mystery of language acquisition. The failure—or at least the only-partial explanation—of behavioristic views of child language causes us to ask more ultimate questions. For language shares attributes of the ultimate; no amount of scientific investigation has thus far revealed its depths and fullness.

There are two types of generative theories which have made their mark in child language research, and they both share the same end of the continuum described in Chapter One. The first type is the *nativist* approach and the second, an outgrowth of the first, is commonly called the *cognitive* approach.

The nativist approach

The term *nativist* is derived from the fundamental assertion that language acquisition is innately determined, that we are born with a built-in device of some kind that predisposes us to language acquisition—to a systematic perception of language around us, resulting in the construction of an internalized system of language. Innateness hypotheses gain support from several sides. Eric Lenneberg (1967) proposed that language is a "species-specific" behavior and that certain modes of perception, categorizing abilities, and other language-related mechanisms are biologically determined. Chomsky

(1965) similarly claimed the existence of innate properties of language to explain the child's mastery of his native language in such a short time despite the highly abstract nature of the rules of language. This innate knowledge, according to Chomsky, is embodied in a "little black box" of sorts, a *language acquisition device* (LAD). McNeill (1966) described LAD as consisting of four innate linguistic properties: (1) the ability to distinguish speech sounds from other sounds in the environment, (2) the ability to organize linguistic events into various classes which can later be refined, (3) knowledge that only a certain kind of linguistic system is possible and that other kinds are not, (4) the ability to engage in constant evaluation of the developing linguistic system so as to construct the simplest possible system out of the linguistic data that are encountered.

McNeill's philosophical arguments were eloquent and to the point. He noted (1968:412) that "because S-R theory is so limited, the problem of language acquisition simply falls beyond its domain." The LAD proposition certainly addresses many of the particularly thorny aspects of language acquisition. Aspects of meaning and abstractness and creativity are accounted for. However, they are accounted for very inexplicitly. They are accounted for in much the same way that the philosophical proposition of the existence of a god accounts for the creation of human life: we do not know how humankind was created, therefore an entity is proposed as creator of life. Similarly we could argue that LAD is an unobserved invention that only superficially accounts for language acquisition, since we know as little about our philosophical god as we do about LAD. In one sense nativists did not come any closer to a solution than the behaviorists did. But in another sense McNeill's proposal led to some very rich possibilities for further research in such ultimate areas as the abstract system of language, linguistic universals, theories of meaning, and the nature of human knowledge. It was a beginning in a positive direction that yielded many possibilities in place of the dead end that behavioristic theory gave us.

A more practical contribution of nativist theories is evident if you look at the kinds of discoveries that have been made about how the *system* of child language works. Chomsky, McNeill, and their colleagues helped us to see that the child's language, at any given point, is a legitimate system in its own right. The child's linguistic development is not a process of developing fewer and fewer "incorrect" structures, not a language in which earlier stages have more "mistakes" than later stages. Rather, the child's language at any stage is systematic in that the child is constantly forming hypotheses on the basis of the input he receives and then testing those hypotheses in his own speech (and comprehension). As the child's language develops, those hypotheses get continually revised, reshaped, or sometimes abandoned.

Of course, the notion of the child as hypothesis tester is not new. Fifteen centuries ago St. Augustine provided in his *Confessions* a self-analysis of his own language learning process:

> For I was no longer a speechless infant, but a speaking boy. This I remember; and have since observed how I learned to speak. It was not that my elders taught me words . . . in any set method; but I, longing by cries and broken accents and various motions of my limbs to express my thoughts, that so I might have my will, and yet unable to express all that I willed, or to whom I willed, did myself, by the understanding which Thou, my God, gavest me, practise the sounds in my memory. . . . And thus by constantly hearing words, as they occurred in various sentences, I collected gradually for what they stood; and having broken in my mouth to these signs, I thereby gave utterance to my will. Thus I exchanged with those about me these current signs of our wills, and so launched deeper into the stormy intercourse of human life.

Before generative linguistics came into vogue, Jean Berko (1958) demonstrated that children learn language not as a series of separate discrete items, but as an integrated system. Using a simple nonsense-word test, Berko discovered that English-speaking children as young as 4 years of age applied rules for the formation of plural, present progressive, past tense, third singular, and possessives. She found, for example, that if a child saw one "wug" he could easily talk about two wug*s*, or if he were presented with a person who knows how to "gling," the child could talk about a person who gling*ed* yesterday, or sometimes who glang.

McNeill and his contemporaries carried out a rash of studies on the systematic nature of child language acquisition. Having thrown off the shackles of behavioristic constraints, researchers were free to construct hypothetical "grammars" of child language, although such grammars were still solidly based on empirical data. These grammars were largely formal representations of the deep structure—the abstract rules underlying surface output, the structure not overtly manifest in speech. Linguists began to examine child language from early forms of "telegraphese" to the complex language of 5- to 10-year-olds. Borrowing one tenet of structural and behavioristic paradigms, they approached the data with few preconceived notions about what the child's language *ought* to be, and probed the data for internally consistent systems, in much the same way that a linguist describes a language in the "field." The use of a generative framework was, of course, a departure from structural methodology.

The generative model enabled researchers of the 1960s to take some giant steps toward understanding the process of first language acquisition. The early grammars of child language were referred to as *pivot grammars*. It was commonly observed that the child's first two-word utterances seemed to manifest two separate word classes, and not simply two words thrown together at random. Consider the following utterances:

My cap
That horsie
Allgone milk
Mommy sock

Linguists noted that the words on the left-hand side seemed to belong to a class which words on the right-hand side generally did not belong to. That is, *my* could co-occur with *cap*, *horsie*, *milk*, or *sock*, but not with *that* or *allgone*. *Mommy* is, in this case, a word that belongs in both classes. The first class of words was called *pivot*, since they could pivot around a number of words in the second, *open* class. Thus the first rule of the generative grammar of the child was described as follows:

Sentence → Pivot word + Open word

Reams of research data gathered in the generative framework yielded hundreds of rules, some rather widely accepted by other researchers, others highly disputed, some very elaborate and others quite simple, some reflecting early "stages" of the child's grammar and others later stages. Some of these rules appear to be *universal*—true for all languages—but we have only just begun to scratch the surface of the question of linguistic universals. Linguistic universals are discussed in more detail in the latter part of this chapter.

Nativistic approaches to child language made at least two important contributions to the understanding of the first language learning process: (1) freedom from the restrictions of the "scientific method" to explore the unseen, unobservable, underlying, invisible, abstract linguistic structures being developed in the child; (2) description of the child's language as a ligitimate, rule-governed, consistent system.

As liberating as the nativist framework was, it still possessed some glaring inadequacies. The late 1960s witnessed a shift in patterns of research, not away from the generative/cognitive side of the continuum, but perhaps better described as a move "deeper" into the essence of language. The generative rules that were proposed under the nativistic framework were abstract, formal, explicit, and quite logical, yet they dealt specifically with the forms of language and not with the very deepest level of language, that level where memory, perception, thought, meaning, and emotion are all interdependently organized in the superstructure of the human mind. Linguists began to see that language was one manifestation of general development, one aspect of the cognitive and affective ability to deal with the world and with self. Linguists also began to see that language was hardly something you could extract and detach from your cognitive and affective framework and consider separately, and that linguistic rules written as mathematical equations failed to capture that ever-elusive facet of language: meaning. The generative rules of nativists were failing to account for the *functions* of language.

Lois Bloom (1971) cogently illustrated the issue in her criticism of pivot grammar when she pointed out that the relationships in which words occur in telegraphic utterances are only superficially similar. For example, in the utterance "Mommy sock," which nativists would describe as a sentence consisting of a pivot word and an open word, Bloom found at least *three* possible underlying relations: agent-action (Mommy is putting the sock on), agent-object (Mommy sees the sock) and possessor-possessed (Mommy's sock . . .). By examining data in reference to contexts, Bloom concluded that children learn underlying structures, and not superficial word order. Thus, depending on the context, "Mommy sock" could mean a number of different things to the child. Those varied meanings were inadequately captured in a pivot grammar approach.

Lewis Carroll aptly captures this charcteristic of language in *Through the Looking Glass* (1872), where Alice argues with Humpty Dumpty about the meanings of words:

> "When I use a word," Humpty Dumpty said, in rather a scornful tone, "it means just what I choose it to mean—neither more nor less."
>
> "The question is," said Alice, "whether you can make words mean so many different things."
>
> "The question is," said Humpty Dumpty, "which is to be master—that's all."

25

Bloom's research, along with that of Jean Piaget, Dan Slobin, and others, paved the way for a new wave of child language study, this time centering on the cognitive prerequisites of linguistic behavior. Piaget described overall development as the result of the child's interaction with his environment, with a complementary interaction between the child's developing perceptual cognitive capacities and his linguistic experience. What the child learns about language is determined by what the child already knows about the world.

Dan Slobin (1971) proposed that in all languages, semantic learning depends on cognitive development and that sequences of development are determined more by semantic complexity than by structural complexity. Bloom (1976:37) noted that "an explanation of language development depends upon an explanation of the cognitive underpinnings of language: what children know will determine what they learn about the code for both speaking and understanding messages."

So child language researchers began to tackle the formulation of the rules of the *functions* of language. At the same time theoretical linguists realized that theoretical grammars in the style of Chomsky's transformational-generative model were inadequate, and offshoots of generative theory began to appear in the form of *generative semantics* and *case grammar*.

In recent years it has become quite clear that language functioning extends well beyond cognitive thought and memory structure. Current investigations of child language are now centering on one of the thorniest areas of linguistic research: the function of language in *discourse*. Since language is used for communication, it is only fitting that one study the communicative functions of language: what do children know and learn about talking with others? about connected pieces of discourse (relations between sentences)? the interaction between hearer and speaker? conversational cues? This newest wave is revolutionizing research on first language acquisition. The very heart of language—its communicative function—is being tackled in all its variability.

But even more revolutionary is the almost paradoxical fact that the most current research on the generative side of the theoretical continuum has focused once again on the *performance* level of language. All those overt responses that were so carefully observed by structuralists and hastily weeded out as "performance variables" by generative linguists in their zeal to get at competence have now returned to the forefront. Hesitations, pauses, backtracking, and the like are indeed significant conversational cues. Even some of the contextual categories described by—of all people—Skinner, in *Verbal*

Behavior, turn out to be relevant! The linguist can no longer deal with abstract, formal rules without dealing with all those minutiae of day-to-day performance which were previously ignored.

Lois Bloom summarized the contrasting approaches described above, referring to them in terms of *linguistic determinism* and *cognitive determinism*. A linguistically determined view holds that "the course of language development depends directly on the nature of the linguistic system and, more specifically, on the nature of those aspects of language that might be universal and represented in an innate, predetermined program for language learning" (1976:37). On the other hand, a cognitively determined view emphasizes "the interaction of the child's perceptual and cognitive development with linguistic and nonlinguistic events in his environment" (ibid.). She then concluded by noting that the question of which type of determinism best describes reality remains to be resolved, but that the development of perception and cognition are keys to the understanding of the process of child language acquisition.

Several theoretical positions have been sketched out here. Perhaps we will never realize a complete, consistent, unified theory of first-language acquisition, but even in its infancy, child language research has manifested some enormous strides toward that ultimate goal. And even if all the answers are far from evident, maybe we are asking more of the right questions.

ISSUES IN FIRST LANGUAGE ACQUISITION

Competence and Performance

For centuries scientists and philosophers have operated with the basic distinction between competence and performance. *Competence* refers to one's underlying knowledge of a system, event, or fact. It is the nonobservable, idealized ability to do something, to perform something. *Performance* is the overtly observable and concrete manifestation or realization of competence. It is the actual doing of something: walking, singing, dancing, speaking. In Western society we have used the competence-performance distinction in all walks of life. In our schools, for example, we have assumed that children possess certain competence in given areas and that this competence can be measured and assessed by means of the observation of elicited samples of performance called "tests" and "examinations."

In reference to language, competence is your underlying knowledge of the system of a language—its rules of grammar, its vocabulary, all the pieces of a language and how those pieces fit together. Performance is actual production (speaking, writing) or the comprehension (listening, reading) of linguistic events. You will recall in Chapter One a reference to Ferdinand de Saussure's (1916) version of the competence/performance construct: a distinction between *langue* and *parole* as two separate phenomena, independent of each other. "*Langue* exists in the form of a sum of impressions deposited in the brain of each member of the community. . . . *Parole* [is] . . . an individual act, . . . willful phonational acts." (Saussure 1916:14-19).

Chomsky (1965) likened competence to an idealized speaker-hearer who does not display such performance variables as memory limitations, distractions, shifts of attention and interest, errors, and hesitation phenomena such as repeats, false starts, pauses, omissions, and additions. (Maclay and Osgood [1959:24] outline a diverse number of hesitation types.) Chomsky's point was that a theory of language had to be a theory of competence lest the linguist vainly try to categorize an infinite number of performance variables which are not reflective of the underlying linguistic ability of the speaker-hearer.

The distinction is one that linguists and psychologists in the generative/cognitive framework have been operating under for some time, a mentalistic construct that structuralists and behaviorists do not deal with. Just *how* does one infer this unobservable, underlying level? How can one be sure that an accurate assessment has been made?

Brown and Bellugi (1964) give us a rather delightful example of the difficulty of attempting to extract underlying grammatical knowledge from children. Unlike adults, who can be asked, for example, whether it is better to say "two foots" or "two feet," children exhibit what is called the "pop-go-weasel" effect, as witnessed in the following dialogue:

Adult interviewer: Now Adam, listen to what I say. Tell me which is better to
                      say . . . *some* water, or *a* water.
Two-year-old child: Pop go weasel.

The researcher is thus forced to devise indirect methods of inferring competence. Among those methods are the tape recording and transcription of countless hours of speech followed by studious analysis, or the direct admission of certain imitation, production, or comprehension tests, all with numerous disadvantages. How is one, for example, to infer some general competence about the linguistic system of a five-year-old, monolingual, English-speaking child whose recounting of an incident viewed on television is transcribed below:

> ... they heared 'em underground ca-cause they went through a hoyle—a hole—and they pulled a rock from underground and then they saw a wave going in—that the hole—and-they brought a table and the wave brought 'em out the k—tunnel and then the—they went away and then—uh—m—ah—back on top and it was—uh—going under a bridge and they went—then the braves hit the—the bridge—they—all of it—th-then they looked there—then they—then they were safe.

On the surface it might appear that this child is severely impaired in his attempts to communicate. In fact, this same transcript was presented without identification of the speaker to a group of speech therapists several years ago and I asked them to analyze the various possible "disorders" manifested in the data. After they cited quite a number of technical manifestations of aphasia, I gleefully informed them of the real source of the data! The point is that every day in our processing of linguistic data we comprehend such strings of speech and comprehend them rather well by attending to the underlying meaning of the utterance and by not allowing ourselves to be distracted by a number of performance variables. Adult talk is often no less fraught with monstrosities, as we can see in the following verbatim transcription of a recorded conversation between television talk-show host Mike Douglas and golfer Tony Jacklin:

Mike Douglas: I think concentration is-is the most important thing for a golfer isn't it?

Tony Jacklin: Concentration is important. But uh—I also—to go with this of course if you're playing well—if you're playing well then you get up tight about your game. You get keyed up and it's easy to concentrate. You know you're playing well and you know ... in with a chance than it's easier, much easier to—to you know get in there and—and start to ... you don't have to think about it. I mean it's got to be automatic.

Perhaps Mr. Jacklin would have been better off if he had simply uttered the very last sentence and omitted all the previous verbiage! If we were to record many more samples of the 5-year-old's speech we would still be faced with the problem of inferring his competence. What is his knowledge of the verb system? of the concept of a "sentence"? Even if we administer rather carefully designed tests of comprehension or production to a child, we are still left with the problem of inferring, as accurately as possible, the child's underlying competence. Often these inferences are mere guesses, and what research is all about is converting the guesswork to accurate measurement.

Comprehension vs. Production

Not to be confused with the competence/performance distinction, *comprehension* and *production* can be aspects of *both* performance *and* competence. One of the myths that has crept into some foreign language teaching materials is that comprehension (listening, reading) can be equated with competence, while production (speaking, writing) is performance. It is important to recognize that this is not the case: production is of course more directly observable, but comprehension is as much performance—a "willful act," to use Saussure's term—as production is.

In child language, both observational and research evidence point to the "superiority" of comprehension over production: children understand "more" than they actually produce. For instance, a child may understand a sentence with an embedded relative in it, but not be able to produce one. W. R. Miller (1963:863) gave us a good example of this phenomenon in phonological development: "Recently a three year old child told me her name was Litha. I answered 'Li*th*a?' 'No, Litha.' 'Oh, Lisa.' 'Yes, Litha.'" The child clearly perceived the contrast between English *s* and *th*, even though she could not produce the contrast herself.

How are we to explain this difference, this well-known "lag" between comprehension and production? We know that even adults understand more vocabulary than they ever use in speech, and also perceive more syntactic variation than they actually produce. Could it be that the same competence accounts for both modes of performance? Or can we speak of comprehension competence as something that is somewhat separately identified from production competence? Because comprehension runs ahead of production, is it more completely indicative of our overall competence? Is production indicative of a smaller portion of competence? Such questions appear to lead to the logical feasibility of making a distinction between production competence and comprehension competence. A theory of language might therefore have to include some accounting of the separation of two types of competence. These are rather fundamental questions that have no answer at the present time, but they remain questions of interest in any attempt to infer what we have commonly referred to as *the* competence a person has in a particular language. It may be wise to hold the possibility that linguistic competence may have several modes or levels, perhaps as many as four, since speaking, listening, reading, and writing are all separate modes of performance.

The Innateness Controversy

Chomsky contended that the child is born with an innate knowledge of or predisposition toward language, and that this innate property (LAD) is universal in all human beings. The innateness hypothesis was a possible resolution of contradiction between the behavioristic notion that language is a set of habits that can be acquired by a process of conditioning and the fact that such conditioning is much too slow and inefficient a process to account for the acquisition of a phenomenon as complex as language. But the innateness hypothesis presented a number of problems itself. One of the difficulties has already been discussed in this chapter: the LAD proposition simply postpones facing the central issue of the nature of the human being's capacity for language acquisition. Having thus "explained" language acquisition, one must now explain LAD. Ambrose Bierce summed it up wryly in *The Devil's Dictionary:* "The doctrine of innate ideas is one of the most admirable faiths of philosophy, being itself an innate idea and therefore inaccessible to disproof" (in Clark and Clark 1977:517).

What, exactly, are the innate properties and predispositions embodied in LAD? How are they genetically transmitted? What has so far been discovered in research on *universals* of language points toward answers, but the discovery of universals does not necessarily imply innateness. Furthermore, research has been an inadequate testing ground in support of the LAD hypothesis; researchers have too often merely assumed the hypothesis to be true when accounting for their data.

Another problem emerges if you consider the complement of innateness: learning. For years psychologists and educators have been embroiled in the "nature-nurture" controversy: what are those behaviors which "nature" provides either innately, in some sort of predetermined biological timetable, and what are those behaviors which are, by environmental exposure—by "nurture," by teaching— learned and internalized? We do observe that language acquisition is universal, that every child acquires language. But how is the efficiency and success of that learning determined by the environment the child is in? Can a child be "taught" his first language? The waters of the innateness hypothesis are considerably muddied by such questions, whose answers are yet to be found.

Closely related to the innateness controversy is the claim that language is universal and universally acquired in the same manner, and, moreover, that the deep structure of language at its deepest level may be common to all languages. Years ago Werner Leopold (1949) who, incidentally, was far ahead of his time, made a rather eloquent case for certain phonological as well as grammatical universals in language. But to this day, except for some rays of hope in research provided by such people as Greenberg (1966) and his colleagues, the quest for substantive universals of language has been like the search for Atlantis. The problem ultimately boils down to the tremendous *variability* across languages and of individuals within a language. Even in English, researchers are not agreed on how to define various "stages" of language acquisition. Certain "typical" patterns appear in child language. For example, it has been found that young children who have not yet mastered the past-tense morpheme tend first to learn past tenses as separate items ("walked," "broke," "drank") without knowledge of the difference between regular and irregular verbs. Then, around the age of 4 or 5, they begin to perceive a system in which the *-ed* morpheme is added to a verb, and at this point all verbs become regularized ("breaked," "drinked," "goed"). Finally, after school age, children perceive that there are two classes of verbs, regular and irregular, and begin to sort out verbs into the two classes, a process which goes on for many years and in some cases persists into young adulthood. But even this tendency is only an instance of what is perhaps a universal cognitive tendency to overgeneralize.

Some research data has been gathered on language acquisition in languages other than English: Russian, Japanese, French, Spanish, German, to name a few. Some commonalities emerge. Pivot grammar, telegraphese, concepts of negation and interrogation are some examples, but not enough data has yet been amassed to form a substantial, systematic set of linguistic universals.

Is it any wonder, though, that universals are hard to find? Consider the variability across speakers within a language group: variability of regional and social dialects, style, and idiolect. Saussure (1916:9) once again puts it rather cogently: "But what is language? . . . It is both a social product of the faculty of speech and a collection of necessary conventions that have been adopted by a social body to permit individuals to exercise that faculty. Taken as a whole, speech is many-sided and heterogeneous; straddling several areas simultaneously—physical, physiological, and psychological—it belongs both to the individual and to society; we cannot put it into any category of human facts, for we cannot discover its unity."

Yet, all human beings do learn a language, and the findings of the last decade of research are encouraging. Joseph Greenberg (1963, 1966) and his associates (see the various issues of *Working Papers on Language Universals*, the results of Stanford University's Language Universals Project under Greenberg's leadership) have made some particularly important advances in the study of linguistic universals. So the next few decades of research may just reveal some of those elusive linguistic universals. Perhaps we are all like the child who told his father he couldn't see any differences between boys and girls, to which the father responded, "The differences are there— if you don't see them, you're just not looking in the right places." We may not yet be looking in all the right places for linguistic universals.

Language and Thought

The relationship between language and thought poses thorny issues and questions. For years researchers have probed the relationship between language and cognition. The behavioristic view that cognition is too mentalistic to be studied by the scientific method is diametrically opposed to such positions as that of Piaget, who claims that cognitive development is at the very center of the human organism and that language is dependent upon and springs from cognitive development. Others choose to emphasize the influence of language on cognitive development. Jerome Bruner (Bruner, Olver, and Greenfield 1966), for example, singled out sources of language-influenced intellectual development: words shaping concepts, dialogues between parent and child or teacher and child serving to orient and educate, and other sources. It is clear that the research of the past decade has pointed to the fact that cognitive and linguistic development are inextricably intertwined with dependencies in both directions.

One of the champions of the position that language affects thought was Benjamin Whorf, who with Edward Sapir formed the well-known Sapir-Whorf hypothesis of linguistic relativity—namely, that each language imposes on its speaker a particular "world view." According to Whorf (1956:213-14):

> We dissect nature along lines laid down by our native languages. The categories and types that we isolate from the world of phenomena we do not find there because they stare every observer in the face; on the contra-

ry, the world is presented in a kaleidoscopic flux of impressions which has to be organized by our minds—and this means largely by the linguistic systems in our minds. We cut nature up, organize it into concepts, and ascribe significances as we do, largely because we are parties to an agreement to organize it in this way—an agreement that holds through our speech community and is codified in the patterns of our language.

The issue at stake in child language acquisition is to determine *how* thought affects language, *how* language affects thought, and *how* linguists can best describe and account for the interaction of the two. Once again we probe the issue of how best to explain both the forms *and* the functions of a language. And again we do not have complete answers. But we do know that language is a way of life, is at the foundation of our being, and interacts simultaneously with thoughts and feelings.

The Role of Imitation

The final three issues focus on more practical questions with answers perhaps not so far removed from possibility as the first five issues presented here.

It is a common, informal observation that children are "good imitators." We think of children typically as imitators and mimics, and then conclude that imitation is one of the important strategies a child uses in the acquisition of language. That conclusion is not inaccurate on a global level. Indeed, research has shown that *echoing* is a particularly salient strategy in early language learning, and an important aspect of early phonological acquisition. Moreover, imitation is consonant with behavioristic principles of language acquisition—principles relevant, at least, to the earliest stages.

But it is important to ask what type of imitation is implied. Behaviorists assume one type of imitation, but there is a deeper level of imitation that is far more important in the process of language acquisition. The first type is surface-structure imitation, where a person repeats or mimics the surface strings, attending to a phonological code rather than a semantic code. It is this level of imitation that enables an adult to repeat random numbers or nonsense syllables, or even to mimic unknown languages. The semantic data, if any, underlying the surface output are neither internalized nor attended to. In foreign language classes, rote pattern drills often evoke surface imitation: a repetition of sounds by the student without the vaguest understanding of what the sounds might possibly mean. The earliest stages of child language acquisition may manifest a good deal of surface imitation, since the baby may not possess the necessary semantic categories to assign "meaning" to utterances. But as the child perceives the importance of the semantic level of language, he attends primarily if not exclusively to that meaningful semantic level—the deep structure of language. He engages in deep-structure imitation. In fact, the imitation of the deep structure of language can literally block his attention to the surface structure so that he becomes, on the face of it, a poor imitator. Consider the following conversation as recorded by McNeill (1966:69);

Child: Nobody don't like me.
Mother: No, say "nobody likes me."
Child: Nobody don't like me.
       (eight repetitions of this dialogue)

    .
    .
    .

Mother: No, now listen carefully; say "nobody likes me."
Child: Oh! Nobody don't likes me.

You can imagine the frustration of both mother and child, for the mother was attending to a rather technical, surface grammatical distinction, and yet the child sought to derive some meaning value. Finally the child perceived some sort of surface distinction between what he was saying and what his mother was saying and made what he thought was an appropriate change.

A similar case in point occurred one day when the teacher of an elementary-school class asked her pupils to write a few sentences on a piece of paper, to which one rather shy pupil responded, "Ain't got no pencil." Disturbed at this nonstandard response the teacher embarked on a barrage of corrective models for the child: "I don't have *any* pencils, you don't have a pencil, they don't have pencils, . . . " When the teacher finally ended her monologue of patterns, the intimated and bewildered child said, "Ain't *nobody* got no pencils?" The teacher's purpose was lost on this child because he too was attending to language as a meaningful and communicative tool, and not to the question of whether certain forms were "correct" and others were not. The child, like all children, was attending to the *truth value* of the utterance.

Research has also shown that children, when explicitly asked to repeat a sentence in a test situation, will often repeat the correct underlying deep structure with a change in the surface rendition. For example, sentences like "The ball that is rolling down the hill is black" and "The boy who's in the sandbox is wearing a red shirt" tend to be repeated back by preschool children as "The black ball is rolling down the hill" and "The red boy is in the sandbox" (Brown 1970).

Children are excellent imitators. It is simply a matter of understanding exactly what it is that they are imitating.

The Role of Practice

Closely related to the notion of imitation is a somewhat broader question, the nature of *practice* in child language. Do children practice their language? If so, how? What is the role of the *frequency* of hearing and producing items in the acquisition of those items? It is common to observe children and conclude that they "practice" language constantly, especially in the early stages of single-word and two-word utterances. A behavioristic model of first language acquisition would claim that practice—repetition and association—is the key to the formation of habits by operant conditioning.

One unique form of practice by a child is recorded by Ruth Weir (1962). She found that her children produced rather long monologues in bed at night before going to sleep. Here is one example:

> *What color*
> *What color blanket*
> *What color mop*
> *What color glass*
> *Mommy's home sick*
> *Mommy's home sick*
> *Where's Mommy home sick*
> *Where's Mikey sick*
> *Mikey sick*

Such monologues are not uncommon among children whose inclination it is to "play" with language just as they do with all objects and events around them. Weir's data show far more structural patterning than has commonly been found in other data. Nevertheless, children's practice seems to be a key to language acquisition.

Practice is usually thought of as referring to speaking only. But one can also think in terms of comprehension practice, which is often considered under the rubric of the *frequency* of linguistic input to the child. Is the acquisition of particular words or structures directly attributable to their frequency in the child's linguistic environment? There is evidence that certain highly frequent forms are acquired first:

wnat questions, irregular past-tense forms, certain common household items and persons. Brown and Hanlon (1970), for example, found that the frequency of occurrence of a linguistic item in the speech of mothers was an overwhelmingly strong predictor of the order of emergence of those items in their children's speech.

There are some conflicting data, however. Telegraphic speech is one case in point. Some of the most frequently occurring words in the language are omitted in such two- and three-word utterances. And McNeill (1968:416) found that a Japanese child produced the Japanese postposition *ga* far more frequently and more correctly than another contrasting postposition *wa*, even though her mother was recorded as using *wa* twice as often as *ga*. McNeill attributed this finding to the fact that *ga* as a subject marker is of more importance, grammatically, to the child, and she therefore acquired the use of that item since it was more meaningful on a deep-structure level. Another feasible explanation, however, for that finding might lie in the easier pronunciation of *ga*.

The jury is still out on the frequency issue. Nativists who claim that "the relative frequency of stimuli is of little importance in language acquisition" (Wardhaugh 1971:12) might, in the face of evidence thus far, be more cautious in their claims. It would appear that frequency of *meaningful* occurrence may well be a more precise refinement of the notion of frequency.

Parental Input

The role of the parents' language in the child's acquisition of language is undeniably crucial. Just as the parents' influence on the child cognitively and affectively is of immeasurable importance, such is also the case in language. Whatever one's position is on the innateness of language, the speech that young children hear is primarily the speech heard in the home, and much of that speech is parental speech or the speech of older siblings. Linguists once claimed that most adult speech is basically semigrammatical (full of performance variables), and that the child is exposed to a chaotic sample of language and only his innate capacities can account for his successful acquisition of language. McNeill, for example, wrote: "The speech of adults from which a child discovers the locally appropriate manifestation of the linguistic universals is a completely random, haphazard sample, in no way contrived to instruct the child on grammar" (1966:73). However, Labov (1970:42) noted that on the basis of his studies the presumed ungrammaticality of everyday speech appears to be a myth, really. Bellugi and Brown (1964) and Drach

(1969) found that the speech addressed to children was carefully grammatical and lacked the usual hesitations and false starts common in adult-to-adult speech. Landes' (1975) summary of a wide range of research on parental input supported their conclusions. Since then, other evidence has accrued to demonstrate the selectivity of parental linguistic input to their children.

At the same time it will be remembered that children react very consistently to the deep structure and the communicative function of language, and they do not react overtly to expansions and grammatical corrections as in the "nobody likes me" dialogue quoted above. Such input is largely ignored unless there is some *truth* or *falsity* which the child can attend to. Thus, if the child says "Dat Harry" and the parent says "No, that's *John*," the child might readily correct himself and say "Oh, dat *John*." But what Landes and others are showing is that in the long run the child will, after consistent, repeated models in meaningful contexts, eventually transfer correct forms to his own speech and thus correct "dat" to "that's."

The importance of the issue lies in the fact that it is clear from more recent research that adult and peer input to the child is far more important than nativists earlier might have believed. Adult input seems to shape the child's acquisition, and the interaction patterns between child and parent change according to the increasing language skill of the child. Nurture and environment in this case are tremendously important, though it remains to be seen just how important parental input is as a proportion of total input.

A number of theories and issues in child language have been explored in this chapter with the purpose of briefly characterizing both the current state of child language research and of highlighting a few of the key concepts which emerge in the formation of an understanding of how babies learn to talk and eventually become sophisticated linguistic beings. There is much to be learned in such an understanding. Every human being who attempts to learn a *second* language has already learned a *first* language. It is said that the second time around on something is always easier. In the case of language this is not true. But in order to understand why it is not, you need to understand the nature of that initial acquisition process, for it may be that some of the keys to the mystery are found therein. That search is continued in the next chapter as we compare and contrast first and second language acquisition.

SUGGESTED READINGS

It would be valuable to read a synopsis of *Skinner*'s (1957) classic work (the whole volume itself is interesting but time-consuming reading). *DeVito* (1971) summarized Skinner, as do a number of introductory books in psychology. *Chomsky*'s (1959) review of Skinner, followed by *MacCorquodale*'s (1970) belated response to Chomsky are both heavy reading but they are eloquent defenses of two contrasting points of view.

Lenneberg (1964) summarized the biological argument for first language acquisition, a point of view which *McNeill* (1968) expanded upon. McNeill also gave a biased but convincing argument against behavioristic theories of language acquisition.

Linguistic and cognitive approaches to the study of first language acquisition are aptly capsulized in *Bloom* (1976), though Bloom's arguments were weighted on the cognitive side of the continuum. Chapter 5 of *Slobin* (1971) also summarized the advantages of a cognitive approach.

Most of the first language acquisition issues dealt with in this chapter are treated in textbooks on child language. A comprehensive treatment of child language acquisition is given by *Clark and Clark* (1977), and *Menyuk* (1971). Other useful general references in child language acquisition are *Bar Adon and Leopold* (1971), *Brown* (1973), and *Bloom* (1978). For more specific information on particular topics, consult the references already given in the chapter.

Berko's (1958) classic study on the child's learning of English morphology is recommended reading. You might want to try to replicate or simulate her study with some young children and see what results you can get.

TOPICS AND QUESTIONS FOR STUDY
AND DISCUSSION

1. Why is it that behavioristic theories can account sufficiently well for the earliest utterances of the child, but not for utterances at the sentence and discourse level? Do nativistic and cognitive approaches provide the necessary tools for accounting for those later, more complex utterances?

2. If you can, try to record samples of young children's speech. A child of about 3 is an ideal subject for you to observe in the study of a human being's growing competence in a language. Transcribe a segment of your recording and see if, inductively, you can determine some of the rules the child is using.

3. Briefly describe the continuum of behavioristic, nativistic, cognitive, and discourse approaches to the study of child language acquisition. In what way do discourse approaches cycle back, in part, to behavioristic approaches?

4. Why do you think Chomsky insisted on weeding out "performance variables" in analyzing language? What does the theorist gain from examining only the "idealized" speaker-hearer? What does he lose?

5. Competence and performance are difficult to define. In what sense are they interdependent? Suppose, for example, that an accomplished pianist suffers an accident in which his hands are cut off: does the pianist still possess the *competence* to play his favorite Mozart concerto? If a person suffers brain damage and can no longer talk, does he still have the competence to talk?

6. Do you think comprehension and production are two separate modes of competence? In what way are they distinctly related? Cite examples supporting their possible unrelatedness.

7. Explain the essential difference between what is referred to as the *forms* of language and the *functions* of language. To which aspect does the child give more conscious attention?

8. The frequency of a linguistic item in the child's input may or may not be an important factor in determining acquisition. What is meant, though, by saying that "frequency of *meaningful* occurrence may well be a more precise refinement of the notion of frequency" (p. 37)?

9. If you can, engage a young child in a conversation and try from time to time to make subtle *grammatical* corrections of his childlike forms. How does the child respond to the corrections?

10. Can you think of ways in which language changes or shapes the thinking of elementary-school children?

3

Comparing and Contrasting First and Second Language Acquisition

The increased pace of research on first language acquisition over the last two decades has attracted the attention not only of linguists of all kinds but also of educators in various language-related fields. In language arts education, for example, it is not uncommon to find teacher trainees studying first language acquisition, particularly acquisition after age 5, in order to improve their understanding of the task of teaching language skills to native speakers. In foreign language education most standard texts and curricula now include some introductory material in first language acquisition. The reasons for this are clear: we have all observed children acquiring their first language easily and well, yet the learning of a second language, particularly in an educational setting, often meets with great difficulty and sometimes failure. We should therefore be able to learn something from a systematic study of that first language learning experience.

What may not be quite as obvious, though, is how the second language teacher should interpret the hundreds of facets of first language research and theory. How does each facet relate to second language learning and teaching? It would be conceivable at this point simply to ask you to make your own interpretations and draw your own conclusions about the implications of theories and research in first language acquisition. But that very process of interpretation invokes so many thorny issues that it is easy to draw false analogies.

The purpose of this chapter is to set forth explicitly some of the parameters for comparing and contrasting the two types of language acquisition.

The first step in that interpretation process might be to dispel some myths about the relationship between first and second language acquisition. H. H. Stern (1970:57-58) summarized some common arguments that have cropped up from time to time to recommend a second language teaching method or procedure on the basis of first language acquisition:

1. In language teaching, we must practice and practice, again and again. Just watch a small child learning his mother tongue. He repeats things over and over again. During the language-learning stage he practices all the time. This is what we must also do when we learn a foreign language.
2. Language learning is mainly a matter of imitation. You must be a mimic. Just like a small child. He imitates everything.
3. First, we practice the separate sounds, then words, then sentences. That is the natural order and is therefore right for learning a foreign language.
4. Watch a small child's speech development. First he listens, then he speaks. Understanding always precedes speaking. Therefore, this must be the right order of presenting the skills in a foreign language.
5. A small child listens and speaks and no one would dream of making him read or write. Reading and writing are advanced stages of language development. The natural order for first and second language learning is listening, speaking, reading, writing.
6. You did not have to translate when you were small. If you were able to learn your own language without translation, you should be able to learn a foreign language in the same way.
7. A small child simply uses language. He does not learn formal grammar. You don't tell him about verbs and nouns. Yet he learns the language perfectly. It is equally unnecessary to use grammatical conceptualization in teaching a foreign language.

These statements represent the views of those who felt that "the first language learner was looked upon as the foreign language teacher's dream: a pupil who mysteriously laps up his vocabulary, whose pronunciation, in spite of occasional lapses, is impeccable, while morphology and syntax, instead of being a constant headache, come to him like a dream" (ibid., p. 58). The statements also tend to represent the views of those who have been dominated by a behavioristic theory of language in which the first language acquisition process is viewed as consisting of rote practice, habit formation, shaping, overlearning, reinforcement, conditioning, association, stimulus and response, and who therefore assume that the second language learning process involves the same constructs.

There are flaws in each view. Sometimes the flaw is in the assumption behind the statement about first language learning and sometimes it is in the analogy or implication that is drawn; sometimes it is in both. The flaws represent some of the misunderstandings that need to be demythologized for the second language teacher. The process of demythologizing requires a broad understanding of first language theory and issues, as well as a keen awareness of the variables that come into play in drawing analogies to second language learning. By characterizing and classifying those variables in this chapter I hope that you will be able, on the one hand, to avoid the pitfalls of these and other false assumptions and analogies, and on the other hand, to draw enlightened, plausible analogies wherever possible, thereby enriching your understanding of the second language learning process itself.

As generative and cognitive research on first language acquisition gathered momentum, second language researchers and foreign language teachers began to recognize the mistakes in drawing direct global analogies between first and second language acquisition. Some of the first warning signals were sent up by the cognitive psychologist David Ausubel (1964). In foreboding terms, Ausubel outlined a number of glaring problems with the very popular audiolingual method, some of whose procedures were derived from notions of "natural" (first) language learning. He warned that the rote learning practice of audiolingual drills lacked the meaningfulness necessary for successful first and second language acquisition, that adults learning a foreign language could, with their full cognitive capacities, benefit from deductive presentations of grammar, that the native language of the learner is not just an interfering factor—it can *facilitate* learning a second language, that the written form of the language could be beneficial, that students could be overwhelmed by language spoken at its "natural speed" and that they, like children, could benefit from more deliberative speech from the teacher. These warnings were derived from Ausubel's cognitive perspective, which ran counter to prevailing behavioristic paradigms on which the audiolingual method was based. But Ausubel's criticism may have been too far ahead of its time, for in 1964 few teachers were ready to entertain doubts about the widely accepted method. (See Chapter Twelve for a further discussion of the audiolingual method.)

By the late 1960s and early 70s generative linguistics was becoming the accepted theoretical mode of thinking, and criticism of earlier direct analogies between first and second language acquisition was mounting. Stern's (1970) article, along with articles by Jakobovits (1968), Cook (1969, 1973), Macnamara (1975), and others began to address the inconsistencies of direct analogies between first and second language learning, but at the same time recognized the legitimate similarities which, if viewed cautiously, allowed one to draw some constructive conclusions about second language learning.

TYPES OF COMPARISON AND CONTRAST

All too often the comparison of first and second language acquisition has been quite carelessly treated. At the very least, one needs to approach the comparison procedure by first considering the differences between *children* and *adults*. It is, in one sense, rather illogical to compare the first language acquisition of a child with the second language acquisition of an adult. This involves trying to draw analogies not only between first and second language learning situations but also between children and adults. It is much more logical to compare first and second language learning in children, or to compare second language learning in children and adults. Nevertheless, child first language acquisition and adult second language acquisition are common and important categories of acquisition to compare. It is reasonable, therefore, to view the latter type of comparison within a matrix of possible comparisons. The figure below represents four possible categories to compare, defined by age and type of acquisition. Note that the vertical shaded line between the "child" and "adult" is "fuzzy" to allow for varying definitions of adulthood. It is generally understood, however, that an adult is one who has reached the age of puberty.

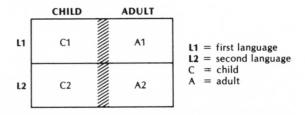

Figure 3-1. First and second language acquisition in adults and children.

Cell A1 is clearly representative of an abnormal situation. There have been few recorded instances of an adult acquiring his first language. Curtiss (1977) has written about Genie, a 13-year-old girl who had been socially isolated all her life until she was discovered, and who was faced with the task of acquiring a first language. Accounts of "wolf children" and other instances of severe retardation fall into this category. Since it is not imperative at this time to deal with abnormal or pathological cases of language acquisition, we can ignore category A1.

That leaves three possible comparisons: C1-C2, C2-A2, and C1-A2. For the sake of considering issues in this chapter the three comparisons will be referred to by type:

Type 1 comparison: first and second language acquisition in children (C1-C2), holding age constant

Type 2 comparison: second language acquisition in children and adults (C2-A2), holding second language constant

Type 3 comparison: first language acquisition in children and second language acquisition in adults (C1-A2)

In the first type of comparison, holding age constant, one is manipulating the language variable. It is important to remember, however, that a 3-year-old and a 9-year-old—both children by definition—exhibit vast cognitive, affective, and physical differences, and that comparisons of all three types must be treated with caution when varying ages of children are being considered. In the second type of comparison one is manipulating the differences between children and adults. In the third type of comparison, of course, both variables are being manipulated. Most of the traditional comparisons have been of Type 3, and such comparisons are difficult to make because of the enormous cognitive, affective, and physical differences between children and adults. That is not to say that Type 3 comparisons ought to be avoided entirely; some valuable insights are to be gained from such comparisons.

DOMAINS OF COMPARISON AND CONTRAST

One way to approach the content of this chapter might be to examine issues within the three types outlined above. A potentially more fruitful approach is taken, however, and that is to consider all three types of comparisons within four general domains of comparison and contrast. In so doing psychological and linguistic issues form the central focus, with types of comparisons serving as subcategories within each domain. The four domains that have been chosen include the three within which educational psychologists have traditionally operated—the physical cognitive, and affective domains—plus a fourth, the linguistic domain. The linguistic domain obviously cuts across all three of the traditional domains, but the separate category seems appropriate for capturing some issues that are unique and otherwise difficult to categorize.

The Physical Domain

The physical domain is a particularly important one in comparisons of Types 2 and 3. Language acquisition has little to do with physical size, large-muscle growth and coordination, body functions, and the like, but it has a lot to do with the brain and the coordination of several hundred small muscles controlling the articulation of speech as well as reading and writing. We will deal in this section with neurological issues and the articulation of speech.

Discussions of first and second language acquisition differences often center on the question of whether there is a *critical period* for language acquisition—a biologically determined period of life when language can be acquired most easily and beyond which time language is increasingly difficult to acquire. Often such discussions involve probing the nature of neurological development. Does the maturation of the brain at some point spell the doom of language acquisition ability? Some scholars have singled out the *lateralization* of the brain as the key to answering such a question. There is evidence in neurological research that as the human brain matures certain functions are assigned to the left hemisphere of the brain and certain other functions to the right hemisphere. Intellectual, logical, and analytic functions appear to be largely located in the left hemisphere while the right hemisphere controls functions related to emotional and social needs. Language functions appear to be controlled mainly in the left hemisphere, though there is a good deal of conflicting evidence. For example, patients who have had left hemispherectomies have been capable of comprehending and producing an amazing amount of language (see Zangwill 1971:220). But generally speaking, a stroke or accident victim who suffers a lesion in the left hemisphere will manifest some degree of language impairment, and such is generally not the case with right-hemisphere lesions.

While one interesting question concerns whether or not language is lateralized and if it is, *how* it is lateralized, the question here is, if language is indeed lateralized, when does this lateralization take place? And how, if at all, does that lateralization affect language acquisition? Eric Lenneberg (1967) and others have suggested that lateralization is a slow process that begins around the age of 2 and is completed around puberty. During this time the child is neurologically assigning functions little by little to one side of the brain or the other; included in these functions, of course, is language. And it has been found that children up to the age of puberty who suffer injury to the left hemisphere are able to relocalize linguistic functions to the right hemisphere, to "relearn" their first language with relatively little impairment. Thomas Scovel (1969) extended these findings to propose a relationship between lateralization and *second* language acquisition. He suggested that the plasticity of the brain prior to puberty enables the child to acquire not only his first language but also a second language, and that possibly it is the very accomplishment of lateralization that makes it difficult for a person to be able ever again to easily acquire fluent control of a second language, or at least to acquire it with what Alexander Guiora et al. (1972a) call "authentic" (nativelike) pronunciation.

While Scovel's suggestion had only marginal experimental basis, it was a suggestion that prompted other researchers to take a careful look at neurological factors in first and second language acquisition with respect to all three types of comparisons. This research has considered the possibility that there is a critical period not only for first language acquisition but also, by extension, for second language acquisition. Much of the neurological argument centers on the *time* of lateralization. While Lenneberg (1967) contended that lateralization is complete around puberty, Norman Geschwind (1970), among others, suggested a much earlier age. Stephen Krashen (1973) believed that the development of lateralization may be complete around age 5. Krashen's suggestion does not grossly conflict with research on first language acquisition if one considers "fluency" in the first language to be achieved by age 5. But Krashen's findings do not square with Scovel's suggestion that lateralization accounts for the inability of persons to acquire fluent, authentic pronunciation of a second language, since we know that children of age 5 on through puberty generally acquire authentic pronunciation of a second language.

We know, too, that some adults—after the age of puberty—have acquired authentic control of a second language. Anthropologist Jane Hill (1970) provided one of the most interesting answers to Scovel's proposal by citing anthropological research on non-Western societies yielding evidence that adults can, in the normal course of their lives, acquire second languages perfectly. One unique instance of second language acquisition in adulthood was reported by Sorenson (1967), who studied the Tukano tribes of South America. At least two dozen languages are spoken among these peoples, and each tribal group, identified by the language it speaks, is an exogamous unit—people must marry outside their group, and hence almost always marry someone who speaks another language. Sorenson reported that during adolescence individuals actively and almost suddenly begin to speak two or three other languages to which they have been exposed at some point. Moreover, "in adulthood [a person] may acquire more languages; as he approaches old age, field observation indicates, he will go on to perfect his knowledge of all the languages at his disposal" (Sorenson 1967:678). In conclusion Hill (1970:247-48) suggests that

> the language acquisition situation seen in adult language learners in the largely monolingual American English middle class speech communities ... may have been inappropriately taken to be a universal situation in proposing an innatist explanation for adult foreign accents. Multilingual speech communities of various types deserve careful study.... We will have to explore the influence of social and cultural roles which language and phonation play, and the role which attitudes about language play, as an alternative or a supplement to the cerebral dominance theory as an explanation of adult foreign accents.

Hill's suggestion has been followed in more recent years. Today researchers are examining the cognitive and affective domains for more relevant evidence of a "critical period," and are less hopeful of finding evidence in the neurological field—a field that remains as much a mystery today as it was a decade ago. More is said about cognitive and affective research in the next two sections of this chapter, and in Chapter Seven I venture to define a culturally based critical period for second language acquisition.

A second area within the physical domain that is significant to touch on is the role of the coordination of "speech muscles" in second language acquisition. We all know that great athletes, great musicians, and others who have become accomplished in a set of skills requiring muscular dexterity have almost always begun to develop that skill in childhood, probably before the age of puberty. We can also appreciate the fact that given the existence of several hundred muscles that are used in the articulation of human speech (throat, larynx, mouth, lips, tongue, and other muscles), a tremendous degree of muscular control is required to achieve the fluency of a native speaker of a language. The physical development of the child must be considered carefully in Type 1 comparisons. At birth the speech muscles are developed only to the extent that the larynx can control sustained cries. These speech muscles gradually develop, and control of some complex sounds in certain languages (in English the *r* and *l* are typical) sometimes is not achieved until after age 5, though virtually complete phonemic control is present in most 5-year-old children. Children who acquire a second language after the age of 5 may have a physical advantage in that phonemic control of a second language is physically possible yet that mysterious plasticity is still present.

Comparisons of Types 2 and 3 may be more significant than Type 1 comparisons in considering the role of muscular coordination. If it is indeed true, and it appears to be so, that starting a physical skill at a young age is advantageous, the same should clearly be true of language with respect to pronunciation of a language. It is no wonder that children acquire authentic pronunciation while adults generally do not, since pronunciation involves the control of so many muscles.

Research on the acquisition of authentic control of the *phonology* of a foreign language supports the notion of a critical period. The evidence thus far indicates that persons beyond the age of puberty do not generally acquire authentic pronunciation of the second language. Such a critical period may have little to do with the lateralization of the brain, though, and much to do with the child's neuromuscular plasticity. Of course, you can cite immediate exceptions to this rule—adults who, well after puberty, learned a second language and now speak it flawlessly. (You can also cite cases of athletes or musicians who started developing their skill relatively late in life and became very proficient.) These, however, appear to be isolated instances. But what is tantalizingly interesting about the isolated instances is that those special people possess somewhere within their competence the ability to override and overcome the general tendency to be less than perfect in the pronunciation of a foreign language. If we could only discover what those unique properties are!

It is important to remember in all these considerations that pronunciation of a language is not by any means the sole criterion for acquisition, nor is it really the most important one. We all know people who have less than perfect pronunciation but who also have magnificent and fluent control of a second language, control that can even exceed that of many native speakers. So, muscular coordination may be of minimal significance in establishing criteria for overall successful acquisition of a second language. The acquisition of the communicative and functional purposes of language is far more important.

All three types of comparisons relate to the cognitive domain of human behavior. Human cognition develops rapidly throughout the first sixteen years of life and less rapidly after adulthood. Some of these changes are critical, others are more gradual and difficult to detect. Jean Piaget outlines the course of intellectual development in a child through various stages: the sensorimotor stage from ages 0 to 2, the preoperational stage from ages 2 to 7, and the operational stage from ages 7 to 16, with a crucial change from the concrete operational stage to the formal operational stage around the age of 11. The most critical stage for a consideration of first and second language acquisition appears to occur, in Piaget's outline, at puberty. It is here that a person becomes capable of abstraction, of formal thinking which transcends concrete experience and direct perception. Cognitively, then, you can make a strong argument for a critical period of language acquisition by connecting language acquisition and the concrete/formal stage transition.

Ausubel (1964) hinted at the relevance of such a connection in noting that adults learning a second language could profit from certain grammatical explanations and deductive thinking that obviously would be pointless for a child. Whether adults do in fact profit from such explanations depends, of course, on the suitability and efficiency of the explanation, the teacher, the context, and other pedagogical variables. We have observed, though, that children do learn second languages well *without* the benefit—or hindrance—of formal operational thought. Adults, possessing superior cognitive capacity, often do not successfully learn a second language. Is this capacity, then, a facilitating or inhibiting effect on language acquisition? Ellen Rosansky (1975:96) offers an explanation noting that initial language acquisition takes place when the child is highly "centered": "He is not only egocentric at this time, but when faced with a problem he can focus (and then only fleetingly) on one dimension at a time. This lack of flexibility and lack of decentration may well be a necessity for language acquisition." The young child is generally not "aware" that he is acquiring a language, nor is he aware of societal values and attitudes placed on one language or another. It is said that "a watched pot never boils"; is it possible that a language learner who is too consciously aware of what he is doing will have difficulty in learning the second language?

You may be tempted to answer that question affirmatively, but there is both logical and anecdotal counterevidence. Logically, a superior intellect should facilitate what is in one sense an intellectual activity. Anecdotal evidence shows that some adults who have been successful language learners have been very much aware of the process they were going through, even to the point of utilizing self-made paradigms and other fabricated linguistic devices to facilitate the learning process. So, if it is true that mature cognition is a liability to successful second language acquisition, clearly some intervening variables are allowing some persons to be quite successful second-language learners after puberty. These variables may in most cases lie outside the cognitive domain entirely, perhaps more centrally in the affective—or, emotional—domain.

The lateralization hypothesis may provide another key to cognitive differences between child and adult language acquisition. As the child matures into adulthood, the left hemisphere (which controls the analytical and intellectual functions) becomes more dominant than the right hemisphere (which controls the emotional functions). It is possible that the dominance of the left hemisphere contributes to a tendency to overanalyze and to be too intellectually centered on the task of second language learning.

Another construct that should be considered in examining the cognitive domain is the Piagetian notion of *equilibration*. Equilibration is defined as "progressive interior organization of knowledge in a stepwise fashion" (Sullivan 1967:12), and is related to the concept of equilibrium. That is, cognition develops as a process of moving from states of doubt and uncertainty (disequilibrium) to states of resolution and certainty (equilibrium) and then back to further doubt which is, in time, also resolved. And so the cycle continues. Piaget claimed that conceptual development is a process of progressively moving from states of disequilibrium to equilibrium and that periods of disequilibrium mark virtually all cognitive development up through age 14 or 15, when formal operations finally are firmly organized and equilibrium is reached.

It is conceivable that disequilibrium may provide the key motivation for language acquisition: language interacts with cognition to achieve equilibrium. Perhaps until that state of final equilibrium is reached, the child is cognitively ready and eager to acquire the language necessary for achieving the cognitive equilibrium of adulthood. That same child is, until that time, decreasingly tolerant of cognitive ambiguities. Children are amazingly indifferent to contradictions, but intellectual growth produces an awareness of ambiguities about them and heightens the need for resolution. Perhaps a general intolerance of contradictions produces an acute awareness of the myriad of differences between two languages and thus perhaps around the age of 14 of 15, the prospect of learning a second language suddenly becomes overwhelming, discouraging the learner from proceeding a step at a time as a younger child would do.

The final consideration in the cognitive domain is the distinction which Ausubel makes between *rote* and *meaningful* learning. Ausubel notes that people of all ages have little need for rote, mechanistic learning that is not related to existing knowledge and experience. Rather, most items are acquired by meaningful learning, by anchoring and relating new items and experiences to knowledge that exists in the cognitive framework. It is a myth to contend that children are good rote learners, that they make good use of meaningless repetition and mimicking. We have already seen in Chapter Two that children's practice and imitation is a very meaningful activity that is contextualized and purposeful. Adults, actually, have developed greater concentration and so have greater ability for rote learning; but rote learning is usually used only for short-term memory or for somewhat artificial purposes. Here, then, one can make a legitimate Type 3 comparison: both adults and children utilize primarily meaningful learning operations. By inference, we may conclude that the foreign language classroom should not become the locus of excessive rote activity—rote drills, pattern practice without context, reciting rules, and other activities that are not in the context of meaningful communication. It is interesting to note that Type 3 comparisons almost always refer in the case of adults (A2), to the *classroom* learning of a second language, but many foreign language classrooms utilize an excessive number of rote-learning procedures. So, naturally if you compare adults learning a foreign language by rote methods with children learning their first language in a natural, meaningful context, you will claim the superiority of the child's learning! The cause of such superiority may not be in the *age* of the person, but in the *context* of learning. The child happens to be learning language meaningfully and the adult is not.

The cognitive domain holds yet other areas of interest for comparing first and second language acquisition. These areas will be treated more fully in Chapters Four and Five. We turn now to what may be the most complex, yet the most illuminating of the four domains: the affective domain.

The Affective Domain

Human beings are emotional creatures. At the heart of all thought and meaning and action is emotion. As "intellectual" as we would like to think we are, we are influenced by our emotions. It is only logical, then, to look at the affective (emotional) domain for some of the most significant answers to the problems of contrasting the differences between first and second language acquisition. Research on the affective domain in second language acquisition has been mounting steadily for a number of years. This research has been inspired by a number of factors. Not the least of these is the fact that linguistic theory is now asking the deepest possible questions about human language, with some linguists and applied linguists examining the inner being of the person to discover if in the affective side of human behavior there lies an explanation to the mysteries of language. A lengthy treatment of affective variables in second language acquisition is provided in Chapters Six and Seven; in this chapter it is important to take a brief look at selected affective factors as they relate to the first and second language issue.

The affective domain includes many factors: empathy, self-esteem, extroversion, inhibition, imitation, anxiety, attitudes—the list could go on for some time. Some of these may seem at first rather far removed from language learning, but when you consider the pervasive nature of language, any affective factor can conceivably be relevant to second language learning.

A case in point is the role of egocentricity in human development. The very young child is totally egocentric. The world revolves about him and he sees all events as focusing on himself. The small baby at first does not even distinguish a separation between himself and the world around him. A rattle held in his hand, for example, is simply an inseparable extension of himself as long as he grasps it; when he drops it or loses sight of it, it ceases to exist. As the child grows older he becomes more aware of himself, more self-conscious as he seeks both to define and understand his self-identity. In pre-adolescence the child develops an acute consciousness of himself as a separate and identifiable entity, but an entity which, in his still-wavering insecurity, needs protecting. He therefore develops *inhibitions* about this self-identity, fearing to expose too much self-doubt. At puberty these inhibitions are heightened in the trauma of undergoing critical physical, cognitive, and emotional changes. The adolescent must acquire a totally new physical, cognitive, and emotional identity. His ego is affected not only in how he understands himself but also in how he reaches out beyond himself, how he relates to others socially, and how he uses the communicative process to bring on affective equilibrium.

Alexander Guiora, a researcher in the study of personality variables in second language learning, proposed what he called the *language ego* (Guiora et al. 1972b) to account for the identity a person develops in reference to the language he speaks. For any monolingual person the language ego involves the interaction of the native language and ego development. Your self-identity is inextricably bound up with your language, for it is in the communicative process—the process of sending out messages and having them "bounced" back—that such identities are confirmed, shaped, and reshaped. Guiora suggested that the language ego may account for the difficulties that adults have in learning a second language. The child's ego is dynamic and growing and flexible through the age of puberty, and thus a new language at this stage does not pose a substantial "threat" or inhibition to the ego and adaptation is made relatively easily as long as there are not undue confounding sociocultural factors such as, for example, a damaging attitude toward a language or language group at a young age. However, the simultaneous physical, emotional, and cognitive changes of puberty give rise to a defensive mechanism in which the language ego becomes protective and defensive. The language ego clings to the security of the native language to protect the fragile ego of the young adult. The language ego, which has now become part and parcel of self-identity, is threatened, and thus a context develops in which you must be willing literally to make a fool of yourself in the trial-and-error struggle of speaking and understanding a foreign language. Younger children are less frightened because they are less aware of language *forms*, and the possibility of making mistakes on those forms—mistakes that one really must make in an attempt to communicate spontaneously—does not concern them greatly.

It is no wonder, then, that the acquisition of a new language ego is an enormous undertaking, not only for young adolescents but also for an adult who has grown comfortable and secure in his own identity, and who possesses inhibitions which serve as a wall of defensive protection around the ego. Making the leap to a new or second identity is no simple matter; it can be successful only when one musters the necessary ego strength to overcome inhibitions. It is possible that the successful adult language learner is someone who can bridge this affective gap. Some of the seeds of success might be sown early in life. In a bilingual setting, for example, if a child has already learned one second language in childhood, then affectively, learning a third language might represent much less of a threat. Or such seeds may be independent of a bilingual setting; they may simply arise out of whatever combination of nature and nurture makes for the development of a strong ego.

In Type 1 comparisons of first and second language acquisition, ego development and identification may be relevant factors. Preadolescent children of 9 or 10, for example, are beginning to develop inhibitions, and it is conceivable, though little research evidence is available, that children of this age who are exposed to a second language will have more difficulty in learning the second language than younger children. Type 2 and 3 comparisons are of course highly relevant. We know from both observational and research evidence that even mature adults are highly inhibited organisms, particularly in Western society. Again, cross-cultural research such as that reported by Hill (1970) is important to consider. These inhibitions surface in modern language classes where the learner's attempts to speak in the foreign language are often fraught with embarrassment. We have also observed the same inhibition in the "natural" setting (a non-classroom setting, such as a learner living in a foreign culture), though in such instances there is the likelihood that the necessity to communicate will soon override the inhibitions.

Other affective factors seem to hinge on the basic notion of ego identification. It would appear that the study of second language learning as the acquisition of a *second identity* might pose a fruitful and important issue in understanding not only some differences between child and adult first and second language learning, but second language learning in general (see Chapter Seven).

Another affectively related variable deserves mention here even though it will be given fuller consideration in Chapter Six: the role of *attitudes* in language learning. From the growing body of literature on attitudes, it seems clear that negative attitudes can affect success in learning a language. Very young children, however, who are not developed enough cognitively to possess "attitudes" toward races, cultures, ethnic groups, classes of people, and languages, are unaffected. Macnamara (1975:79) notes that "a child suddenly transported from Montreal to Berlin will rapidly learn German no matter what he thinks of the Germans." But as a child reaches school age, he also begins to acquire certain attitudes toward types and stereotypes of people. Most of these attitudes are "taught," consciously or unconsciously, by parents, other adults, and peers. The learning of negative attitudes toward the people who speak the second language or toward the second language itself has been shown to affect the success of language learning in persons from school age on up.

Finally, *peer pressure* is a particularly important variable in Type 2 and Type 3 comparisons. The peer pressure children encounter in language learning is quite unlike what the adult experiences. Children usually have strong constraints upon them to conform. They are told in words, thoughts, and actions that they had better "be like the rest of the kids." Such peer pressure extends to language. Adults experience some peer pressure, but of a different kind. Adults tend to tolerate linguistic differences more than children, and therefore errors in speech are more easily excused. If an adult can *understand* a second language speaker, for example, he will usually provide positive cognitive and affective feedback, a level of tolerance which might encourage some adult learners to "get by." Children are harsher critics of one another's actions and words and may thus provide a necessary and sufficient degree of pressure to learn the second language.

The Linguistic Domain

The linguistic "domain" is not a part of traditional categorizing of human behavior, but since language is such a specialized and pervading aspect of all of behavior and of all three previous domains, and since it is the very subject matter with which we are dealing, it deserves unique consideration. We have so far looked at the *organism* and considered a number of different types of comparisons; now we look at the subject matter itself. What are some of the *linguistic* differences between first and second language learning?

A growing number of research studies are now available to shed some light on the linguistic processes of second language learning, and how those processes differ between children and adults. A good deal of this research will be treated in Chapters Eight, Nine, and Ten, but at this point we can look briefly at some of the linguistic findings, particularly in the child's acquisition of a second language (Type 1 comparison).

It is clear that children learning two languages simultaneously acquire them by the use of similar strategies. They are, in essence, learning two first languages, and the key to success is in distinguishing separate contexts for the two languages. This children do with amazing dexterity. Usually there are two distinct contexts such as home/neighborhood, home/school, or mother/father. Children generally do not have difficulty discerning the separateness of such contexts, though sometimes acquisition in both languages is slightly slower than the normal schedule of first language acquisition. It was shown by Wallace Lambert (1962) that such bilingualism does *not* retard intelligence. If anything, bilinguals may be slightly superior; as Lambert notes, "they have a language asset, are more facile at concept formation, and have a greater mental flexibility" (p. 155).

Nonsimultaneous second language acquisition is difficult to define within the limits of childhood. One could refer to a child who is acquiring a second language soon after he has begun to learn his first language (say at age 3 or 4), or as late as age 10. For the most part, research confirms that the linguistic and cognitive processes of second language learning in children are in general similar to first language processes. Ravem (1968), Milon (1974), Natalicio and Natalicio (1971), Dulay and Burt (1974a), Ervin-Tripp (1974), and Hansen-Bede (1975), among others, concluded that similar strategies and linguistic features are present in both first and second language learning in children. Dulay and Burt (1974a) found, for example, that in an examination of over 500 errors made by Spanish-speaking children learning English, 86 percent of the errors reflected normal developmental characteristics—that is, expected intralingual strategies, not interference errors from the first language. Hansen-Bede (1975) examined such linguistic structures as possession, gender, word order, verb forms, questions, and negation in an English-speaking 3-year-old child who learned Urdu upon moving to Pakistan. In spite of some marked linguistic contrasts between English and Urdu, the child's acquisition did not appear to show first language interference and, except for negation, showed similar strategies and rules for both the first and the second language.

Adult second language linguistic processes are more difficult to pin down. Only a few detailed studies have been carried out on the natural, untutored acquisition of a second language by adults. So much of adult second language acquisition in Western culture is tempered and shaped by classroom variables—textbooks, methods, and the like—that it is difficult to conclude much about the natural process. While other chapters in this book will touch on this issue, what can be said here is that adults do approach a second language systematically and attempt to formulate linguistic rules on the basis of whatever linguistic information is available to them—information from both the native language and from the second language itself. The nature and sequencing of these systems is the subject of a good deal of second language research today. What we have learned above all else from this research is that the saliency of interference from the first language does not imply that interference is the most relevant or most crucial factor in adult second language acquisition. Adults learning a second language manifest some of the same types of errors found in children learning their first language.

One of the first steps demonstrating the importance of factors other than first language interference was taken in a series of research studies by Heidi Dulay and Marina Burt (1972, 1974a, 1974b, 1976). They even went so far at one point as to claim that "transfer of L1 syntactic patterns *rarely* occurs" (italics mine) in child second language acquisition (1976:72). They claimed that children learning a second language use a *creative construction* process, just as they do in their first language. This conclusion was supported by some massive research data collected on the acquisition order of eleven English morphemes in children learning English as a second language. Dulay and Burt found a common order of acquisition among children of several native language backgrounds, an order very similar to that found by Roger Brown (1973) using the same morphemes but for children acquiring English as their first language.

There are logical and methodological arguments about the validity of Dulay and Burt's findings. Rosansky (1976) argued that the statistical procedures used were suspect, and others (Larsen-Freeman 1976, Andersen 1978) noted that eleven English morphemes constitute only a minute portion of English syntax. Nevertheless, the assertion that children do not appear to be as distracted by the first language as do adults is upheld by other research on children's second language acquisition, though the assertion that first language interference is "rare" is an overstatement. It may be more prudent to assert that the first language, for cognitive and affective reasons already discussed, does not pose the same degree of interference in children learning a second language as it does in adults.

Adults, more cognitively secure, appear to operate from the solid foundation of the first language and thus manifest more interference. But it was pointed out earlier that adults, too, manifest errors not unlike some of the errors children make, the result of creative perception of the second language and an attempt to discover its rules apart from the rules of the first language. The first language, however, may be more readily used to bridge gaps that the adult learner cannot fill by generalization within the second language. In this case we do well to remember that first language can be a facilitating factor, and not just an interfering factor.

We have touched on four domains that hold significant factors for the comparison of first and second language acquisition. In all four, though, it is important to maintain the distinction among the three types of comparisons between first and second language acquisition. Beware of the pitfalls of merely comparing "first" and "second" language acquisition! By considering the three logically possible comparisons, unnecessary loopholes in logic should be minimized. Once again, final answers have not been provided, but parameters for considering the comparisons have been set forth. By operating on them you can construct your own personal integrated understanding of what the relationship is between first and second language acquisition, and how that relationship might hold fruitful implications for second language teaching.

ISSUES IN FIRST LANGUAGE ACQUISITION REVISITED

Having examined the comparison of first and second language acquisition in four general domains of human behavior, we turn in this final section to a brief consideration of the eight issues in first language acquisition that were presented in Chapter Two. In most cases the implications of these issues are already clear, from the comments in the previous chapter, from your own logical thinking, or from comments in this chapter. Therefore what follows is a way of highlighting the implications of the issues for second language learning.

Competence-performance

It is as difficult to "get at" linguistic competence in a second language as it is in a first. For children, judgments of grammaticality may elicit a second language "pop-go-weasel" effect. For adults you can be a little more direct in inferring competence; adults can make choices between two alternative forms and sometimes they manifest an awareness of grammaticality in a second language. But you must remember that adults are not generally able to verbalize "rules" and paradigms consciously even in their native language. Furthermore, in judging utterances in the modern language classroom and responses on various tests, teachers need to be cautiously attentive to the discrepancy between performance on a given day or in a given context and competence in a second language in general. Remember that one isolated sample of second language speech may on the surface appear to be rather malformed until you consider that sample in comparison with the everyday mistakes and errors of native speakers.

Comprehension vs. production

Whether comprehension is derived from a separate level of competence or not, there is a universal distinction between comprehension and production. Learning a second language usually means learning to speak it *and* to comprehend it! When we say "Do you speak English?" or "Parlez-vous français?" we usually mean ". . . and do you *understand* it too?" Learning involves both modes (unless you are interested only in, say, learning to read in the second language). So teaching involves attending to both comprehension and production and the full consideration of the gaps and differences between the two. Adult second language learners will, like children, often *hear* a distinction and not be able to produce it. The inability to produce an item, therefore, should not be taken to mean that the learner cannot comprehend the item.

Innateness

What happens to the magic "little black box" called LAD after puberty? Does the adult suffer from linguistic "hardening of the arteries"? Does LAD "grow up" somehow? Does lateralization signal the death of LAD? We do not have the answers to these questions, but there have been some hints in the discussion of physical, cognitive, and affective factors. What we do know is that adults and children alike appear to have the capacity to acquire a second language at any age. If a person does not acquire a second language successfully it is probably because of intervening cognitive or affective variables and not the absence of innate capacities. Defining those intervening variables appears to be more relevant than probing the properties of innateness.

Universals

Is there a universal deep structure, common to all languages? If so, then second language learning is merely the learning of a new surface structure, a new set of forms for the basic meanings already established. However, there seems to be little evidence that deep structures are all so universal. Meaning and thought seem to be as culturally determined as surface structures are. So the quest for universals is a slow and tedious process, something to look toward in the distant future, but we should not expect immediately applicable results soon. The best we can do in applying universals to second language learning may be to look for commonalities between the first and the second language itself and to examine the process of acquisition. Learners may all use similar strategies at similar stages in their acquisition process. If there is a universally successful way to learn a second language, detailed studies of the characteristics of "good language learners" around the world may begin to open up some new vistas.

Language and thought

Another mind-boggling issue in both first and second language acquisition is the precise relationship between language and thought. We can see that surely language helps to shape thinking and that thinking helps to shape language. What happens to this interdependence when a second language is acquired? Does the bilingual person's memory consist of one storage system or two? The second language learner is clearly presented with a tremendous task in sorting out new meanings from old, distinguishing thoughts and concepts in one language that are similar but not quite parallel to the second language, perhaps really acquiring a whole new system of conceptualization. The second language teacher needs to be acutely aware of cultural thought patterns that may be as interfering as the linguistic patterns themselves.

Imitation

While children are good deep-structure imitators, adults can fare much better in imitating surface structure if they are explicitly directed either internally or externally to do so. Sometimes their ability to center on surface distinctions is a distracting factor; at other times it is helpful. Adults learning a second language might do well to attend consciously to truth value and to be less aware of surface structure as they communicate. The implication is that *meaningful* contexts for language learning are necessary; second language learners ought not to become too preoccupied with form lest they lose sight of the function and purpose of language.

Practice

Too many language classes are filled with rote practice that centers on surface forms. If Ausubel is correct in his theory of learning, the *frequency* of stimuli and the number of times spent practicing a form are not highly important in learning an item. What is important is meaningfulness. Contextualized, appropriate, meaningful communication in the second language seems to be the best possible practice the second language learner could engage in.

Input

In the case of adult second language learning, parental input is replaced by peer and/or teacher input. The teacher might do well to be as deliberate, but meaningful, in his communications with students as the parent is to the child, since input is as important to the second language learner as it is to the first language learner. And that input should foster meaningful communicative use of the language.

Can you now more adequately dispel the myths represented in the statements cited by H. H. Stern at the beginning of the chapter? It is probably apparent why you cannot, in simple statements, compare first and second language acquisition. The fallacies of many of such statements should be more clearly perceived with carefully integrated considerations of the several types and domains of comparison and some of the implications of the issues of first language acquisition.

SUGGESTED READINGS

There are several well-known articles that have compared first and second language acquisition. *Ausubel* (1964), *Cook* (1969), and *Stern* (1970) were some of the first to deal with the issue. *Dulay and Burt* (1972) and *Macnamara* (1975) added some important arguments to the comparison.

The discussion of the effects of lateralization on first and second language acquisition is an interesting topic of debate. *Lenneberg* (1967) gave the classic position, then *Scovel's* (1969) article related lateralization to foreign accents. *Krashen's* (1973) work on the notion of a critical period for language acquisition extended the argument further. *Hill's* (1970) response to Scovel was an intriguing account of language learning in non-Western contexts.

Since cognition is so central to the comparison of children and adults in language acquisition, it is worthwhile to read some of *Piaget's* monumental works. An excellent short summary of Piaget's theory of intellectual development was given by *Sullivan* (1967). *Rosansky* (1975) discussed the application of Piaget's notion of equilibration to second language learning.

The series of studies by *Dulay and Burt* (1972, 1974a, 1974b, 1976) are widely known as being among the first few attempts to demonstrate empirically that children learning a second language do not manifest the same degree of interference attributed to adults. *Larsen-Freeman's* (1976) study provided an important commentary on Dulay and Burt's data.

TOPICS AND QUESTIONS FOR STUDY AND DISCUSSION

1. Read over each of the common arguments (p. 42) cited by Stern (1970) which have been used to justify analogies between first language learning and second language teaching. For each statement determine what is assumed or presupposed. Then decide whether the analogy is correct or not. If so, why? If not, why not?

2. What are the implications of including cell A1 in the possible comparisons on page 44? You might speculate a little on what the speech therapist has to face in getting a person to relearn his first language, if he has lost the ability to use language through a stroke or accident.

3. This chapter is organized around physical, cognitive, affective, and linguistic considerations in making various types of comparisons. To review the arguments, turn the procedure around and list the separate physical, cognitive, af-

fective, and linguistic arguments within *each* of the three major types of comparisons.

4. Cite anecdotal evidence in your own experience of a *critical period* for the acquisition of a second language phonology (pronunciation).

5. The notion of a critical period is important in considering first and second language acquisition. Summarize *cognitive* arguments for an optimal critical period for second language acquisition. Next, summarize *affective* and then *physical* arguments. Which set of arguments do you consider the most powerful for distinguishing between children and adults in second language learning (Type 2)? Does the combination of arguments begin to achieve explanatory power in distinguishing child and adult second language learning abilities?

6. It was noted on page 47 that "the *saliency* of interference . . . from the first language does not imply that interference is the most relevant . . . factor in adult language acquisition." Explain what is meant by that statement.

7. Summarize the eight "revisited" issues in your own words. How does your understanding of those issues, as they apply to second language learning, help you to formulate a better understanding of the total process of second language acquisition? Cite what you think might be some practical classroom implications of the eight issues.

8. Do you think it is worthwhile at all to *teach* children a second language in the classroom? If so, how might approaches and methods differ between a class of children and a class of adults?

9. Review some of the arguments and issues in this chapter in view of their possible bias toward Western society. Do you think all the same arguments would hold for non-Western cultures?

4

Human Learning

Thus far in the search for a theory of second language acquisition we have discovered that the cognitive domain of human behavior is of key importance in the acquisition of both a first and a second language. The processes of perceiving, judging, knowing, and remembering are central to the task of internalizing a language. One could, of course, argue that virtually all of second language learning is cognitive in character, for after all, language comprehension and production is one of the highest forms of cognitive functioning among living organisms. This chapter and Chapter Five, however, treat variables that are more *centrally* cognitive in character and more traditionally the concern of the cognitive domain.

In this chapter we examine the general nature of human learning as it is defined by four different learning theories. Each of these theories is related to the learning of a second language. Chapter Five will then view learning from the perspective of cognitive variations in learning: the *types* of learning involved in human cognition, *stragegies* of learning, and individual *styles* of learning, which vary tremendously across and within human beings. You will no doubt detect some omissions from the ensuing discussion of cognition and language learning. I have not dealt separately and extensively, for example, with intellectual development, memory systems, and language and thought. Nevertheless the essence of these subfields is captured under the rubric of related topics. Intellectual development and language and thought have both been introduced in previous chapters; the area of memory is considered in this chapter as a part of theories of learning. The choice of emphasis does not necessarily mean that in *your* teaching you will find, say, intellectual development an unimportant variable; it does mean, though, that the integration of intellectual development into your theory of second language acquisition can be derived from your general understanding of a cluster of related issues presented throughout this book.

OF MICE AND MEN

How do human beings learn? Are there certain basic principles of learning that apply to all learning acts? Is one theory of learning "better" than another? If so, how can you evaluate the usefulness of a theory? These and other important questions need to be answered in order to achieve an integrated understanding of second language acquisition.

Before tackling theories of human learning directly, consider for a moment the following situation as an illustration of the awesome task of sorting out cognitive considerations in any task in which you are trying to determine what it means to conclude that an organism has *learned* something. Suppose you have been asked to train a mouse to walk backward in a circle in an open space (without barriers or guiding markers). Overwhelming? Yes indeed, unless you are an expert mouse trainer. Nevertheless, you might be able to begin to identify some of the pertinent questions you would need to have answered before you attempt the training program. What would those questions be?

First, you will need to specify *entry behavior*: what the organism already "knows." What abilities does it possess upon which you, the trainer, can build? What are its drives, needs, motivations, limitations? Next, the *goals* of the task would need to be formulated explicitly. You have a general directive; what are the specific objectives? How many times and how fast must the mouse walk backward in the circle? With what percentage of regularity? In what differing environments or contexts? You would also need to devise some *methods of training*. Based on what you know about entry behavior and goals of the task, how would you go about the training program? Where would you begin? Would you use some external stimuli—some goading or pushing? Would you construct a circular guide as a beginning stimulus—to be removed later when behavior is "achieved"? Would you use rewards? Punishment? What alternatives would you have ready if the mouse failed to learn? Finally, you would need some sort of *evaluation procedure*. How would you determine whether or not the mouse had indeed learned what you set out to teach? You would need to determine short-term and long-term evaluation measures. If it performs correctly within one day of training, what will happen one month from your training session? That is, how will the organism *maintain* what it has learned?

Already a somewhat simple task has become quite complex with technical questions that require considerable expertise to answer. But we are talking only about a mouse! If we talk about human beings learning a second language, the task is clearly mind-boggling! Not only is the task itself anything but simple; the organism is a highly complex cognitive being. Nevertheless, the questions and procedures that apply to you, the language teacher, are akin to those that applied to the mouse trainer. You must have a comprehensive knowledge of the entry behavior of a person, of objectives you wish to reach, of possible methods that follow from your understanding of the first two factors, and of an evaluation procedure. All this hinges on your conception of how human beings learn, and that is what this chapter is all about.

In turning now to varied theories of how human beings learn, consider once again the definition of learning given in Chapter One: "acquiring or getting of knowledge of a subject or a skill by study, experience, or instruction," or "a relatively permanent change in a behavioral tendency, . . . the result of reinforced practice." When we consider such definitions it is clear that one can understand learning in many different ways, which is why there are so many different theories—extended definitions—of learning. The polarized distinction between cognitive and behavioristic theories of human behavior has become apparent in the topics covered in the first three chapters. We now focus on how psychologists have defined *learning*, and I have chosen to look at these theories through the eyes of four psychologists, representing *classical behaviorism, neobehaviorism, cognitive learning theory*, and *humanistic psychology*. The first two views represent theories on the behavioristic side of the continuum described in Chapter One, and the latter two the cognitive side. The four positions should enable you to catch a glimpse not only of the history of learning theory, but of the diverse perspectives which form the foundations of varying language teaching approaches and methods.

CLASSICAL BEHAVIORISM

Certainly the best-known classical behaviorist is the Russian psychologist Ivan Pavlov, who at the turn of the century conducted a series of experiments in which he trained a dog to salivate to the tone of a tuning fork through a procedure that has come to be labeled *classical conditioning*. For Pavlov the learning process consisted of the formation of associations between stimuli and reflexive responses. All of us are aware that certain stimuli automatically produce or elicit rather specific responses or reflexes, and we have also observed that sometimes that reflex occurs in response to stimuli that appear to be indirectly related to the reflex. Pavlov used the salivation response to the sight or smell of food (an unconditioned response) in many of his pioneering experiments. In the classical experiment he trained a dog, by repeated occurrences, to associate the sound of a tuning-fork tone with salivation until the dog acquired a *conditioned response*: salivation at the sound of the tuning fork. A previously neutral stimulus (the sound of the tuning fork) had acquired the power to elicit a response (salivation) that was originally elicited by another stimulus (the smell of meat).

Drawing on Pavlov's findings, John B. Watson (1913) coined the term *behaviorism*. In the empirical tradition of John Locke, Watson contended that human behavior should be studied *objectively*, rejecting mentalistic notions of innateness and instinct. Taking an "environmentalist" position, following Pavlov, he adopted classical conditioning theory as the explanation for all learning: by the process of conditioning, we build an array of stimulus-response connections, and more complex behaviors are learned by building up series or chains of responses. Watson's emphasis on the study of overt behavior and his rigorous adherence to the scientific method had a tremendous influence on learning theories for decades. Language teaching methods likewise for many years followed a behavioristic tradition.

NEOBEHAVIORISM

In 1938 B. F. Skinner published his *Behavior of Organisms* and in so doing established himself as one of the leading behaviorists in the United States. He followed the tradition of Watson, but other psychologists (see Anderson and Ausubel 1965:5) have called Skinner a *neo*behaviorist because he added a unique dimension to behavioristic psychology. The classical conditioning of Pavlov was, according to Skinner, a highly specialized form of learning utilized mainly by animals and playing little part in human conditioning. Skinner called Pavlovian conditioning *respondent conditioning* since it was concerned with respondent behavior—that is, behavior that is *elicited* by a preceding stimulus. Skinner's *operant conditioning* attempts to account for most of human learning and behavior. Operant behavior is behavior in which one "operates" on the environment; within this model the importance of stimuli is de-emphasized. For example, we cannot identify a specific stimulus leading a small baby to pull himself to a standing position or to take his first step; we therefore need not be concerned about that stimulus, but we should be concerned about the *consequences*—the stimuli that follow the response. Skinner, stressing Thorndike's Law of Effect, demonstrated the importance of those events which follow a response. Suppose that a baby accidentally touches an object near him in his crib and a tinkling bell-sound occurs. The infant may look in the direction from which the sound came, become curious about it, and after several such "accidental" responses discover exactly which toy it is that makes the sound and how to produce that sound. The baby operated on his environment. His responses were *reinforced* until finally a particular concept or behavior was learned.

According to Skinner, the events or stimuli—the reinforcers—that follow a response and that tend to strengthen behavior or increase the probability of a recurrence of that response constitute a powerful force in the control of human behavior. Reinforcers are far stronger aspects of learning than mere association of a prior stimulus with a following response, as in the classical conditioning model. We are governed by the consequences of our behavior, and therefore Skinner felt we ought, in studying human behavior, to study the effect of those consequences. And if we wish to control behavior, say, to teach someone something, we ought to attend carefully to reinforcers.

Operants are classes of responses. Crying, sitting down, walking, and batting a baseball are operants. They are sets of responses that are *emitted* and governed by the consequences they produce. In contrast, *respondents* are sets of responses that are *elicited* by identifiable stimuli. Certain physical reflex actions are respondents. Crying can be respondent or operant behavior. Sometimes crying is elicited in direct reaction to a hurt. Often, however, it is an *emitted* response which produces the consequences of getting fed, cuddled, played with, comforted, and so forth. Such operant crying can be controlled. If a parent waits until a child's crying reaches a certain intensity before responding, loud crying is more likely to appear in the future. If a parent ignores crying (when he is certain that it is operant crying), eventually the absence of reinforcers will extinguish the behavior. Operant crying depends on its *effect* on the parents and is maintained or changed according to their response to it.

Skinner believes that, in keeping with the above principle, punishment "works to the disadvantage of both the punished organism and the punishing agency" (1953:183). Punishment can be both the withdrawal of a positive reinforcer or the presentation of an aversive stimulus. More commonly we think of punishment as the latter—a spanking, a harsh reprimand—but the removal of certain positive reinforcers, a privilege, for example, can also be considered a form of punishment. Skinner feels that in the long run punishment does not actually eliminate behavior, but that mild punishment may be necessary for temporary suppression of an undesired response, although no punishment of such a kind should be meted out without positively reinforcing *alternate* responses. The best method of extinction, says Skinner, is the absence of reinforcement entirely; however, the active reinforcement of alternate responses hastens that extinction. So if a parent wishes the children would not kick a football in the living room, Skinner would maintain that instead of punishing them adversively for such behavior when it occurs the parent should refrain from any negative reaction and should provide positive reinforcement for kicking footballs outside instead; in this way the undesired behavior will be effectively extinguished. Such a procedure is, of course, easier said than done, especially if the children break your best table lamp in the absence of any punishment!

Skinner, as you can see, was extremely methodical and empirical in his theory of learning, to the point of being preoccupied with scientific controls. While many of his experiments were performed on lower animals, his theories have had an impact on our understanding of human learning and on education. His book *The Technology of Teaching* (1968) is a classic in the field of programmed instruction. Following Skinner's model, one is led to believe that virtually any subject matter can be taught effectively and successfully by a carefully designed program of step-by-step reinforcement. Programmed instruction has had its impact on foreign language teaching, though language is such complex behavior, penetrating so deeply into both cognitive and affective domains of persons, that programmed instruction in languages is limited to very specialized subsets of language.

The impact of Skinnerian psychology on foreign language teaching has extended well beyond programmed instruction. Skinner's

Verbal Behavior (1957) described language as a system of verbal operants, and his understanding of the role of conditioning led to a whole new era in language teaching around the middle of the century. A Skinnerian view of both language and language learning dominated foreign language teaching methodology for several decades, leading to a heavy reliance in the classroom on the controlled practice of verbal operants under carefully designed schedules of reinforcement. A discussion of the popular audiolingual method in Chapter Twelve will elucidate Skinner's impact on American language teaching practices in the decades of the 50s, 60s, and early 70s.

There is no doubt that behavioristic and Skinnerian learning theory have had a lasting impact on our understanding of the process of human learning. There is much in the theory that is true and valuable. There is another side to the coin, however. We have looked at the side that claims that human behavior can be predicted and controlled and scientifically studied and validated. We have not looked at the side that views human behavior as essentially abstract in nature, as being composed of such a complex of variables that behavior, except in its extreme abnormality, simply cannot be predicted or easily controlled. That is not to say, though, that lack of prediction means that the behavior of people cannot be nevertheless lawful and dependable, with abiding characteristics and tendencies that can indeed be studied. We turn now to two representatives of this other side of the coin—David Ausubel's cognitive learning theory and Carl Rogers' humanistic psychology.

COGNITIVE LEARNING THEORY

David Ausubel contends that learning takes place in the human organism through a meaningful process of relating new events or items to already existing cognitive concepts or propositions—hanging new items on existing cognitive pegs. Meaning is not an implicit *response*, but a "clearly articulated and precisely differentiated conscious *experience* [my italics] that emerges when potentially meaningful signs, symbols, concepts, or propositions are related to and incorporated within a given individual's cognitive structure on a nonarbitrary and substantive basis" (Anderson and Ausubel 1965:8). It is this relatability that, according to Ausubel, accounts for a number of phenomena: the acquisition of new meanings (knowledge), retention, the psychological organization of knowledge as a hierarchical structure, and the eventual occurrence of forgetting.

The cognitive theory of learning as put forth by Ausubel is perhaps best understood by contrasting *rote* and *meaningful* learning.

In the perspective of rote learning the concept of meaningful learning takes on new significance. Ausubel described rote learning as the process of acquiring material as "discrete and relatively isolated entities that are relatable to cognitive structure only in an arbitrary and verbatim fashion, not permitting the establishment of [meaningful] relationships" (1968:108). That is, rote learning involves the mental storage of items having little or no association with existing cognitive structure. Most of us, for example, can rotely learn a few necessary phone numbers and zip codes without reference to cognitive hierarchical organization.

Meaningful learning, on the other hand, may be described as a process of relating and anchoring new material to relevant established entities in cognitive structure. As new material enters the cognitive field, it interacts with, and is appropriately "subsumed" under, a more inclusive conceptual system. The very fact that material is sub-subsumable—that is, relatable to stable elements in cognitive structure—accounts for its meaningfulness. If we can conceive of cognitive structure as a system of building blocks, then rote learning is the process of acquiring isolated blocks with no particular function in the building of a structure, and therefore with no relationship to other blocks. Meaningful learning is the process whereby blocks become an integral part of already established categories or systematic clusters of blocks. For the sake of a visual picture of the distinction, consider the graphic representation which I have depicted in Figures 4-1 and 4-2.

Any learning situation can be meaningful if (a) the learner has a meaningful learning set—that is, a disposition to relate the new learning task to what he already knows; and (b) the learning task itself is potentially meaningful to the learner—that is, relatable to the learner's structure of knowledge. The second (b) method of establishing meaningfulness, one which Frank Smith (1975:162)

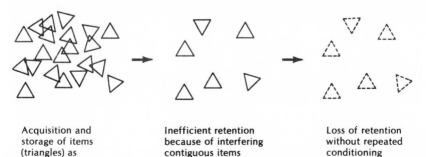

| Acquisition and storage of items (triangles) as arbitrary entities | Inefficient retention because of interfering contiguous items | Loss of retention without repeated conditioning |

Figure 4-1. Schematic representation of rote learning and retention.

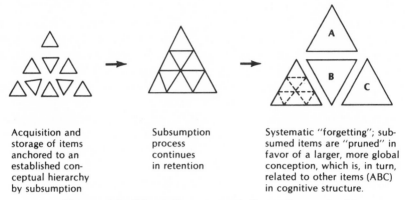

| Acquisition and storage of items anchored to an established conceptual hierarchy by subsumption | Subsumption process continues in retention | Systematic "forgetting"; subsumed items are "pruned" in favor of a larger, more global conception, which is, in turn, related to other items (ABC) in cognitive structure. |

Figure 4-2. Schematic representation of meaningful learning and retention.

has called "manufacturing meaningfulness," is a potentially powerful factor in human learning. We can make things meaningful if necessary, and if we are strongly motivated to do so. Common among students cramming for an examination is the invention of a mnemonic device for remembering a list of items; the meaningful retention of the device successfully retrieves the whole list of items. Frank Smith (1975) noted that similar strategies can be used in parlor games in which, for example, you are called upon to remember for a few moments several items presented to you. By associating items either in groups or with some external stimuli, retention is enhanced. Imagine "putting" each object in a different location on your person: a safety pin in your pocket, a toothpick in your mouth, a marble in your shoe. By later "taking a tour around your person" you can "feel" the objects there in your imagination. Nearly a century ago William James (1890:662) described meaningful learning:

> In mental terms, the more other facts a fact is associated with in the mind, the better possession of it our memory retains. Each of its associates becomes a hook to which it hangs, a means to fish it up by when sunk beneath the surface. Together, they form a network of attachments by which it is woven into the entire tissue of our thought. The "secret of good memory" is thus the secret of forming diverse and multiple associations with every fact we care to retain. . . . Briefly, then, of two men with the same outward experiences and the same amount of mere native tenacity, the one who thinks over his experiences most, and weaves them into systematic relation with each other, will be the one with the best memory.

The distinction between rote and meaningful learning may not at first appear to be important since in either case material can be acquired or learned. But the significance of the distinction becomes clear when we consider the relative efficiency of the two kinds of learning in terms of retention, or long-term memory. We are often tempted to examine learning from the perspective of acquisition alone, failing to consider the uselessness of a learned item that is not retained. Human beings are capable of learning almost any given item within the so-called "magic seven, plus or minus two" (Miller 1956) for perhaps a few seconds, but long-term memory is a different matter. We can remember an unfamiliar phone number, for example, long enough to dial the number, after which point it is usually extinguished by interfering factors. But a meaningfully learned, subsumed item has far greater potential for retention. Try, for example, to recall all your previous phone numbers (assuming you have moved a number of times in your life). It is doubtful you will be very successful; a phone number is quite arbitrary, bearing little meaningful relationship to reality (other than perhaps area codes and other such numerical systematization). But previous street addresses, for example, are sometimes more efficiently retained, since they bear some meaningful relationship to the reality of physical images, directions, streets, houses, and the rest of the town, and are therefore more suitable for long-term retention without concerted reinforcement.

Ausubel provides a plausible explanation for this apparently universal nature of forgetting. Since rotely learned materials do not interact with cognitive structure in a substantive fashion, they are learned in conformity with the laws of association, and their retention is influenced primarily by the interfering effects of similar rote materials learned immediately before or after the learning task (commonly referred to as *proactive* and *retroactive inhibition*). In the case of meaningfully learned material, retention is influenced primarily by the properties of "relevant and cumulatively established ideational systems in cognitive structure with which the learning task interacts" (Ausubel 1968:108). Compared to this kind of extended interaction, concurrent interfering effects have relatively little influence on meaningful learning, and retention is highly efficient. Hence, addresses are retained as part of a meaningful set, while phone numbers, as self-contained, isolated entities, are easily forgotten.

We cannot say, of course, that meaningfully learned material is never forgotten. However, in the case of such learning, forgetting takes place in a much more intentional and purposeful manner because it is a continuation of the very process of subsumption by which one learns; forgetting is really a second or "obliterative" stage of subsumption, characterized as "memorial reduction to the least common denominator" (Ausubel 1963:218). Because it is more economical and less burdensome to retain a single inclusive concept than to remember a large number of more specific items, the importance of a specific item tends to be incorporated into the generalized meaning of the larger item. In this obliterative stage of subsumption the specific items become progressively less identifiable as entities in their own right until they are finally no longer available and are said to be forgotten (see Figure 4-2). It is this second stage of subsumption that operates through what I have called "cognitive pruning" procedures (Brown 1972). Pruning is the elimination of unnecessary clutter and a clearing of the way for more material to enter the cognitive field, in the same way that pruning a tree ultimately allows greater and fuller growth. Using the building-block analogy, you might say that, at the outset, a structure made of blocks is seen as a few individual blocks, but as "nucleation" begins to give the structure a perceived shape, some of the single blocks achieve less and less identity in their own right, and become subsumed into the larger structure. Finally the single blocks are lost to perception, or "pruned" out, to use the metaphor, and the total structure is perceived as a single whole without clearly defined parts.

An example of such pruning may be found in a child's learning of the concept of "hot"—that is, excessive heat capable of burning someone. A small child's first exposure to such heat may be either direct contact with or verbally mediated exposure to hot coffee, a pan of boiling water, a stove, an iron, a candle. That first exposure may be readily recalled for some time as the child maintains a meaningful association between his parent's hot coffee and hurting. After a number of exposures to things that are very hot, the child begins to form a concept of "hotness" by clustering his experiences together and forming a generalization. In so doing the bits and pieces of experience that actually built the concept are slowly forgotten— "pruned"—in favor of the general concept which, in the years that follow, enable the child to extrapolate to future experiences and to avoid burning fingers on hot objects.

An important aspect of the pruning stage of learning is that subsumptive forgetting, or pruning, is not haphazard or chance—it is systematic. Thus by promoting optimal pruning procedures, we have a potential learning situation that will produce retention beyond that normally expected under more traditional theories of forgetting.

Ausubel's theory of learning has important implications for second language learning and teaching. The importance of meaning in language and of meaningful contexts for linguistic communication has been discussed in the first three chapters. Too much rote activity, at the expense of meaningful communication in language classes, could stifle the learning process.

Subsumption theory provides a strong theoretical basis for the rejection of conditioning models of practice and repetition in language teaching. In a meaningful process like second language learning, mindless repetition, imitation, and other rotely oriented practices in the language classroom have no place. The audiolingual method, which has emerged as a widely used and accepted method of foreign language teaching, is based almost exclusively on a behavioristic theory of conditioning which relies heavily on rote learning. The mechanical "stamping in" of the language through saturation with little reference to meaning is seriously challenged by subsumption theory. Rote learning can be effective on a short-term basis, but for any long-term retention it fails because of the tremendous buildup of interference. In those cases in which efficient long-term retention *is* attained in rote-learning situations like those often found in the audiolingual method, it would appear that by sheer dogged determination, the learner has somehow subsumed the material meaningfully *in spite of* the method!

The notion that forgetting is systematic also has important implications for language learning and teaching. In the early stages of language learning, certain devices (definitions, paradigms, illustrations, or rules) are often used to facilitate subsumption. These devices can be made initially meaningful by assigning or "manufacturing" meaningfulness. But in the process of making language automatic, the devices serve only as interim entities, meaningful at a low level of subsumption, and then they are systematically pruned out at later stages of language learning. We might thus better achieve the goal of communicative competence by removing unnecessary barriers to automaticity. A definition or a paraphrase, for example, might be initially facilitative, but as its need is minimized by larger and more global conceptualizations, it is pruned.

While we are all fully aware of the decreasing dependence upon such devices in language learning, Ausubel's theory of learning may help to give explanatory adequacy to the notion. Language teachers might consider urging students to "forget" these interim, mechanical items as they make progress in a language, and instead to focus only on the communicative use (comprehension or production) of language.

Ausubel's conception of meaningful learning provides valuable insights, but it also presents a number of problems. We do not know, especially in early "nucleation" stages, exactly how subsumption occurs in human learning in general, much less in second language acquisition in particular. Also, while meaningful learning of all kinds is certainly facilitated linguistically, it is not clear whether language acquisition should be explained in terms of the acquisition of added subsumers, the reshaping of existing subsumers, or perhaps some other cognitive change. And the "meaningfulness" of hypothetical grammatical rules is yet to be determined; we can only assume that semantic processes which grammatical rules attempt to explain are of prime importance in that they clearly relate to cognitive functioning. Despite these questions and problems, there is a good deal of promise in cognitively oriented models for understanding second language learning, a promise earlier psychological theories were not able to offer.

HUMANISTIC PSYCHOLOGY

Carl Rogers is not traditionally thought of as a "learning" psychologist, yet he and his colleagues and followers have had a significant impact on our present understanding of learning, particularly learning in an educational or pedagogical context. Rogers' humanistic psychology has more of an affective focus than a cognitive one, and so the impact of his thought may be more fully appreciated in the context of discussion on personality and sociocultural variables (Chapters Six and Seven). For the present, however, we take a brief look here at the contribution of Rogers' viewpoint to our understanding of learning, for his perspective gives us a fuller picture of the depth and breadth of human learning.

Rogers has devoted most of his professional life to clinical work in an attempt to be of therapeutic help to individuals. In his classic work *Client-Centered Therapy* (1951), Rogers carefully analyzed human behavior in general, including the learning process, by means of the presentation of nineteen formal principles of human behavior. All nineteen principles are concerned with learning to some degree, from a "phenomenological" perspective, a perspective that is in sharp contrast to that of Skinner. Rogers studied the "whole person" as a physical and cognitive, but primarily emotional, being. His formal principles focused on the development of an individual's self-concept and his personal sense of reality, those internal forces which cause a person to act. Rogers felt that inherent in principles of behavior is the human being's ability to adapt and to grow in the direction that enhances his existence. Given a nonthreatening environment, a person will form a picture of reality that is indeed congruent with reality, and will grow and learn.

The "fully functioning person," according to Rogers, lives at peace with all of his feelings and reactions; he is able to be what he potentially is; he exists as a process of being and becoming himself.

This fully functioning person, in his self-knowledge, is fully open to his experience, is without defensiveness, and creates himself anew at each moment in every action taken and in every decision made.

Rogers' thinking has important implications for education. The focus is away from "teaching" and toward "learning." The goal of education is the facilitation of change and learning. Learning how to learn is more important than being "taught" something from the "superior" vantage point of a teacher who unilaterally decides what shall be taught. Our present system of education, in prescribing curricular goals and dictating what shall be learned, denies persons both freedom and dignity. What is needed, according to Rogers, is real facilitators of learning, and one can only facilitate by establishing an interpersonal relationship with the learner. The teacher, to be a facilitator, must first of all be real and genuine, discarding masks of superiority and ommiscience. Second, the teacher needs to have genuine trust, acceptance, and a prizing of the other person—the student—as a worthy, valuable individual. And third, the teacher needs to communicate openly and empathically with his students and vice versa. A teacher with these characteristics will not only understand himself better but also be an effective teacher, who, having set the optimal stage and context for learning, will succeed in the goals of education.

We can see in the Rogers' humanism quite a departure from the scientific analysis of Skinnerian psychology, and even from Ausubel's rationalistic theory. Rogers is not as concerned about the actual cognitive process of learning since, he feels, if the *context* for learning is properly created, then human beings will, in fact, learn everything they need to.

Rogers' position has come under some attack by those who uphold more traditional theories of teaching and education. Nevertheless, his emphasis on student-centered teaching has contributed significantly in recent years to a redefinition of the educational process. In adapting Rogers' ideas to language teaching and learning, we need to understand that the learner is an organism who needs to understand himself and to communicate this self to others freely and nondefensively. The teacher as facilitator must therefore provide the nurturing context for learning and not to see his mission as one of rather programmatically feeding students quantities of knowledge which they subsequently devour. The latter practice fosters a climate of *defensive* learning in which the learner learns to protect himself from failure, from criticism, from competition with fellow students, and possibly from punishment. Classroom activities and materials in language learning should therefore utilize meaningful contexts of genuine communication with persons together engaged in the process of becoming persons.

We have much to gain from the understanding of all four learning theories that have been presented here. There are aspects of language learning which may call upon a conditioning process and other aspects which require a meaningful cognitive process and yet others which depend upon the security of supportive fellow learners interacting freely and willingly with one another. Each context will involve optimal dosages of each kind of learning. No one can give you an exact formula for that dosage; it must remain as a rather intuitive process that will be facilitated by an integrated understanding of the appropriateness and of the strengths and weaknesses of each theory of learning.

SUGGESTED READINGS

Most introductory psychology textbooks will provide useful summaries of behavioristic and cognitive theories of psychology. Such summaries can help to flesh out your understanding beyond what has been gained in this and preceding chapters.

For a reasonably concise statement of *Ausubel*'s subsumption theory you should consult two articles in *Anderson and Ausubel* (1965) found consecutively on pages 87-115. *Ausubel*'s (1968) textbook on educational psychology is an invaluable source of information on pedagogical applications of a great variety of psychological principles.

Smith (1975) is a very readable text relating a number of psychological perspectives to learning with particular reference to language. Chapters 4 and 5 make informative supplementary reading.

Rogers' (1951) classic is serious and difficult reading at times but contains valuable insights. Rogers provides a "counterpoint" in learning theory.

TOPICS AND QUESTIONS FOR STUDY AND DISCUSSION

1. At the beginning of the chapter a sketch was made of considerations that must be given to training a mouse to walk backward in a circle. Go through the same procedure (that is, specify entry behavior, explicit goals, methods of training, and an evaluation procedure) for the following three general tasks:

    a. Train an aardvark (anteater) to find hidden anthills in an apartment.

    b. Train a 10-month-old baby to clap hands together in rhythm to nursery rhymes.

    c. Train an adult to put together a do-it-yourself radio kit (that he has never seen before) without an instruction sheet.

Compare and contrast the tasks. What types of learning theory do you think would be differentially helpful for the three tasks? How effective do you think various possible methods of training would be?

2. Think of some of the language teaching methods you have been exposed to (or perhaps have used in your own teaching). Evaluate those teaching methods in reference to the different types of learning theories presented in this chapter. How might you justify certain practices? or reject certain other practices?

3. Summarize the distinction between *elicited* and *emitted* behavior and between *respondent* and *operant* conditioning. Can you specify some operants that are emitted by the learner in a foreign language class? and some responses that are elicited? Specify some of the *reinforcers* that are present in language classes. How effective are certain reinforcers? Can you pinpoint examples of *punishment* in foreign language classes? How effective are those forms of punishment for short-term and long-term retention?

4. In foreign language classes you have taken (or are teaching), identify some practices you could consider *rote* and others that are *meaningful*. Evaluate the effectiveness of those practices.

5. Is Ausubel's distinction between rote and meaningful learning clearly demarcated? Explain how there might be some "fuzzy" areas in between.

6. Explain the notion of "cognitive pruning." Give examples of necessary systematic forgetting in the foreign language classroom. How can you promote such forgetting, or can you really promote it at all?

7. In one sense Skinner, Ausubel, and Rogers represent quite different points of view—at least they focus on different facets of human learning. Do you think it is possible to *synthesize* the three points of view? In what way are all three psychologists expressing the "truth"? In what way do they differ substantially? Try to formulate an integrated understanding of human learning by taking the best of all three points of view. Does your integrated theory tell you something about how people learn a second language? or how you should teach a second language?

5

Cognitive Variations
in Language Learning

Theories of learning are generalized in nature. They seek to explain globally how people learn, what common characteristics there are in all learning. Such theories do not account for the plethora of differing contexts of learning, differences across individuals in the way they learn items, or differences within any one individual. While we all exhibit inherently human traits of learning, every individual approaches a problem or learns a set of facts or organizes a combination of feelings from a unique perspective. The three major sections of this chapter deal with categories of variation in human learning: variation in *types* of learning inherent in cognitive tasks, variation in *strategies* individuals employ, and variation in personal cognitive *styles* of learning. Second language learning involves complex cognitive processes that consist of many types of learning, and every individual utilizes a variety of strategies and styles in order to master the language. It is important to understand these processes so that you can teach effectively.

TYPES OF LEARNING

In his classic work on the conditions of learning, Robert Gagné (1965) ably demonstrated the importance of identifying a number of different types of learning which all humans use. Types of learning vary according to the context and subject matter to be learned, but a complex task such as language learning involves every one of Gagné's types of learning—from simple signal learning to problem solving. Gagné (1965:58-59) identified eight types of learning:

1. *Signal learning*. The individual learns to make a general diffuse response to a signal. This is the classical conditioned response of Pavlov.

2. *Stimulus-response learning*. The learner acquires a precise response to a discriminated stimulus. What is learned is a connection or, in Skinnerian terms, a discriminated operant, sometimes called an instrumental response.

3. *Chaining*. What is acquired is a chain of two or more stimulus-response connections. The conditions for such learning have also been described by Skinner.

4. *Verbal association*. Verbal association is the learning of chains that are verbal. Basically, the conditions resemble those for other (motor) chains. However, the presence of language in the human being makes this a special type because internal links may be selected from the individual's previously learned repertoire of language.

5. *Multiple discrimination*. The individual learns to make a number of different identifying responses to many different stimuli, which may resemble each other in physical appearance to a greater or lesser degree. Although the learning of each stimulus-response connection is a simple occurrence, the connections tend to interfere with one another.

6. *Concept learning*. The learner acquires the ability to make a common response to a class of stimuli even though the individual members of that class may differ widely from each other. The learner is able to make a response that identifies an entire class of objects or events.

7. *Principle learning*. In simplest terms, a principle is a chain of two or more concepts. It functions to organize behavior and experience. In Ausubel's terminology, a principle is a "subsumer"—a cluster of related concepts.

8. *Problem solving*. Problem solving is a kind of learning that requires the internal events usually referred to as "thinking." Previously acquired concepts and principles are combined in a conscious focus on an unresolved or ambiguous set of events.

It is apparent from just a cursory definition of these eight types of learning that some types are better explained by certain theories than others. For example, the first five types seem to fit easily into a behavioristic framework, while the last three are better explained by Ausubel's or Rogers' theories of learning. Since all eight types of learning are relevant to second language learning, the implication is that certain "lower"-level aspects of second language learning may be more adequately treated by behavioristic approaches and methods, while certain "higher"-order types of learning are more effectively taught by methods derived from a cognitive approach to learning.

The second language learning process can be rather efficiently categorized and sequenced in cognitive terms by means of the eight types of learning. Signal learning generally occurs in the total language process: human beings make a general response of some kind (emotional, cognitive, verbal, or nonverbal) to language. Stimulus-response learning is quite evident in the acquisition of the sound system of a foreign language in which, through a process of conditioning and trial and error, the learner makes closer and closer approximations to nativelike pronunciation. Simple lexical items are, in one sense, acquired by stimulus-response connections; in another sense they are related to higher-order types of learning. Chaining is evident in the acquisition of phonological sequences and syntactic patterns—the stringing together of several responses—though we should not be misled into believing that verbal chains are necessarily *linear*; generative linguists (like McNeill, as we saw in Chapter 2) have wisely shown that sentence structure is *hierarchical*. The fourth type of learning involves Gagné's distinction between verbal and nonverbal chains, and is not really therefore a separate type of language learning. Multiple discriminations are necessary particularly in second language learning where, for example, a word has to take on several meanings, or a rule in the native language is reshaped to fit a second language context. Concept learning includes the notion that language and cognition are inextricably interrelated, also that rules themselves—rules of syntax, rules of conversation—are linguistic concepts that have to be acquired. Principle learning is the extension of concept learning to the formation of a linguistic system, in which rules are not isolated in rote memory but conjoined and subsumed in a total system. Finally, problem solving is clearly evident in second language learning as the learner is continually faced with sets of events that are truly problems to be solved—problems every bit as difficult as algebra problems or other "intellectual" problems. Solutions to the problems involve the creative interaction of all eight types of learning as the learner sifts and weighs previous information and knowledge in order to correctly determine the meaning of a word, the interpretation of an utterance, the rule that governs a common class of linguistic items, or a conversationally appropriate response.

It is not difficult, upon some reflection, to discern the importance of varied types of learning in the second language acquisition process. Teachers and researchers have all too often dismissed certain theories of learning as irrelevant or useless because of the misperception that language learning consists of only one type of learning. "Language is concept learning" say some, "Language is a conditioning process" say others. Both are correct in that part of language learning consists of each of the above. But both are incorrect to assume that all of language learning can be so simply classified. Methods of teaching, in recognizing different levels of learning, need to be consonant with whichever aspect of language is being taught at a particular time while also recognizing the interrelatedness of all levels of language learning.

STRATEGIES OF LEARNING

The highest levels of learning in Gagné's hierarchy imply active cognitive *operating* upon items—upon concepts, principles, and problems. Just exactly how does the learner operate upon the problem of language? How does he "attack" the material at hand? Second language teachers and researchers have commonly spoken of language learning "strategies" in referring to the all-encompassing and highest of Gagné's levels of learning. A *strategy* may be defined as a particular method of approaching a problem or task, a mode of operation for achieving a particular end, a planned design for controlling and manipulating certain information.

In language learning we can distinguish two basic categories of strategies: *learning* strategies and *communication* strategies. A learning strategy is a method of perceiving and storing particular items for later recall. A communication strategy is a method of achieving communication, of encoding or expressing meaning in a language. The two types of strategies are quite different in their manifestation, though there is obviously a strong relationship between them. For example, transfer of a native language false cognate in the learning process might result in some instances in the actual productive use of the false cognate in the second language, but in other instances—where the learner perceives the falsity of the cognate—he might utilize an avoidance strategy (avoiding use of the particular word and substituting an alternate) in the communicative process, even though the basis for avoidance is transfer. We turn now to a consideration of these two kinds of strategies.

Learning Strategies

The human organism approaches any new problem with an existing set of cognitive structures, and through insight, logical thinking, and various forms of hypothesis testing, calls upon whatever prior experiences he has had and whatever cognitive structures he possesses to attempt a solution. At the beginning of this century

John Dewey (1910) described problem solving in a model which really has not been appreciably improved upon in three-quarters of a century. He described the problem-solving process as a series of five successive temporal stages:

1. A state of doubt, cognitive perplexity, frustration, or awareness of difficulty.
2. An attempt to identify the problem, including a rather nonspecific designation of the ends that are sought, the gap to be filled, or the goal to be reached, as defined by the situation that sets the problem.
3. Relating these problem-setting propositions to cognitive structure, thereby activating relevant background ideas and previously achieved problem solutions which, in turn, are reorganized (transformed) in the form of problem-solving propositions or hypotheses.
4. Successive testing of the hypotheses and reformulation of the problem if necessary.
5. Incorporating the successful solution into cognitive structure (understanding it) and then applying it both to the problem at hand and to other exemplars of the same problem.

While both children and adults utilize the five general stages of problem solving outlined by Dewey, children exhibit different problem-solving strategies from those of adults. Increasing maturity brings on more abstract, complex thinking. Accordingly, language teaching methods need to be appropriately geared to age levels even though both child and adult are going through the same five stages and are, in a sense, solving the same problem: learning the second language.

In the literature on language learning strategies, four terms have commonly been singled out for explication: *transfer*, *interference*, *generalization*, and *simplification*. The four terms have too often been considered as separate strategies; they are more correctly understood as several manifestations of one principle of learning—the interaction of previously learned material with a present learning event. From the beginning of life the human organism, or any organism for that matter, builds a structure of knowledge by the accumulation of experiences and by the storage of aspects of those experiences in memory. Let us consider these common terms in two associated pairs.

Transfer and interference

Transfer is a general term describing the carryover of previous performance or knowledge to subsequent learning. Positive transfer occurs when the prior knowledge benefits the learning task—that is, when a previous item is correctly applied to present subject matter. Negative transfer occurs when the previous performance disrupts the performance on a second task. The latter can be referred to as *interference*, in that previously learned material interferes with subsequent material—a previous item is incorrectly transferred or incorrectly associated with an item to be learned.

It has been common in second language teaching to stress the role of interference—that is, the interfering effects of the native language on the target (the second) language. It is of course not surprising that this strategy has been so singled out, for native-language interference is surely the most immediately noticeable source of error among second-language learners. The saliency of interference has been so strong that some have viewed second language learning as exclusively involving the overcoming of the effects of the native language. It is clear from learning theory that a person will use whatever previous experience he has had with *language* in order to facilitate the *second* language learning process. The native language is an obvious set of prior experiences. Sometimes the native language is negatively transferred, and we say then that interference has occurred. For example, a French native speaker might say in English "I am in New York since January," a perfectly logical transfer of the comparable French sentence "Je suis à New York depuis janvier." Because of the negative transfer of the French verb form to English, the French system has, in this case, interfered with the person's production of a correct English form.

It is exceedingly important to remember, however, that the native language of a second language learner is often *positively* transferred, in which case the learner benefits from the *facilitating* effects of the first language. In the above sentence, for example, the correct one-to-one word order correspondence, the personal pronoun, and the preposition have been positively transferred from French to English. We often mistakenly overlook the facilitating effects of the native language in our penchant for analyzing errors in the second language and for overstressing the interfering effects of the first language. A more detailed discussion of this syndrome is provided in Chapter Eight.

Generalization and simplification

In the literature on second language acquisition, interference is almost as frequent a term as *overgeneralization*, which is, of course, a particular subset of *generalization*. Generalization is a crucially important and pervading strategy in human learning. To generalize means to infer or derive a law, rule, or conclusion, usually from the observation of particular instances. The principle of generalization can be explained by Ausubel's concept of meaningful learning. Meaningful learning is, in fact, generalization: items are subsumed (generalized) under high-order categories for meaningful retention. Much of human learning involves generalization. The learning of concepts in early childhood is a process of generalizing. A child who has been exposed to various kinds of animals gradually acquires a generalized concept of "animal." That same child, however, at an early stage of generalization, might in his familiarity with dogs see a horse for the first time and *overgeneralize* the concept of "dog" and call the horse a dog. Similarly, a number of animals might be placed into a category of "dog" until the general attributes of a larger category, "animal," have been learned.

Inductive and *deductive* reasoning are two polar aspects of the generalization process. In the case of inductive reasoning, one stores a number of specific instances and induces a general law or rule or conclusion which governs or subsumes the specific instances. Deductive reasoning is a movement from a generalization to specific instances: specific subsumed facts are inferred or deduced from a general principle. Second language learning in the "field" (natural, untutored language learning), as well as first language learning, involve a largely inductive process, in which the learner must infer from all the data around him certain rules and meanings. Classroom learning usually involves a mixture of both types of reasoning. Deductive reasoning is commonly used in cases in which, for example, a grammatical rule is presented and the student is subsequently required, through drills and exercises, to supply instances of that rule. Inductive reasoning is necessary to infer superordinate principles or rules from the day-to-day linguistic input the learner receives. Inductive and deductive teaching methods have both advantages and disadvantages, depending upon the situation, the goals of the learner, the age of the learner (children are not as adept at deductive thinking as adults), the subject matter, and other variables.

Simplification is a term that has also been used in the literature on second language acquisition. In one sense all human learning is simplification: the process of "uncomplicating," of reducing events to a common denominator, to as few parts of features as possible. Meaningful learning is simplification, a process of storing items so that a few higher-order features lead to more and more lower-order features. Simplification is synonymous with generalization. But simplification can be contrasted with *complexification*, the act of discovering many varied parts of a whole, or even parts that do not fit into a whole. Complexification is necessary at times in order to counteract a tendency to *over*simplify, to overgeneralize to the point of omitting essential parts of the whole.

In second language acquisition it has been common to refer to overgeneralization as a strategy that occurs as the second language learner acts *within* the target language, generalizing a particular rule or item in the second language—irrespective of the native language—beyond ligitimate bounds. We have already observed that children, at a particular stage of learning English as a native language, overgeneralize regular past-tense endings (walked, opened) as applicable to all past-tense forms (goed, flied) until they recognize a subset of verbs that belong in an "irregular" category. After gaining some exposure and familarity with the second language, second language learners similarly will overgeneralize within the target language. Typical examples in learning English as a second language are past-tense regularization and utterances like "John doesn't can study" (negativization requires insertion of the *do* auxiliary before verbs) or "He told me when should I get off the train" (indirect discourse requires normal word order, not question word order, after the *wh*-word). Unaware that these rules have special constraints, the learner overgeneralizes. Such overgeneralization is committed by learners of English from almost any native language background. (Chapter Nine gives a more detailed discussion of linguistic overgeneralization.)

Many have been led to believe that there are *two* "strategies" of second language acquisition: interference and overgeneralization. This is obviously a misconception. First, interference and overgeneralization are the negative counterparts of the facilitating strategies of transfer and generalization. Second, while they are indeed aspects of somewhat different strategies, they represent fundamental and interrelated components of all human learning, and when applied to second language acquisition, are simply extensions of general psychological principles. Interference of the first language in the second is simply a form of generalizing that takes prior *first* language experiences and applies them incorrectly. Overgeneralization is the incorrect application—negative transfer—of previously learned *second* language material to a present second language context. All generalizing involves transfer, and all transfer involves generalizing.

Communication Strategies

We now turn to another type or category of strategy: communication strategies. Communication is the output modality and learning is the input modality of language acquisition. While strategies of communication are related to strategies of learning, it is nevertheless appropriate to consider the two types separately, since we know from earlier discussions (Chapters Two and Three) that receptive and productive competence may be separate. Our discussion here will be brief, serving as an introduction to later consideration of communication strategies in Chapter Nine.

Communication strategies are systematic attempts to express meaning in the target language in which the speaker must attend to both the *form* (the surface structure) of language and the *function* (the intended purpose of the utterances) of language. In order to communicate in the target language, the speaker (the learner) must assess the total context of communication, perceive the cognitive, affective, and linguistic set of the hearer, personally organize his intended meaning, then draw upon whatever existing structures he possesses to effect that communication. The resulting utterance will vary from learner to learner depending, among other things, upon the way linguistic material has been organized, stored, and recalled. Sometimes a communication strategy will enable the learner to fill in some gaps where he is uncertain of the correct or appropriate linguistic form. Most of the time, in a proficient speaker, communication strategies that have become virtually subconscious will result in correct and unambiguous output in the target language.

Generally, in communicating productively in a second language we use the same fundamental strategies that we use in "learning" a second language. For example, in a situation in which a learner discerns either correctly or incorrectly from stored knowledge that it is appropriate to transfer a first language thought or rule or pattern, he will do so and in his utterance will reflect that transfer. Positive transfer cannot be overtly detected in an utterance since one can only guess at the underlying causes of correctness; negative transfer is often manifested overtly and the hearer cognitively and affectively reacts to such evidence of interference. Generalization within the target language is also a common production strategy that stems from generalization in the learning or receptive stage. Again, correct generalization is not readily discerned, while overgeneralization (incorrect generalization) is. Various forms of generalization production strategies are discussed in Chapter Nine.

The strategy of *avoidance* is a most interesting one both psychologically and linguistically. Avoidance has cognitive and semantic manifestations when a learner avoids a whole topic of conversation about which perhaps he feels linguistically uncomfortable. Or a learner may for similar reasons abandon a particular message he has started because of difficulty in expressing certain ideas in the target language. Linguistic manifestations of syntactic avoidance occur when a person opts for a simpler structure that gives enough information by way of presupposition for communication to continue. Syntactic avoidance is often manifested by a strategy of paraphrasing. As a last resort, second language learners sometimes actually switch languages, reverting entirely to the native language in an effort to communicate an idea.

While a fuller treatment of communication strategies is provided in Chapter Nine, the notion is introduced here to provide a link between learning and production strategies and eventually to integrate productive communication with a comprehensive understanding of all the cognitive processes that interrelate in the acquisition of a second language.

STYLES OF LEARNING

Suppose you are being held captive in an airplane by a deranged gunman who tells you in no uncertain terms that he plans to kill you and the other passengers. You have emerged as the leader of this group of captives. What will you do? There is clearly no single solution to the problem. One solution may be as effective as another. Your solution will be based to a great extent on the *cognitive styles* you happen to bring to bear. For example, if you are *reflective* you will exercise patience, and not jump quickly to a conclusion about how to approach the situation; if you are *field-independent* you will focus on the necessary and relevant details and not be distracted by surrounding but irrelevant details.

The way we learn things in general and the particular attack we make on a problem seem to hinge on a rather amorphous link between personality and cognition; this link is referred to as *cognitive style*. In the enormous task of learning a second language, one which so deeply involves affective factors, a study of cognitive style brings very important variables to the forefront. Such styles can contribute significantly to the construction of a unified theory of second language acquisition.

If I were to try to enumerate all the cognitive styles that educators and psychologists have identified, a very long list would emerge. Ausubel (1968:171) identified at least 18 different styles. Joseph Hill (1972) defines some 29 different factors which make up the cognitive-style "map" of a learner; these include just about every imaginable sensory, communicative, cultural, affective, cognitive, and intellectual factor. I have chosen not to deal with cognitive style here as a construct that can be described comprehensively; rather,

we will look at five major styles, chosen because of their compre-
hensiveness (they subsume a number of different other styles) and
their relevance to language learning.

Ausubel (1968:170) defines cognitive style as "self-consistent
and enduring individual differences in cognitive organization and
functioning. The term refers both to individual differences in general
principles of cognitive organization . . . , and to various self-consistent idiosyncratic tendencies . . . that are not reflective of human
cognitive functioning in general." It is difficult to argue that cognitive
style is strictly a cognitive matter. It really mediates between emotion
and cognition, as you will soon discover. For example, a reflective
cognitive style invariably grows out of a reflective personality or a
reflective mood. An impulsive cognitive style, on the other hand,
usually arises out of an impulsive emotional state. A person's cognitive
style is determined by the way he internalizes his total environment,
and since that internalization process is not strictly cognitive, we
find that physical, affective, and cognitive domains merge in cognitive
style. Some would claim that cognitive styles are stable traits in
adults. This is a questionable view. It would appear that individuals
show general tendencies toward one style or another, but that
differing contexts will evoke differing styles in one individual.
Perhaps the person who is more intelligent and more successful in
learning is the person who is "bi-cognitive"—one who can manipulate
both ends of a cognitive style continuum.

We turn now to an examination of five cognitive styles that are
particularly relevant to second language learning.

Field Independence and Dependence

Do you remember, in those coloring books you pored over as a
child, a picture of a forest scene with exotic trees and flowers, and a
caption under the picture saying "Find the hidden monkeys in the
trees"? If you looked carefully, you soon began to spot them, some
upside-down, some sideways, some high and some low, a dozen or
so monkeys camouflaged by the lines of what at first sight looked like
just leaves and trees. The ability to find those hidden monkeys
hinged upon your *field-independent* style: your ability to perceive a
particular, relevant item or factor in a "field" of distracting items. In
general psychological terms, that "field" may be perceptual or it
may be more abstract in referring to a set of thoughts, ideas, or
feelings from which your task is to perceive specific relevant subsets.
Field dependence is, conversely, the tendency to be "dependent"
on the total field such that the parts embedded within the field are

not easily perceived, though that total field is perceived more clearly as a unified whole.

There are positive and negative characteristics to both field independence and field dependence. A field-independent style enables you to distinguish parts from a whole, to concentrate on something (like reading a book in a noisy train station), to analyze separate variables without the contamination of neighboring variables. On the other hand, *too much* field independence can backfire: cognitive "tunnel vision" forces you to see only the parts and fail to see their relationship to a whole. "You can't see the forest for the trees," as the saying goes. Seen in this light, development of a field-dependent style has positive effects: you perceive the whole picture, the larger view, the general configuration of a problem or idea or event. It is clear, then, that some degree of *both* field independence and field dependence is necessary for most of the cognitive and affective problems we face.

The literature on field independence-dependence has shown that persons tend to be dominant in one mode of field independence-dependence or the other, that field independence-dependence is a relatively stable trait, and that field independence increases as a child matures to adulthood. It has been found in Western culture that males tend to be more field-independent, and that field independence is related to one of the three main factors used to define intelligence (the analytical factor), but not to the other two factors (verbal-comprehension and attention-concentration). Cross-culturally, the extent of the development of a field-independent style as children mature is a factor of the type of society and home in which the child is reared. Authoritarian or agrarian societies, which are usually highly socialized and utilize strict rearing practices, tend to produce more field dependence. A democratic, industrialized, competitive society with freer rearing norms tends to produce more field-independent persons.

Affectively, persons who are more predominantly field-independent tend to be generally more independent, competitive, and self-confident. Field-dependent persons tend to be more socialized, tend to derive their self-identity from persons around them, and are usually more empathic and perceptive of the feelings and thoughts of others.

How does all this relate to second language learning? Two conflicting hypotheses can be proposed. First, we could conclude that a primarily field-dependent person will, by virtue of his empathy, his social outreach, and his perception of other people, be successful in learning a second language, an endeavor that has at its very foundation effective and motivated communication. But a second hypothesis seems to be supported by some recent research. Naiman, Fröhlich, and Stern (1975) found in a study of English-speaking eighth-, tenth-, and twelfth-graders learning French as a second language in Toronto that field independence correlated positively and significantly with language "success" in the classroom. This would seem reasonable if one argued that success necessitated focusing on the relevant variables in the distracting and ambiguous field of stimuli produced within the classroom context. One must be analytical and precise in distinguishing phonological and syntactic patterns in language and the rules that underlie them. Moreover, in a classroom in particular, one needs to be able to master exercises, drills, and other analytical oral and written activities.

The two hypotheses appear to present a paradox: how could field dependence be most important on the one hand, and field independence equally important? The answer to the paradox would appear to be that clearly *both* styles are important. The two hypotheses deal with two different kinds of language learning. One kind of learning implies natural, face-to-face communication, the kind of communication that occurs too rarely in the average language classroom. The second kind of learning involves the familiar classroom activities: drills, exercises, tests, and so forth. It could well be that "natural" language learning in the "field," beyond the constraints of the classroom, requires a field-dependent style and the classroom type of learning requires, conversely, a field-independent style.

There is some research to support such a conclusion. Guiora et al. (1972b) showed that empathy is related to language acquisition, and though one could argue with some of his experimental design factors (see H. D. Brown 1973), the conclusion seems highly reasonable and also supportable by observational evidence and intuition. Some pilot studies of field independence-dependence (Brown 1977a) indicated that field dependence correlated quite highly with a test of language proficiency in the case of adult English-learners in the United States. And so it would appear that field independence-dependence might provide one construct which differentiates "classroom" (tutored) second language learning from "natural" (untutored) second language learning.

Field independence-dependence may also prove to be a valuable tool for differentiating child and adult language acquisition. The child, more predominantly field-dependent, may have a cognitive style advantage over the more field-independent adult. Stephen Krashen (1977) has suggested that adults use more "monitoring," or "learning," strategies (conscious attention to forms) for language acquisition while children utilize strategies of "acquisition" (subconscious attention to functions). This distinction between acquisition and learning could well be explicated by the field independence-dependence dichotomy. (See Chapter Nine for further discussion of Krashen's Monitor model.)

Field independence-dependence has been conceived by psychological researchers as a construct in which a person turns out to be relatively stable. Unfortunately, there seems to be little room in such research for considering the possibility that field independence-dependence is contextualized and variable. Logically and observationally, field independence-dependence is quite variable within one person. Depending upon the context of learning, the learner can vary his utilization of field independence or field dependence. If a task requires field independence, a person may invoke his field-independent style; if it requires field dependence, he may invoke a field-dependent style. It is a misconception to view field dependence and field independence in complementary distribution; some persons might be both highly field-dependent and highly field-independent as contexts vary. Such variability is not without its parallels in almost every other psychological construct. A generally extroverted person might, for example, be relatively introverted at certain times. In second language learning, then, it may be incorrect to assume that learners should be *either* field-independent *or* field-dependent; it is more likely that persons have general inclinations, but, given certain contexts, can exercise a sufficient degree of an appropriate style. The burden on the learner is to invoke the appropriate style for the context. The burden on the teacher is to understand the preferred styles of each learner and to sow the seeds for flexibility in the learner.

Reflectivity and Impulsivity

It is common for us to show in our personalities certain tendencies toward *reflectivity* sometimes and at other times *impulsivity*. Psychological studies have been conducted to determine the degree to which, in the cognitive domain, a person tends to make either a quick, or gambling (impulsive) guess at an answer to a problem, or a slower, more calculated (reflective) decision. David Ewing (1977) refers to two styles that are closely related to the reflectivity-impulsivity dimension: systematic and intuitive styles. An intuitive style implies an approach in which a person makes a number of different gambles on the basis of "hunches," with possibly several successive gambles before a solution is achieved. Systematic thinkers tend to weigh all the considerations in a problem, work out all the loopholes, then, after extensive reflection, carefully venture a solution.

The implications for language acquisition are numerous. It has been found that children who are conceptually reflective tend to make fewer errors in reading than impulsive children (Kagan 1965); however, impulsive persons are usually faster readers, and eventually master the "psycholinguistic guessing game" (Goodman 1970) of reading such that their impulsive style of reading may not necessarily deter comprehension. In another study inductive reasoning was found to be more effective with reflective persons (Kagan, Pearson, and Welch 1966), suggesting that generally reflective persons could benefit more from inductive learning situations. In second language learning, little research has been conducted. Doron (1973) sought to examine the relationship between reflectivity-impulsivity and reading proficiency in adult learners of English as a second language. Her study revealed that reflective students were slower but more accurate than impulsive students in reading.

Reflectivity-impulsivity has some important considerations for classroom second language learning and teaching. Teachers tend to judge mistakes too harshly, especially in the case of a learner with an impulsive style who may be more willing than a reflective person to gamble at a correct answer. On the other hand, a reflective person may require patience from the teacher, who must allow more time for the student to struggle with responses. It is also quite conceivable that those with impulsive styles may go through a number of rapid transitions of semigrammatical stages of interlanguage, with reflective persons tending to remain longer at a particular stage with "larger" leaps from stage to stage.

Tolerance and Intolerance of Ambiguity

A third cognitive style concerns the degree to which you are cognitively willing to tolerate ideas and propositions that run counter to your own belief system or structure of knowledge. Some people are, for example, relatively "open-minded" in accepting ideologies and events and facts that contradict their own views; they are more content than others to entertain and even internalize contradictory propositions. Others, more "closed-minded," more dogmatic, tend to reject items that are contradictory or slightly incongruent with their existing system; they wish to see every proposition fit into an acceptable place in their cognitive organization, and if it does not fit, it is rejected.

Again, advantages and disadvantages are present in each style. The person who is tolerant of ambiguity is free to entertain a number of innovative and creative possibilities, and not be cognitively or affectively disturbed by ambiguity and uncertainty. In second language learning a great amount of apparently contradictory information is encountered: words that differ from the native language, rules that not only differ but that are internally inconsistent because of certain "exceptions," and sometimes a whole cultural system that is distant from that of the native culture. Successful language learning necessitates tolerance of such ambiguities, at least for interim periods or stages, during which time ambiguous items are given a chance to become resolved. On the other hand, too much tolerance of ambiguity can have a detrimental effect. A person can become "wishy-washy," accepting virtually every proposition before him, not efficiently subsuming necessary facts into his cognitive organizational structure. Such excess tolerance has the effect of hampering or preventing meaningful subsumption of ideas. Linguistic rules, for example, might not be effectively integrated into a whole system; rather, they may be gulped down in rotely learned, meaningless chunks.

Intolerance of ambiguity also has its advantages and disadvantages. A certain intolerance at an optimal level enables one to guard against the wishy-washiness referred to above, to close off avenues of hopeless possibilities, to reject entirely contradictory material, and to deal with the reality of the system that one has built. But clearly intolerance can close the mind too soon, especially if ambiguity is perceived as a threat; the result is a rigid, dogmatic, brittle mind that is too narrow to be creative. This may be particularly harmful in second language learning.

Few conclusive research findings are available on this style in second language learning, but one rather important finding was reported by Naiman, Fröhlich, and Stern (1975). They found that tolerance of ambiguity was one of only two significant factors in predicting the success of their high school learners of French in Toronto. Their finding suggests that tolerance of ambiguity, inasmuch as it can be accurately measured by existing instruments, is an important factor in second language learning. The finding has intuitive appeal, of course, since it is hard to imagine a compartmentalizer—a person who sees everything in black and white with no shades of gray —ever being successful in the overwhelmingly amorphous process of second language learning.

Broad and Narrow Category Width

Somewhat related to all three of the previously discussed cognitive styles is the tendency that persons have to categorize items either broadly or narrowly. Narrow categorizers, like impulsive learners, are more often willing to take the risk of being wrong in problem-solving situations by attending to "smaller" subordinate concepts, while broad categorizers may choose a larger slice of the pie in an attempt to encompass more possibilities. Category-width preference can be illustrated by a typical question on an instrument designed to measure this style: "Usually about 58 ships arrive in New York City harbor every day. What do you guess is the largest number of ships ever to arrive in New York in one day? . . . the smallest number of ships?" Those who are relatively broad categorizers will tend to give a large range, while narrow categorizers will give a smaller range.

Evidence of shifting from narrow to broad categorizing is found in first language acquisition in English—in the example mentioned earlier—when children first produce past-tense forms of verbs as separate, narrowly categorized items, but then shift to a broad classification of all verbs in a regularized category. Eventually with subsequent narrowing, verbs are subclassified into regular and irregular forms. Similar strategies may play a part in adult second language acquisition, but since adults tend to be more rigid and less likely to manifest the same degree of style shifting, the intraindividual variation may not be quite as prevalent. While the relationship of broad and narrow categorization to second language acquisition has scarcely begun to be researched, the Toronto study (Naiman, Fröhlich, and Stern 1975) did examine category width and found virtually no statistical support for a relationship between this style and success in French as a second language. However, in the case of category width it may be argued that successful language learning has little to do with *general* tendencies—as measured by standard instruments—and a great deal to do with the flexibility of a person in a given context to apply broad and narrow categorizing appropriately as the situation demands.

Skeletonization and Embroidery

Another little-researched cognitive style involves the tendency for some individuals to skeletonize and others to embroider in the recall of cognitive material, not unrelated to the distinction between simplification and complexification strategies discussed earlier. The need to simplify the representation and storage of information in cognitive structure is probably universal. But some studies (Holzman and Gardner 1960, Uhlmann and Saltz 1965) support the notion that simplification strategies have interindividual variations. In the recall of narrative material, for example, *skeletonizing* involves "pruning" out some particulars by retaining a substantive core of general facts which subsume the details; *embroidering*, on the other hand, involves "importing," or adding some material in order to retain original details that otherwise might be forgotten. Embroidery is a natural offshoot of the human intellectual tendency toward *closure*; sometimes one will perceive something that is not present in the data simply because he extrapolates beyond the overt stimuli. Carmichael, Hogan, and Walter (1932) showed how embroidery can be verbally stimulated; the recall of simple visual line designs varied depending upon the verbal stimulus attached to the visual stimulus. (See Chapter Seven for a description of that study.) Evidence of skeletonization and embroidery is also found in production styles. We have all known "yarn spinners" who can conjure up countless exaggerated additions in telling or retelling a story. It is also common to find people who provide only the bare facts of an event.

Such preferences could play an important role in the assessment of comprehension as well as production in second language learning. Writing skill might be a particularly fruitful area in which to try to discover how the tendency to embroider or skeletonize relates to style, efficiency, and teachability of writing. Some tests of oral production require a testee to retell a previously read story; the interpretation of the results of such tests could be biased toward embroiderers, who appear proficient if only because of the sheer quantity of output. Either style can be quite efficient; it is appropriate to judge embroidery as more desirable in some situations and skeletonizing as more appropriate in others. A more careful study of this feature of cognitive style might help to indicate how such preferences may influence actual language acquisition or our judgment of language proficiency.

In this chapter we have looked at a number of both relevant and salient cognitive variables in the learning of a foreign language. It should by now be apparent that cognitive variables alone represent a quagmire of factors which must be channeled into an understanding of the total second-language acquisition process. An awareness of these factors will help you, the teacher, to perceive in the learners you encounter some wide-ranging individual differences. Not all learners are alike! No one can be neatly pigeon-holed into a cognitive type. Five cognitive styles, several strategies, and eight types of learning—and those are not exhaustive—yield over a hundred possible combinations! If we could discover some overriding and all-pervading variable that classifies learners neatly into categories of "successful" and "unsuccessful," then of course we could then make a case for typing language learners. But such is not the case; the "good language learner" has not yet been defined. And until the utopian era when that definition is found, the teacher needs to recognize and understand a multiplicity of cognitive variables active in the second language learning process and to make appropriate judgments about each individual, meeting the learner where he is and providing him with optimal opportunities for learning.

SUGGESTED READINGS

Gagné's (1965) hierarchy of types of learning is summarized in Chapter Two of his book. The rest of the book then gives details on each type of learning, but a reading of at least that one chapter would give you a firmer grasp of what is meant by the eight levels of learning.

Again, a standard introductory psychology textbook will give summaries of such notions as transfer, interference, and generalization. Consult something convenient and current.

Taylor's (1975) work on overgeneralization and interference in second language learning is an excellent source to read in detail. It is a good example of a carefully executed empirical study with implications for a general understanding of learning variables in second language acquisition.

Richards (1975) expounded on the construct of simplification and develops the notion in reference to second language acquisition.

Many pages have been written on cognitive styles, and it is difficult to know exactly what to recommend. Some information is available in *Naiman, Fröhlich, and Stern* (1975)—the "Toronto study"—on good language learners. You could also consult *Ausubel* (1968:170-74) for descriptive information on cognitive styles. *Witkin* et al. (1971) gave, in very clearly written terms, an excellent synopsis of research on field independence.

Smith (1975) is also a good general source on learning variables in language acquisition.

TOPICS AND QUESTIONS FOR STUDY
AND DISCUSSION

1. Some linguistic examples were given of Gagné's eight types of learning. Give further examples of the use of these types of learning in the foreign language classroom. Identify certain aspects of the learning process which

are more readily explained by "lower" levels of learning and certain others which relate to "higher" levels. Does such categorizing help to resolve certain apparent contradictions between Skinner's and Ausubel's theories of learning?

2. People sometimes regard second language "processes" as virtually synonymous with "strategies." That has not been the case here. Process has been used in a generalized sense to refer to all second language acquisition. In that perspective, then, what is a *strategy*? How are learning strategies and communication strategies separable? In what way are they interconnected?

3. Relate Dewey's five stages of problem solving specifically to the "problem" of second language learning. Give examples. How would children and adults differ in respect to these five stages?

4. Review the concepts of transfer and generalization by defining them for yourself as succinctly as possible. Give examples of each phenomenon in the speech of a second language learner.

5. What are some advantages and disadvantages of inductive and deductive learning in the classroom? Consider the variables of situation, goals, age of the learner, and language skill (speaking, reading, etc.). How could each type be pushed too far? How can a teacher avoid pushing each type of learning too far?

6. It was noted on page 88 that "positive transfer cannot be overtly detected in an utterance . . . ." Explain what that means, and why such a phenomenon leads teachers to focus on the *errors* of learners.

7. What is the difference between strategies of learning and styles of learning as the terms have been used here?

8. In a class or conversation group of second language learners, observe the varying cognitive styles. Do you see evidence of degrees of field independence, reflectivity, or tolerance of ambiguity? What is that evidence? Is it linguistic or behavioral evidence? Is there a connection between such styles and the apparent success of the learner?

9. Someone once claimed (source unknown) that field dependence is related to farsightedness. That is, farsighted people tend to be more field-dependent, and vice versa. If that is true, how would you theoretically justify such a finding?

10. Review the argument that the field-independence-dependence dichotomy helps give explanatory power to the differentiation between natural (untutored) language learning and classroom (tutored) learning. How does this pose a dilemma for the foreign language teacher? Can you compromise between the two styles in the classroom?

6

Personality
and Language Learning

The previous two chapters dealt with two facets of the cognitive domain of language learning—human learning in general, and particular types, strategies, and styles of learning. Similarly, this chapter and the following chapter deal with two facets of the affective domain of second language acquisition. The first of these is the intrinsic side of affectivity: personality factors within a person that contribute in some way to the success of language learning. The second facet, treated in Chapter Seven, encompasses extrinsic factors—sociocultural variables that emerge as the second language learner brings not just two languages into contact, but two cultures, and in some sense must learn a second culture along with a second language.

If we were to devise theories of second language acquisition or teaching methods which were based only on cognitive considerations, we would be omitting the most fundamental side of human behavior. Nearly two decades ago Ernest Hilgard, well known for his study of human learning and cognition, noted that "purely cognitive theories of learning will be rejected unless a role is assigned to affectivity" (1963:267). In recent years there has been an increasing awareness of the necessity in second language research and teaching to examine human personality in order to find solutions to perplexing problems.

The affective domain is impossible to describe within definable limits. An overwhelming set of variables is implied in considering the emotional side of human behavior in the second language learning process. One difficulty in striving for affective explanations of

100

language success is presented by the task of subdividing and categorizing the factors of the affective domain. We are often guilty of using rather sweeping terms as if they were carefully defined. For example, it is easy enough to say that "culture conflict" accounts for most language learning problems, or that "motivation" is the key to success in a foreign language; but it is quite another matter to define such terms with precision. Psychologists also experience a difficulty in defining terms. Abstract concepts such as empathy, aggression, extroversion, and other common terms are difficult to define operationally. Standardized psychological tests often form an empirical definition of such concepts, but constant revisions are evidence of an ongoing struggle for validity. Nevertheless, the elusive nature of affective and cognitive concepts need not deter us from seeking answers to questions. Careful, systematic study of the role of personality in second language acquisition has already led to a greater understanding of the language learning process and to improved language teaching methods.

THE AFFECTIVE DOMAIN

What is the affective domain? How is it to be delimited and understood? *Affect* refers to emotion or feeling. The affective domain is the emotional side of human behavior, and it may be juxtaposed to the cognitive side. The development of affective states or feelings involves a variety of personality factors, feelings both about ourselves and about others with whom we come into contact.

Benjamin Bloom and his colleagues (Krathwohl, Bloom, and Masia 1964) provided a useful extended definition of the affective domain, outlining five levels of affectivity.

1. At the first and fundamental level, the development of affectivity begins with *receiving*. A person must be aware of the environment surrounding him, be conscious of situations, phenomena, people, objects; be willing to receive, willing to tolerate a stimulus, not avoid it, and give a stimulus his controlled or selected attention.

2. Next, a person must go beyond receiving to *responding*, committing himself in at least some small measure to a phenomenon or a person. Such responding in one dimension may be in acquiescence, but in another, higher, dimension the person is willing to respond voluntarily without coercion, and then to receive satisfaction from that response.

3. The third level of affectivity involves *valuing*, placing worth on a thing, a behavior, or a person. Valuing takes on the characteristics of beliefs or attitudes as values are internalized. A person does not merely accept a

value to the point of being willing to be identified with it, but commits himself to the value to pursue it, seek it out, and to want it, finally to the point of conviction.

4. The fourth level of the affective domain is the *organization* of values into a system of beliefs, determining interrelationships among them, and establishing a hierarchy of values within the system.

5. Finally, an individual becomes characterized by and understands himself in terms of his *value system*. The individual acts consistently in accordance with the values he has internalized and integrates beliefs, ideas, and attitudes into a total philosophy or world view. It is at this level that problem solving, for example, is approached on the basis of a total, self-consistent system.

Bloom's taxonomy was devised for educational purposes, but it has been widely used for a general understanding of the affective domain in human behavior. The fundamental notions of receiving, responding, and valuing are universal. In second language acquisition the learner needs to be receptive both to those with whom he is communicating and to the language itself, responsive to persons and to the context of communication, and to place a certain value on the communicative act of interpersonal exchange.

Lest you feel at this point that the affective domain as described by Bloom is just a bit too far removed from the essence of language, it is appropriate to recall that language is inextricably bound up in virtually every aspect of human behavior. Language is so pervasive a phenomenon in our humanity that it cannot be separated from the larger whole—from the whole persons that live and breathe and think and feel. Kenneth Pike (1967:26) said that

> language is behavior, that is, a phase of human activity which must not be treated in essence as structurally divorced from the structure of nonverbal human activity. The activity of man constitutes a structural whole in such a way that it cannot be subdivided into neat "parts" or "levels" or "compartments" with language in a behavioral compartment insulated in character, content, and organization from other behavior.

Understanding how human beings feel and respond and believe and value is an exceedingly important aspect of a theory of second language acquisition.

We turn now to a consideration of specific personality factors in human behavior and how they relate to second language acquisition. I have chosen to examine these factors by looking at four general categories: (1) *egocentric* factors—one's view of self and its relevance to language learning; (2) *transactional* factors—how the self is transacted to others; (3) *motivational* factors; and (4) a sketch of Community Language Learning as an instance of an affectively based teaching method.

EGOCENTRIC FACTORS

Self-Esteem

Self-esteem is probably the most pervasive aspect of any human behavior. It could easily be claimed that no successful cognitive or affective activity can be carried out without some degree of self-esteem, self-confidence, knowledge of yourself and belief in your own capabilities for that activity. Malinowski (1923) noted that all human beings have a need for *phatic communion*—defining oneself and finding acceptance in expressing that self in relation to valued others. Personality development universally involves the growth of a person's concept of self, acceptance of self, and reflection of self as seen in the interaction between self and others.

Carl Rogers (1951:136-37) offered the following definition of self-esteem:

> The self-concept or self-structure may be thought of as an organized configuration of perceptions of the self which are admissible to awareness. It is composed of such elements as the perceptions of one's characteristics and abilities; the precepts and concepts of the self in relation to others and to the environment; the value qualities which are perceived as associated with experiences and objects; and goals and ideals which are perceived as having a positive or negative valence.

A similar definition was given by Coopersmith (1967:4-5):

> By self-esteem, we refer to the evaluation which the individual makes and customarily maintains with regard to himself; it expresses an attitude of approval or disapproval, and indicates the extent to which an individual believes himself to be capable, significant, successful and worthy. In short, self-esteem is a personal judgement of worthiness that is expressed in the attitudes that the individual holds towards himself. It is a subjective experience which the individual conveys to others by verbal reports and other overt expressive behavior.

A person derives his sense of self-esteem from the accumulation of experiences with himself and with others and from assessments of the external world around him. General, or *global*, self-esteem is thought to be relatively stable in a mature adult, and is resistant to change except by active and extended therapy. But since no personality or cognitive trait is predictably stable for all situations and at all times, self-esteem has been categorized into three levels, only the first of which is global self-esteem. *Situational* or *specific* self-esteem is a second level of self-esteem, referring to one's appraisals of oneself in certain life situations, such as social interaction, work, education, home, or on certain relatively discretely defined traits—intelligence, communicative ability, athletic ability, or personality traits like gregariousness, empathy, and flexibility. The degree of specific self-esteem a person has may vary depending upon the situation or the trait in question. The third level, *task* self-esteem, relates to particular tasks within specific situations. For example, within the educational domain task self-esteem might refer to particular subject-matter areas. In an athletic context, skill in a particular sport—or even a facet of a sport such as net play in tennis or pitching in baseball— would be evaluated on the level of task self-esteem. Specific self-esteem might refer to second language acquisition in general, and task self-esteem might appropriately refer to one's self-evaluation of a particular aspect of the process: speaking, writing, a particular class in a second language, or even a special kind of classroom exercise.

Little research has been carried out on the relationship between self-esteem and second language acquisition. Most recently Adelaide Heyde (1979) studied the effects of the three levels of self-esteem on performance of an oral production task by American college students learning French as a foreign language. She found that all three levels of self-esteem correlated positively with performance on the oral production measure, with the highest correlation occurring between task self-esteem and performance in oral production. That is, students with high self-esteem actually performed better in the foreign language.

Brodkey and Shore (1976) and Gardner and Lambert (1972) both included measures of self-esteem in their studies of success in language learning. While no conclusive statistical evidence emerged from these studies, the results of both revealed that self-esteem appears to be an important variable in second language acquisition, particularly in view of cross-cultural factors of second language learning which will be discussed in the next chapter.

What we do not know at this time is the answer to the classic chicken-or-egg question: does high self-esteem cause language success or does language success cause high self-esteem? Clearly, both are interacting factors. It is difficult to say whether teachers should try to "improve" global self-esteem or simply improve a learner's proficiency and let self-esteem take care of itself. Heyde (1979) found that certain sections of French 101 (sections made up of randomly assigned students) manifested better oral production and self-esteem scores than other sections—after only eight weeks of instruction. This finding suggests that teachers really can have a positive and influential effect on both the linguistic performance and the emotional well-being of the student. Perhaps those "good" teachers succeeded because they gave optimal attention to linguistic goals and to the personhood of their students.

Inhibition

Closely related to and in some cases subsumed under the notion of self-esteem is the concept of inhibition. All human beings, in their understanding of themselves, build sets of defenses to protect the ego. The newborn baby has no concept of his own self; gradually he learns to identify a self that is distinct from others. Then in childhood, the growing degrees of awareness, responding, and valuing begin to create a system of affective traits which the person identifies with himself. In adolescence, the physical, emotional, and cognitive changes of the preteenager and teenager bring on mounting defensive inhibitions to protect a fragile ego, to ward off ideas, experiences, and feelings that threaten to dismantle the organization of values and beliefs on which appraisals of self-esteem have been founded. The process of building defenses continues on into adulthood. Some persons—those with higher self-esteem and ego strength—are more able to withstand threats to their existence and thus their defenses are lower. Those with weaker self-esteem maintain walls of inhibition to protect what is self-perceived to be a weak or fragile ego, or a lack of self-confidence in a situation or task.

The human ego encompasses what Guiora has called the *language ego* to refer to the very personal, egoistic nature of second language acquisition. Meaningful language acquisition involves some degree of identity conflict as the language learner takes on a new identity with his newly acquired competence. An adaptive language ego enables the learner to lower the inhibitions that may impede success. Guiora et al. (1972a) produced one of the few studies on inhibition in relation to second language learning. Claiming that the notion of ego boundaries is relevant to language learning, Guiora designed an experiment using small quantities of alcohol to induce temporary states of less than normal inhibition in an experimental group of subjects. The performance on a pronunciation test in Thai of subjects given the alcohol was significantly better than the performance of a control group. Guiora concluded that a direct relationship existed between inhibition (a component of language ego) and pronunciation ability in a second language. But there were some serious problems in his conclusion. Alcohol may lower inhibitions, but alcohol also tends to affect muscular tension, and while "mind" and "body" in this instance may not be clearly separable, the physical effect of the alcohol may have been a more important factor than the mental effect in accounting for the superior pronunciation performance of the subjects given alcohol. Furthermore, pronunciation may be a rather poor indicator of overall language competence. Nevertheless, Guiora has provided an important hypothesis which has tremendous intuitive—if not experimental—support.

Some have facetiously suggested that the moral to Guiora's alcohol experiment is that we should pass out cocktails during every foreign language class! While many students would certainly take delight in such a proposal, the experiments have highlighted a most interesting possibility: that the inhibitions, the defenses, which we place between ourselves and others can prevent us from communicating in a foreign language. Since Guiora's experiments were conducted, a number of giant steps have been taken in foreign language teaching methodology to create methods that reduce these defenses. Language teaching methods in the last quarter of this century have been characterized by the creation of contexts for meaningful classroom communication such that the interpersonal ego barriers are lowered to pave the way for free, unfettered communication (see Chapter Twelve).

Anyone who has learned a foreign language is acutely aware that second language learning actually necessitates the making of mistakes. We test out hypotheses about language by trial and many errors; children learning their first language and adults learning a second can really only make progress by learning from making mistakes. If we never ventured to speak a sentence until we were absolutely certain of its total correctness, we would likely never communicate productively at all. But mistakes can be viewed as threats to one's ego. They pose both internal and external threats. Internally, one's critical self and one's performing self can be in conflict: the learner performs something "wrong" and he becomes critical of his own mistake. Externally, the learner perceives others exercising their critical selves, even judging his very person when he blunders in a second language. Earl Stevick (1976b) spoke of language learning as involving a number of forms of *alienation*, alienation between the critical me and the performing me, between my native culture and my target culture, between me and my teacher, and between me and my fellow students. This alienation arises from the defenses that we build around ourselves. These defenses do not facilitate learning; rather they inhibit learning, and their removal therefore can promote language learning, which involves self-exposure to a degree manifested in few other endeavors.

TRANSACTIONAL FACTORS

The human being is a social animal and the chief mechanism for maintaining the bonds of society is language. Some highly sophisticated methods of language teaching have failed to accomplish the goal of communicativity in the learner by overlooking the social nature of language. While we tend to recognize the importance of the social aspect of language, we also tend to oversimplify that aspect by not recognizing the complexity of the relation between language and society, or by considering socially oriented problems in language learning as a simple matter of "acculturation." Chapter Seven demonstrates that acculturation is no simple process, and it will become clear in this chapter that the social *transactions* which the second language learner is called upon to make constitute complex endeavors.

Transaction is the process of reaching out beyond the self to others. The tools of language help to accomplish these feats. A variety of transactional variables comes to bear on second language learning: imitation, modeling, identification, empathy, extroversion, aggression, styles of communication, and others. Three of these variables, chosen for their relevance to a global understanding of second language acquisition, will be treated here: empathy, extroversion, and aggression.

Empathy

Empathy, like so many personality variables, defies adequate definition. In common terminology, empathy is the process of "putting yourself into someone else's shoes," of reaching beyond the self and understanding and feeling what another person is understanding or feeling. It is probably the major factor in the harmonious coexistence of individuals in society. Language is one of the primary means of empathizing, but nonverbal communication facilitates the process of empathizing and must not be overlooked.

In more sophisticated terms, empathy is usually described as the projection of one's own personality into the personality of

another in order to understand him better. Empathy is not synonymous with *sympathy*. Empathy implies more possibility of detach-
ment; sympathy connotes an agreement or harmony between
individuals. Guiora (1972b:142) defined empathy as "a process of
comprehending in which a temporary fusion of self-object boundaries
permits an immediate emotional apprehension of the affective
experience of another." The affective side of that definition could
apply to the cognitive as well. Psychologists have found it difficult
to define empathy. Hogan (1969:309), one of the leading researchers
in empathy, at one point defined empathy as "a relatively discrete
social phenomenon recognizable in the experience of laymen and psychologists alike." The circularity of this definition is reminiscent of
the zoologist's definition of a *dog* as a four-legged animal recognizable as a dog by other dogs! Despite the difficulty of defining the
concept, there is general consensus on what empathy is. Psychologists
generally agree with Guiora's definition above, and add that there are
two necessary aspects to the development and exercising of empathy:
first, an awareness and knowledge of one's own feelings, and second,
identification with another person (Hogan 1969). In other words,
you cannot fully empathize—or know someone else—until you
adequately know yourself.

Communication requires a sophisticated degree of empathy. In
order to communicate effectively you need to be able to understand
the other person's affective and cognitive states; communication
breaks down when false presuppositions or assumptions are made
about the other person's state. From the very mechanical, syntactic
level of language to the most abstract, meaningful level, we assume
certain structures of knowledge and certain emotional states in any
communicative act. In order to make those assumptions correctly
we need to transcend our own ego boundaries, or using Guiora's
term, to "permeate" our ego boundaries so that we can send and
receive messages clearly.

Oral communication is a case in which, cognitively at least, it is
easier to achieve empathic communication since there is immediate
feedback from the hearer. A misunderstood word, phrase, or idea
can be questioned by the hearer, and then rephrased by the speaker
until a clear message is interpreted. Written communication requires
a special kind of empathy—a cognitive empathy in which the writer,
without the benefit of immediate feedback from the reader, must
communicate ideas by means of a very clear empathic intuition and
judgment of the reader's state of mind and structure of knowledge.

So in a second language learning situation the problem of
empathy becomes acute. Not only must the learner-speaker correctly

identify cognitive and affective sets in the hearer, but he must do so in a language in which he is insecure. Then, the learner-hearer, attempting to comprehend a second language, often discovers that his own states of thought are misinterpreted by a native speaker, and the result is that linguistic, cognitive, and affective information easily passes "in one ear and out the other."

Guiora and his colleagues (1972a, 1972b) found that a modified version of the Micro-Momentary Expression (MME) test, a test claiming to measure degrees of empathy, successfully predicted authenticity of pronunciation of a foreign language. Naiman, Fröhlich, and Stern (1975) included an empathy measure (Hogan's Empathy Scale—see Hogan 1969) in their battery of tests used to try to discover characteristics of the "good language learner," but found no significant correlation between empathy and language success as measured by an imitation test and a listening test. However, their finding was not unexpected since they found field independence to be positively correlated with language success; the presumed antithesis of field independence—field dependence—has been shown to correlate highly with empathy (Witkin et al. 1971). But a great deal of the problem of the study of most personality variables lies in the accuracy of the tests used to measure traits. Serious methodological problems surround such measurement; the MME and Hogan's Empathy Scale are cases in point. It has been shown that such tests accurately identify personality *extremes* (schizophrenic, paranoid, or psychotic behavior, for example) but fail to differentiate among the vast "normal" population.

If indeed a high degree of empathy is predictive of success in language learning, it would be invaluable to discover how one could capitalize on that possibility in language teaching. It is one thing to claim to be able to predict success and quite another matter to cause success by fostering empathy in the language classroom. One would need to determine if empathy is something one can "learn" in the adult years, especially cross-culturally. If so, then it would not be unreasonable to incorporate empathy in language teaching methods. What kinds of drills and exercises could be devised which require a person to predict or guess another person's response? How worthwhile would it be to attempt to organize foreign language classes which operate on a high-empathy basis, as in Community Language Learning, in which principles of T-group therapy are used to aid the language learning process? These and other questions give rise to some creative issues in language teaching methodology.

Probably the most interesting implication of the study of empathy is the need to define empathy cross-culturally—to understand how different cultures express empathy. Most of the empathy tests devised in the United States are culture-bound to Western North American middle-class society. Chapter Seven will deal more specifically with empathy in cross-cultural settings, particularly with the role of empathy in defining the concept of acculturation.

Extroversion

Extroversion, and its antithesis, introversion, are also interesting and salient variables in the acquisition of a second language. Again, the construct is beyond adequate definition, but there is general intuitive consensus on what is meant by extroversion. It is a common belief among teachers in general, particularly in Western society, that introversion is an undesirable behavior. The outgoing, amiable, talkative personality tends to be held up as axiomatically desirable and ideal. This valuing of extroversion carries over into the language classroom as well. Quiet, reserved personalities are treated as "problems" and language teachers seek ways of encouraging extroversion. The syndrome is further complicated by the tendency in modern language teaching to emphasize speaking in the classroom, with all too little emphasis on aural comprehension.

Educational psychologists tend to agree that a child's introversion and extroversion may be "a grossly misleading index of social adjustment" (Ausubel 1968:413). The role of introversion and extroversion may be misinterpreted in language classes. Is it indeed true that the "proficiency" of a more introverted person is qualitatively lower than his extroverted counterpart? And do those students a teacher assumes to be introverted actually classify as such, if cultural variations are taken fully into account? Teachers are prone to stereotype certain people as introverted or extroverted on the basis of their cultural background. However, a careful analysis of the sociolinguistic and extralinguistic expectations of that culture could significantly change such judgments.

Extroversion is commonly thought to be related to empathy, but such may not be the case. The extroverted person may actually behave in an extroverted manner in order to protect his own ego, with extroverted behavior being symptomatic of defensive barriers and high ego boundaries. At the same time the introverted, quieter, more reserved person may show high empathy—an intuitive understanding and apprehension of others—and simply be more reserved in the outward and overt expression of empathy.

It is not clear then, that extroversion or introversion helps or hinders the process of second language acquisition. The Toronto study (Naiman, Fröhlich, and Stern 1975—found no significant effect for extroversion in characterizing the "good language learner." It is quite conceivable that extroversion may be a factor in the *speaking* of a foreign language, but not in aural and reading comprehension, nor in writing. It is also readily apparent that cross-cultural norms of non-verbal and verbal interaction vary widely, and what in one culture (say, the United States) may appear as introversion is in another culture (say, Japan) respect and politeness. Nevertheless, on a practical level, the facilitating or interfering effects of certain methods which invoke extroversion need to be carefully considered. How effective are methods that incorporate drama, pantomime, humor, role plays, and overt personality exposure? A teacher needs to develop an awareness of the role of kinesic and other nonverbal factors in communication and the degree of extroversion that is optimal within the context of a particular culture and particular communicative situations.

Aggression

Aggression is a third transactional variable in language learning which has received only minor attention; yet it could be an important factor in a theory of language acquisition. Studies in child development take the question of aggression quite seriously, and a description of any adult personality would be inadequate if the notion of aggression were omitted from consideration. Aggression can be defined in a number of different ways, ranging from "a sequence of behavior the goal of which . . . is injury of the person toward whom it is directed" (Dollard, Doob, Miller, Mowrer, and Sears 1939:9) to more general definitions that include reference to responses that could injure or damage if aimed at a vulnerable object (Bandura and Walters 1963:114). There is also some debate about the relationship of *frustration* to aggression; Freud's early theory of aggression, for example, maintained that aggression is a "primordial reaction" to frustration (Freud 1920). Nevertheless, aggressive behavior appears in every human organism, and depending upon the individual and his society, different manifestations and expressions of aggression will be observed. But aggression should not be defined only in a negative context. Aggression, even in the "injurious" sense, is a behavior necessary for survival; for example, consistent refusal to be aggressive in mere self-defense, physically and emotionally, could result in physical or mental illness and/or death. However, *assertiveness* is perhaps a more positive notion that is related to the construct of aggression.

How does aggression relate to language learning? Even the exhaustive questionnaires of Gardner and Lambert (1972) did not deal directly with aggression. Some reference to aggression was made indirectly by LaForge (1971) in his discussion of the manifestation of hostility in his experimental language classes; he noted that the overt display, and thus eventual release, of hostility seemed to facilitate communication and to lead toward less inhibited and freer, albeit semigrammatical, conversation. In other words, when students got angry with each other, they communicated more freely. The potential disadvantage of thwarted aggressive instincts is of course intuitively understood by most teachers. However, a number of other questions related to aggression are not yet answered. To what extent does the basic aggressiveness of the individual indicate his probable success in learning a foreign language? Because of its negative connotations, aggressive behavior may be considered undesirable; yet there is intuitive evidence of the facilitating effect of aggression (or at least assertiveness). Aggression could be a central factor determining motivation to learn a language, and foreign language teaching methods indeed ought to capitalize on positive and constructive aggressive behavior.

MOTIVATION

Motivation is probably the most often used catch-all term for explaining the success or failure of virtually any complex task. It is easy to figure that success in a task is due simply to the fact that someone is "motivated." It is easy in second language learning to claim that a learner will be successful with the proper motivation. Such claims are of course not erroneous, for countless studies and experiments in human learning have shown that motivation is a key to learning. But these claims gloss over a detailed understanding of exactly what motivation is and what the subcomponents of motivation are. What does it mean to say that someone is motivated? How do you create, foster, and maintain motivation?

Basic Needs and Drives

Motivation is commonly thought of as an inner drive, impulse, emotion, or desire that moves one to a particular action. More specifically, human beings universally have needs or drives that are more or less innate, yet their intensity is environmentally conditioned. Six desires or needs of human organisms are commonly identified (see Ausubel 1968:368-79) which undergird the construct of motivation: (1) the need for *exploration*, for seeing "the other side of the mountain," for probing the unknown; (2) the need for *manipulation*, for operating—to use Skinner's term—on the environment and causing change; (3) the need for *activity*, for movement and exercise, both physical and mental; (4) the need for *stimulation*, the need to be stimulated by the environment, by other people, or by ideas, thoughts, and feelings; (5) the need for *knowledge*, the need to process and internalize the results of exploration, manipulation, activity, and stimulation, to resolve contradictions, to quest for solutions to problems and for self-consistent systems of knowledge; (6) finally, the need for *ego enhancement*, for the self to be known and to be accepted and approved of by others.

There are other possible factors that could be listed in accounting for motivation. Maslow (1970) listed hierarchical human needs, from fundamental physical necessities (air, water, food) to higher needs of security, identity, and self-esteem, the fulfillment of which leads to *self-actualization*. Other psychologists have noted further basic needs: achievement, autonomy, affiliation, order, change, endurance, aggression, and other needs. The six needs listed above appear to capture the essence of most general categories of needs, and are especially relevant to second language acquisition.

Examples abound to illustrate the sixfold concept of motivation. Consider the child who is "motivated" to learn to read. He is motivated because certain needs are important to him, perhaps all six of the needs mentioned above, particularly exploration, stimulation, and knowledge. The child who is not motivated to read sees no way in which reading meets the needs he has. The adult who learns to ski and learns to do so well no doubt is motivated by a need for exploration and stimulation and activity and maybe even ego enhancement. The foreign language learner who is either intrinsically or extrinsically meeting needs in learning the language will be positively motivated to learn.

Motivation, then, is an inner drive or stimulus which can, like self-esteem, be global, situational, or task-oriented. Learning a foreign language clearly requires some of all three levels of motivation. For example, a learner may possess high "global" motivation but low "task" motivation to perform well on, say, the written mode of the language. It is easy to see how virtually any aspect of second-language learning can be related to motivation. Nelson and Jakobovits (1970), in a lengthy report on motivation in foreign language learning, cited just about every possible factor as relevant to the role of motivation in second language learning. A number of instructional, individual, and sociocultural factors were considered which could enhance or deter motivation. Among learner factors, for example, were included intelligence, aptitude, perseverance, learning strategies, interference, and self-evaluation! It is not difficult to see how all of those factors could contribute either positively or negatively to motivation. But it is fruitless merely to list a host of variables which can be subsumed under motivation without examining the relationship of each variable to the basic needs underlying motivation. Why, for example, does a learner persevere in his task? Or how can the less intelligent person appeal to his inner needs and enhance motivation? How can a teacher provide extrinsic motivation where intrinsic motivation is lacking? Answers to these questions necessitate probing the fundamental nature of human psychology, but such probing will ultimately lead to a deeper and richer understanding of both motivation and the second language learning process in general.

Motivation, seen as the fulfillment of needs, is closely connected to behavioristic reinforcement theory. Inasmuch as certain needs are being satisfactorily met in a person, reinforcement occurs. If learning to speak a foreign language enhances one's ego, for example, the ego enhancement is in itself an internal reinforcer of the desired behavior.

Instrumental and Integrative Motivation

One of the best-known studies of motivation in second language learning was carried out by Robert Gardner and Wallace Lambert (1972). Over a period of twelve years they extensively studied foreign language learners in Canada, several parts of the United States, and the Philippines in an effort to determine how attitudinal and motivational factors affect language learning success. Motivation was examined as a factor of a number of different kinds of attitudes. Two different clusters of attitudes divided two basic types of motivation: instrumental and integrative motivation. *Instrumental* motivation refers to motivation to acquire a language as means for attaining instrumental goals: furthering a career, reading technical material, translation, and so forth. An *integrative* motive is employed when a learner wishes to integrate himself within the culture of the second language group, to identify himself with and become a part of that society. Many of Lambert's studies (see Lambert 1972) and one study by Spolsky (1969) found that integrative motivation generally accompanied higher scores on proficiency tests in a foreign language. The conclusion from these studies was that integrative motivation may indeed be an important requirement for successful language learning. And some teachers and researchers have even gone so far as to claim that integrative motivation is absolutely essential for successful second language learning.

In recent years evidence has begun to accumulate which challenges such a claim. Yasmeen Lukmani (1972) demonstrated that among Marathi-speaking Indian students learning English in India, those with higher *instrumental* motivation scored higher in tests of English proficiency. Braj Kachru (1977) has noted that Indian English is but one example of a variety of English*es*, which, especially in Third World countries where English has become an international language, can be acquired very successfully for instrumental reasons alone.

The more recent findings are not necessarily contradictory to Lambert's. They point out once again that there is no single means of learning a second language: some learners in some contexts are more successful in learning a language if they are integratively oriented, and others in different contexts benefit from an instrumental orientation. The findings also suggest that the two types of motivation are not necessarily mutually exclusive. Second language learning is rarely motivated by attitudes that are exclusively instrumental or exclusively integrative. Most situations involve a mixture of each type of motivation. An Arabic speaker learning English in the United States for academic purposes may be relatively balanced in his desire to learn English both for academic (instrumental) purposes and to understand and become somewhat integrated with the culture and people of the United States. Macnamara (1973:64) noted that the dichotomy is not as important as searching "for the really important part of motivation in the act of communication itself, in the student's effort to make his own meaning clear."

The instrumental/integrative construct does, however, help to put some of the recent interest in affective variables into some perspective. It is easy to conclude that second language learning is an emotional activity involving countless affective variables, or to assert that learning a second language involves taking on a new identity (see Chapter Seven). But the findings of studies like those of Lukmani and Kachru warn us that while perhaps some contexts of foreign language learning involve an identity crisis, there are a good many legitimate language learning contexts in which that identity crisis may be minimized, or at least seen as less of a personal affective crisis and more of a cognitive crisis. Does the child in French-speaking Africa, who must learn French in order to succeed in educational settings, and who is quite instrumentally motivated to do so, meet with an identity crisis? Must he take on a "French" identity? It is possible that he does not, just as the child learning English in India tends to learn *Indian* English as an integral part of his own culture. In some cases, then, the foreign language does not carry with it the heavy cultural loading that some have assumed to be characteristic of all language learning contexts.

COMMUNITY LANGUAGE LEARNING

The importance of the affective domain has been recently stressed in most of the literature on language teaching methods and techniques. A number of methods have been devised in the last decade—and some used successfully—which claim to capitalize on humanistic factors in language learning. The Silent Way, Suggest-opedia, Total Physical Response, Community Language Learning, and others have emerged as methods which attempt to provide the humanistic context and affective support necessary to meet the egocentric, transactional, and motivational necessities of second language acquisition. While this is not a textbook on methodology, it seems appropriate here to give a brief description of a method that has arisen out of a primary concern for the role of affectivity in communication. Many of the abstract variables outlined in this chapter are brought into a practical focus in a relatively successful method called Community Language Learning. A brief description and analysis is offered here.

In his "Counseling-Learning" model of education Charles Curran (1972) was inspired by Carl Rogers' view of education in which learners in a classroom are regarded as a "group" rather than a "class"—a group in need of certain therapy and counseling. The social dynamics of such a group are of primary importance. In order for any learning to take place, as has already been noted in Carl Rogers' model, what is first needed is for the members to interact in an interpersonal relationship in which students and teacher join together to facilitate learning in a context of valuing and prizing each individual in the group. In such a surrounding each person lowers the defenses that prevent open interpersonal communication. The anxiety caused by the educational context is lessened by means of the supportive community. The teacher's presence is not perceived as a threat, nor is it the teacher's purpose to impose limits and boundaries, but rather, as a true counselor, to center his attention on the client (the student) and his needs. "Defensive" learning is made unnecessary by the empathic relationship between teacher and students. Curran's Counseling-Learning model of education thus capitalizes on the primacy of the needs of the learners—clients—who have gathered together in the educational community to be counseled.

Curran's Counseling-learning model of education has been extended to language learning contexts in the form of Community Language Learning (CLL). While particular adaptations of CLL are numerous, the basic methodogy is explicit. The group of clients (learners), having first established in their native language an interpersonal relationship and trust, are seated in a circle with the counselor (teacher) on the outside of the circle. The clients may be complete beginners in the foreign language. When one of the clients wishes to say something to the group or to an individual, he says it in his native language (say, English) and the counselor translates the utterance back to the learner in the second language (say, Japanese). The learner then repeats that Japanese sentence as accurately as he can. Another client responds, in English; the utterance is translated by the counselor; the client repeats it; and the conversation continues. If possible the conversation is taped for later listening, and at the end of each session the learners inductively attempt together to glean information about the new language. If he wishes, the counselor may take a more directive role and provide some explanation of certain linguistic rules or items.

The first stage of intense struggle and confusion may continue for many sessions, but always with the support of the counselor and of the fellow clients. Gradually the learner becomes able to speak a word or phrase directly in the foreign language, without translation. This is the first sign of the learner's moving away from complete dependence upon the counselor. As the learners gain more and more familiarity with the foreign language, more and more direct communication can take place with the counselor providing less and less direct translation and information, until after many sessions, perhaps months later, the learner acquires fluency in the spoken language. The movement from total dependence to independence in the foreign language is illustrated by Curran's (1976:53) own diagram (Figure 6-1), depicting a five-stage process of learning. CLL thus reflects not only the principles of Carl Rogers' view of education but also basic principles of the dynamics of counseling, in which the counselor, through careful attention to the client's needs, aids the client in moving from dependence and helplessness to independence and self-assurance.

There are advantages and disadvantages to a method like CLL. The affective advantages are evident. CLL is an attempt to put Carl Rogers' philosophy into action and to overcome some of the threatening affective factors in second language learning. The threat of the all-knowing teacher, of making blunders in the foreign language in front of classmates, of competing against peers—all threats which can lead to a feeling of alienation and inadequacy—are presumably removed. The counselor allows the learner to determine the type of conversation and to analyze the foreign language inductively. It is interesting to note that the teacher can also become a client at times: in situations in which explanation or translation seems to be impossi-

I
Total dependence on language counselor. Idea said in English, then said to group in foreign language, as counselor slowly and sensitively gives each word to the client.

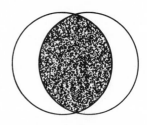

II
Beginning courage to make some attempts to speak in the foreign language as words and phrases are picked up and retained.

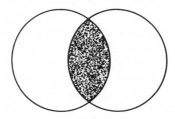

III
Growing independence with mistakes that are immediately corrected by counselor.

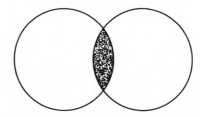

IV
Needing counselor now only for idioms and more subtle expressions and grammar.

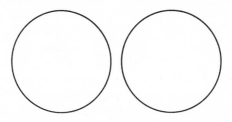

V
Independent and free communication in the foreign language. Counselor's *silent* presence reinforces correctness of grammar and pronunciation.

Figure 6-1. Stages in language counselor-client relationship from dependency to independence. (from Curran 1976:53)

ble, it is often the client-learner who steps in and becomes a counselor to aid the teacher. The student-centered nature of the method can provide extrinsic motivation and capitalize on intrinsic motivation.

But there are some practical and theoretical problems with CLL. The counselor-teacher can become *too* nondirective. The

118

student often needs direction, especially in the first stage, in which there is such seemingly endless struggle within the foreign language. Supportive but assertive direction from the counselor could strengthen the method. Another problem with CLL is its reliance upon an inductive strategy of learning. I have already noted in Chapter Five that deductive learning is both a viable and efficient strategy of learning, and that adults particularly can benefit from deduction as well as induction. While some intense inductive struggle is a necessary component of second language learning, the initial grueling days and weeks of floundering in ignorance in CLL could be alleviated by more directed, deductive, learning "by being told." Perhaps only in the second or third stage, when the learner has moved to more independence, is an inductive strategy really successful. Finally, the success of CLL depends largely on the translation expertise of the counselor. Translation is an intricate and complex process that is often "easier said than done"; if subtle aspects of language are mistranslated, there could be a less than effective understanding of the target language.

Despite its weaknesses, however, CLL has emerged as a most interesting method of language teaching, useful in varied contexts if the teacher adapts aspects of CLL for his own use. That adaptation requires an understanding of the many variables that are at play in language acquisition, a recognition of not only the salient variables but the relevant variables in second language learning in given contexts. Some of these variables have been defined in this and previous chapters, and still others are yet to be defined in the chapters ahead.

SUGGESTED READINGS

Bloom's (Krathwohl, Bloom, and Masia 1964) classic taxonomy of the affective domain has been widely used in educational circles for a number of years. You will find that reading portions of it, especially pages 95-185, will provide a more technical understanding of levels of affectivity.

Schumann (1975) and *Naiman, Fröhlich, and Stern* (1975) dealt at length with affective factors in second language acquisition. Schumann's article is particularly readable and little technical knowledge is required to understand it.

Because it is one of the earliest experiments on affective variables in second language acquisition, *Guiora*'s (1972a) study of the effect of alcohol-induced inhibition on second language pronunciation is recommended reading. *Guiora*'s (1972b) article on empathy in second language learning is also informative.

Stevick's (1976b) highly readable article on the alienation felt by language learners is an excellent resource for understanding the affective nature of language learning.

Gardner and Lambert's (1972) work on attitudes and motivation in second language learning has been widely read and quoted in recent years. If you are interested in the instruments they used to measure attitudes and motivation or even in one or two of the experiments they conducted, you may wish to become familiar with the book.

More information on Community Language Learning is available in *LaForge* (1971) and *Curran* (1976). The latter is a comprehensive treatment of the theory behind Community Language Learning. *Brown*'s (1977b) critique of Community Language Learning put the method into some perspective.

TOPICS AND QUESTIONS FOR STUDY AND DISCUSSION

1. How would you relate Bloom's levels of affectivity to the second language learning process? Do you see the levels manifested in the classroom or in a conversation group?

2. Restate the chicken-or-egg question in relating self-esteem to second language learning. Can you *teach* self-esteem? What can a teacher do with a student who apparently has very low self-esteem?

3. Give some examples of the manifestation of inhibition in children. How about adults? And yourself? How might these inhibitions hamper language acquisition? In your own experience in language learning, have you ever been troubled by your own inhibitions? How can a person overcome those inhibitions?

4. Distinguish between empathy and sympathy. Give an example of a language learner empathizing with a native speaker but not sympathizing.

5. What is meant by "cognitive empathy" (p. 108)? Why does written communication require a different kind of empathy than oral communication? Which mode of communication might therefore more readily reveal a person's degree of empathy?

6. How is empathy expressed in cultures other than your own? Can empathy be defined cross-culturally? How might different manifestations of empathy be misunderstood in second language learning contexts?

7. How can the expression of aggression be used creatively and constructively in the foreign language classroom?

8. Can a teacher provide extrinsic motivation to learn a language when intrinsic motivation is lacking? In foreign language classes where students are simply taking a course to pass a language requirement, can the teacher appeal to

any of the six levels (pp. 112-13) of motivation? What are your personal feelings about the advisability of a foreign language *requirement* in universities and high schools?

9. Explain the connection between motivation and reinforcement.

10. Distinguish between integrative and instrumental motivation to learn a language. In the case of your second language, do you feel you were more instrumentally or more integratively motivated? Why? Why does it appear that instrumental and integrative orientations are not mutually exclusive?

11. What is meant by "defensive" learning (p. 116)? Give some examples of defensive learning from your own educational experiences. How might foreign language classes minimize defensive learning?

12. In a conversation group or foreign language class, make an attempt to follow the procedures of Community Language Learning (if the right ingredients are present: a translator, one native language, small group, flexible program). If possible, carry through with the method for a couple of hours. How did the group react? How did you feel as the counselor-teacher? What was your assessment? What were advantages and disadvantages?

7

Sociocultural Variables

The previous chapter examined one aspect of the affective domain of second language acquisition: how those very personal variables within oneself and the reflection of that self to other people affect our communicative interaction. This chapter touches on a major and very crucial aspect of the communicative process, an aspect that is still very much a part of the egocentric self in a transactional process, but a specialized subset of that process: the learning of another culture, the overcoming of the personal and transactional barriers presented by two cultures in contact, and the relationship of culture learning to second language learning.

Culture is a way of life. Culture is the context within which we exist, think, feel, and relate to others. It is the "glue" that binds a group of people together. John Donne wrote: "No man is an island entire of itself; every man is a piece of the continent, a part of the main" (Devotions, XVII). Culture is our continent, the collective identity of which each of us is a part.

Larson and Smalley (1972:39) described culture as a "blueprint" that "guides the behavior of people in a community and is incubated in family life. It governs our behavior in groups, makes us sensitive to matters of status, and helps us know what others expect of us and what will happen if we do not live up to their expectations. Culture helps us to know how far we can go as individuals and what our responsibility is to the group. Different cultures are the underlying structures which make Round community round and Square community square."

Culture might be defined as the ideas, customs, skills, arts, and tools which characterize a given group of people in a given period of time. But culture is more than the sum of its parts. "It is a system of integrated patterns, most of which remain below the threshold of consciousness, yet all of which govern human behavior just as surely as the manipulated strings of a puppet control its motions" (Condon 1973:4). The fact that no society exists without a culture reflects the need for culture to fulfill certain biological and psychological needs in human beings. Consider the bewildering host of confusing and contradictory facts and propositions and ideas that present themselves every day to any human being; some organization of these facts is necessary to provide some order to potential chaos, and therefore conceptual networks of reality evolve within a group of people for such organization. The mental constructs that enable us thus to survive are a way of life which we call "culture."

These constructs are infinitely diverse and therefore cultures have widely differing characteristics. Nevertheless, such patterns for living have, in the view of some anthropologists, universal characteristics. George Peter Murdock (1961:45-54) cites seven "universals" of cultural patterns of behavior: (1) they originate in the human mind; (2) they facilitate human and environmental interactions; (3) they satisfy basic human needs; (4) they are cumulative and adjust to changes in external and internal conditions; (5) they tend to form a consistent structure; (6) they are learned and shared by all the members of a society; and (7) they are transmitted to new generations.

Culture thus establishes for each person a context of cognitive and affective behavior, a blueprint for personal and social existence. But we tend to perceive reality strictly within the context of our own culture; this is a reality which we have "created," not necessarily "objective" reality, if indeed there is any such thing as objectivity in its ultimate sense. "The meaningful universe in which each human being exists is not a universal reality, but 'a category of reality' consisting of selectively organized features considered significant by the society in which he lives" (Condon 1973:17). Although the opportunities for world travel in the last quarter of this century are increasing, there is still a tendency for us to believe that our own reality is the "correct" perception. Perception, though, is always quite subjective. Perception involves the filtering of information even before it is stored in memory, resulting in a selective form of consciousness. What appears to you to be an accurate and objective perception of a person, a custom, and idea, is sometimes "jaded," or "stilted" in the view of someone from another culture. Misunderstandings are therefore likely to occur between members of different cultures. We will probably never be able to answer the question of how perception came to be shaped in different ways by different cultural groups; it is another chicken-or-egg question. But differences are real and we must learn to deal with them in any situation in which two cultures come into contact.

It is apparent that culture, as an ingrained set of behaviors and modes of perception, becomes highly important in the learning of a second language. A language is a part of a culture and a culture is a part of a language; the two are intricately interwoven such that one cannot separate the two without losing the significance of either language or culture. The acquisition of a second language, except for specialized, instrumental acquisition (as may be the case, say, in "Indian" English), is also the acquisition of a second culture. Both linguists (see Lado 1957) and anthropoligists (see Burling 1970) bear ample testimony to this observation.

The sections of this chapter attempt to capture some of the important aspects of the relationship between learning a second language and learning the cultural context of the second language. An examination of the notion of cultural stereotypes and attitudes will precede a discussion of what it means to "learn" another culture, followed by a section on the relationship among language, thought, and culture.

CULTURAL STEREOTYPES

Mark Twain gave us a delightfully biased view of other cultures and other languages in *The Innocents Abroad*. In reference to the French language, Twain comments that Frenchmen "always tangle up everything to that degree that when you start into a sentence you never know whether you are going to come out alive or not." In *A Tramp Abroad*, Twain notes that German is a most difficult language: "A gifted person ought to learn English (barring spelling and pronouncing) in 30 hours, French in 30 days, and German in 30 years." So he proposed to reform the German language, for "if it is to remain as it is, it ought to be gently and reverently set aside among the dead languages, for only the dead have time to learn it."

Twain, like all of us at times, has expressed caricatures of certain languages. Such caricatures are not unlike linguistic and cultural stereotypes. In the bias of our own culture-bound world view, we picture other cultures in an oversimplified manner, lumping cultural differences into exaggerated categories, and then we view every person in a culture as possessing corresponding stereotypical traits. Thus Americans are all rich, informal, materialistic, and overly friendly. Italians are passionate and demonstrative. The British are reserved, polite, thrifty, and drink tea. Germans are stubborn, industrious, methodical, and drink beer. Orientals are reserved, wise, cunning, and "inscrutable." François Lierres, writing in the Paris newsmagazine *Le Point*, gave some tongue-in-cheek advice to Frenchmen on how to get along with Americans: "They are the Vikings of the world economy, descending upon it in their jets as the Vikings once did in their *drakars*. They have money, technology, and nerve. . . . We would be wise to get acquainted with them." Upon which he offered some *do's* and *don't's*. Among the *do's*: Greet them, but after you have been introduced once, don't shake hands, merely emit a brief cluck of joy—"hi." Speak without emotion, with self-assurance, giving the impression you have a command of the subject even if you haven't. Check the collar of your jacket—nothing is uglier in the eyes of an American than dandruff. Radiate congeniality and show a good disposition—a big smile and a warm expression are essential. Learn how to play golf. Then, among the *don't's*: Don't tamper with your accent—Maurice Chevalier is well liked in America. And don't allow the slightest smell of perspiration to reach the offending nostrils of your American friends.

How do stereotypes form? Our cultural milieu shapes our world view—our *Weltanschauung*—in such a way that reality is thought to be objectively perceived through our own cultural pattern, and a differing perception is seen as either false or "strange" and is thus oversimplified. If a person recognizes and understands differing world views, he will usually adopt a positive and open-minded attitude toward cross-cultural differences. A closed-minded view of such differences often results in the maintenance of a *stereotype*—an oversimplification and blanket assumption. A stereotype is a category that singles out an individual as sharing assumed characteristics on the basis of his group membership. The stereotype may be accurate in depicting the "typical" member of a culture, but it is inaccurate for describing a particular person, simply because every person is a unique individual and all of a person's behavioral characteristics cannot be accurately predicted on the basis of cultural norms.

Cross-cultural research has shown that there are indeed characteristics of culture that make one culture different from another. Condon (1973) concluded from cross-cultural research that American, French, and Hispanic world views are quite different in their concept of time and space. Americans tend to be dominated by a "psychomotor" view of time and space that is dynamic, diffuse, and nominalistic. French orientation is more "cognitive" with a static, centralized, and universalistic view. The Hispanic orientation is more "affectively" centered with a passive, relational, and intuitive world view. It is from these general but reasonably accurate descriptions that stereotypes emerge.

Are cultural stereotypes "bad"? Not necessarily, if a person recognizes positive effects of stereotyping. It was noted in Chapter Four that all human beings organize the environment by means of systematic and meaningful storage. Having developed one particular world view—one set of tools for storing experiences and for reacting to others in our culture—we place incongruous or different world views into categories for meaningful understanding. Since one person is not an integral part of another world view, that other world view is simplified. Sometimes these perceptions are accurate. To say that Americans think of distances in relatively broad categories (60 miles is an easy jaunt) and that the French view distances in narrower categories (60 miles, or 100 kilometers, is a considerable travel distance) is reasonably accurate. So the cautious accumulation of stereotyped images can help a person to understand another culture in general and the differences between that culture and his own.

But there are obvious negative connotations of stereotyping. One is the idea that all persons in a culture fit neatly into a group of rigid categories. Clearly not all Americans are rich, friendly, and materialistic, even though that may be a fairly accurate stereotype of an American in general. And to judge a single member of a culture by overall traits of the culture is both to prejudge and to misjudge that person. The most destructive aspect of stereotyping is that which is derogatory or falls short of valuing and prizing people from different cultures. Mark Twain's comments about the French and German languages, while written in a humorous vein and without any malice, could be interpreted by some to be insulting.

False stereotyping is another negative aspect of cultural stereotyping. Sometimes our oversimplified concepts of members of another culture are downright false. Americans sometimes think of Japanese as being unfriendly because of their cultural norms of respect and politeness. The false view that members of another culture are "dirty" or "smelly"—with verbal and nonverbal messages conveying that view—in fact usually stems merely from different customs of so-called cleanliness. Muriel Saville-Troike (1976:51) notes that "Middle-class whites may objectively note that the lower socioeconomic classes frequently lack proper bathing facilities or changes of clothing, but may be surprised to discover that a common stereotype Blacks hold of whites is that they 'smell like dogs coming in out of the rain." Asians have a similar stereotype of Caucasians."

Both learners and teachers of a second language need to understand cultural differences, to recognize openly that everyone in the world is not "just like me," that people are *not* all the same beneath the skin. There are real differences between groups and cultures. We can learn to perceive those differences, appreciate them, and above all to respect, value, and prize the personhood of every human being.

ATTITUDES

Stereotyping usually implies some type of *attitude* toward the culture or language in question. I recently happened upon an incredible example of a negative attitude stemming from a stereotype; the following passage is an excerpt from an item on "Chinese literature" in the *New Standard Encyclopedia* published in 1940:

> The Chinese Language is monosyllabic and uninflectional. . . . With a language so incapable of variation, a literature cannot be produced which possesses the qualities we look for and admire in literary works. Elegance, variety, beauty of imagery—these must all be lacking. A monotonous and wearisome language must give rise to a forced and formal literature lacking in originality and interesting in its subject matter only. Moreover, a conservative people . . . , profoundly reverencing all that is old and formal, and hating innovation, must leave the impress of its own character upon its literature. (Volume VI)

Fortunately, one would probably not find such views expressed in encyclopedias today. Such biased attitudes are based on insufficient knowledge, misinformed stereotyping, and extreme ethnocentric thinking.

Attitudes, like all aspects of the development of cognition and affect in human beings, develop early in childhood and are the result of parents' and peers' attitudes, contact with people who are "different" in any number of ways, and interacting affective factors in the human experience. These attitudes form a part of one's perception of self, of others, and of the culture in which one is living.

Gardner and Lambert's (1972) extensive studies were systematic attempts to examine the effect of attitudes on language learning. After studying the interrelationships of a number of different types of attitudes, they defined motivation as a construct made up of certain attitudes. The most important of these is group-specific, the attitude the learner has toward the members of the cultural group whose language he is learning. Thus, in Gardner and Lambert's model, an English-speaking Canadian's positive attitude toward French-Canadians—a desire to understand them, and to empathize with them—will lead to high integrative motivation to learn French. That attitude is a factor of the learner's attitudes toward his own native culture, his degree of ethnocentrism, and the extent to which he prefers his own language over the one he is learning as a second language. Among the Canadian subjects Gardner and Lambert distinguished between attitudes toward French-Canadians and attitudes toward people from France.

John Oller and his colleagues (see Oller, Hudson, and Liu 1977; Chihara and Oller 1978; Oller, Baca, and Vigil 1978) conducted several large-scale studies of the relationship between attitudes and language success. They looked at the relationship of Chinese, Japanese, and Mexican students' achievement in English to their attitudes toward self, the native language group, the target language group, their reasons for learning English, and their reasons for traveling to the United States. The researchers were able to identify a few meaningful clusters of attitudinal variables that correlated positively with attained proficiency. Each of the three studies yielded slightly differing conclusions, but for the most part, positive attitudes toward self, the native language group, and the target language group enhanced proficiency. There were mixed results on the relative advantages and disadvantages of integrative and instrumental motivation. For example, in one study they found that better proficiency was attained by students who did not want to stay in the United States permanently.

It seems clear that the second language learner benefits from positive attitudes and that negative attitudes may lead to decreased motivation and in all likelihood unsuccessful attainment of proficiency. Yet the teacher needs to be aware that everyone has both positive and negative attitudes. The negative attitudes *can* be changed, often by exposure to reality, by encounters with actual persons from other cultures. Negative attitudes usually emerge either from false stereotyping or from undue ethnocentrism. The quotation from the encyclopedia above might lead one to stereotype Chinese incorrectly, and therefore to develop a negative attitude toward learning a language that reportedly lacks "elegance, variety, beauty of imagery." Teachers can aid in dispelling what are often myths about other cultures, and replace those myths with a realistic understanding of the other culture as one that is different from one's own, yet to be respected and valued. Learners can thus move through the hierarchy of affectivity as described by Bloom in the preceding chapter, through awareness and responding, to valuing, and finally to an organized and systematic understanding and appreciation of the foreign culture.

LEARNING A SECOND CULTURE

In Chapter Six we saw that second language learning in some respects involves the acquisition of a second identity. Guiora introduced the concept of language ego to capture the deeply seated affective nature of second language learning, stressing the necessity for permeable ego boundaries in order to successfully overcome the trauma of second language learning. Guiora and others have placed strong emphasis on affective characteristics of second language learning because of the highly *social* context of language. Second language learning is often second culture learning. In order to understand just what second culture learning is, one needs to understand the nature of acculturation, culture shock, and social distance.

Acculturation

If a French person is primarily cognitive-oriented and an American is psychomotor-oriented and a Spanish speaker is affective-oriented, as claimed by Condon (1973:22), it is not difficult on this plane alone to understand the complexity of *acculturation*, the process of becoming adapted to a new culture. A reorientation of thinking and feeling, not to mention communication, is necessary.

> For instance, to a European or a South American, the overall impression created by American culture is that of a frantic, perpetual round of actions which leave practically no time for personal feeling and reflection. But, to an American, the reasonable and orderly tempo of French life conveys a sense of hopeless backwardness and ineffectuality; and the leisurely time-lessness of Spanish activities represents an appalling waste of time and human potential. And, to a Spanish speaker, the methodical essense of planned change in France may seem cold-blooded, just as much as his own proclivity toward spur-of-the-moment decisions may strike his French counterpart as recklessly irresponsible. (Condon 1973:25)

The process of acculturation runs even deeper when language is brought into the picture. To be sure, culture is a deeply ingrained part of the very fiber of our being, but language—the means for communication among members of a culture—is the most visible and available expression of that culture. And so a person's world view, self-identity, his systems of thinking, acting, feeling, and communicating, are disrupted by a change from one culture to another.

In considering the relationship between second language learning and second culture learning, it is very important to consider several different types of second language learning contexts. (1) One context is technically referred to as the learning of a *second* language, or learning another language either (a) within the culture of that second language (for example, an Arabic speaker learning English in the United States) or (b) within one's own native culture where the second language is an accepted *lingua franca* used for education, government, or business within the country (for example, learning English in the Philippines or India). (2) Another context for learning another language is technically called *foreign* language learning—that is, learning a non-native language in one's own culture with few immediate and widespread opportunities to use the language within the environment of one's own culture (for example, learning French or German in the United States). It should be pointed out that in this book no such restricted or technical connotations have been implied in the use of the term "second language learning." "Second" language learning and "foreign" language learning have been used interchangeably.

Each type of second language situation involves different degrees of acculturation. Second language learning in a foreign culture (type 1a) clearly involves the deepest form of acculturation. The learner must survive within a strange culture as well as learn a language on which he is totally dependent for communication. Second language learning in the native culture (1b) varies in the severity of acculturation experienced by the learner, depending upon the country, the cultural and sociopolitical status of the language, and the motivations or aspirations of the learner. Kachru (1976) noted that learning English in India really does not involve taking on a new culture, since one is acquiring *Indian* English in India. As was noted earlier, a child learning French in grammar school in French-speaking Africa may not be faced with a difficult cultural conflict; he is faced more with a cognitive or "educational" conflict caused by the necessity for the acquisition of new modes of communication within an educational setting. The foreignness of the educational context may cause extreme conflict, akin to cultural conflict, but not in itself cultural conflict.

The *foreign* language context (type 2) produces the most variable degrees of acculturation since people attempt to learn foreign languages for such a variety of reasons. A person may learn a foreign language in order to communicate someday with the people in another culture; others learn foreign languages for instrumental purposes—for example, fulfilling a foreign language requirement in a university or gaining a reading knowledge within a field of specialization. Still others learn a foreign language simply out of an interest in languages, ranging from passing curiosity to highly technical linguistic interest in the language. Generally, however, the foreign language situation is more culturally loaded than second language learning in the native culture (1b), since the language is almost always learned in a context of understanding the people of another culture. Foreign language curricula therefore commonly attempt to deal with the cultural connotations of the foreign language.

Culture Shock

Culture shock is a common experience for a person learning a second language in a second culture. Culture shock refers to phenomena ranging from mild irritability to deep psychological panic and crisis. Generally culture shock will be experienced only in the first of the second language contexts above (1a), and in the foreign language situation only upon actually entering the second culture (which is tantamount, at that point, to a second language [1a] situation). Culture shock is associated with feelings in the learner of estrangement, anger, hostility, indecision, frustration, unhappiness, sadness, loneliness, homesickness, and even physical illness. The person undergoing culture shock views his new world out of resentment, and alternates between being angry at others for not understanding him and being filled with self-pity. Edward Hall (1959:59) describes a hypothetical example of an American living abroad for the first time:

> At first, things in the cities look pretty much alike. There are taxis, hotels with hot and cold running water, theatres, neon lights, even tall buildings with elevators and a few people who can speak English. But pretty soon the American discovers that underneath the familiar exterior there are vast differences. When someone says "yes" it often doesn't mean yes at all, and when people smile it doesn't always mean they are pleased. When the American visitor makes a helpful gesture he may be rebuffed; when he tries to be friendly nothing happens. People tell him that they will do things and don't. The longer he stays, the more enigmatic the new country looks. . . .

This case of an American in Japan illustrates the point that initially the person in a foreign culture is comfortable and delighted with the "exotic" surroundings. As long as he can perceptually filter his surroundings and internalize the environment in his *own* world view, he feels at ease. As soon as this newness wears off, and the cognitive and affective contradictions of the foreign culture mount up, he becomes disoriented.

Peter Adler (1972:8) describes culture shock in more technical psychological terms:

> Culture shock, then, is thought to be a form of anxiety that results from the loss of commonly perceived and understood signs and symbols of social intercourse. The individual undergoing culture shock reflects his anxiety and nervousness with cultural differences through any number of defense mechanisms: repression, regression, isolation and rejection. These defensive attitudes speak, in behavioral terms, of a basic underlying insecurity which may encompass loneliness, anger, frustration and self-questioning of competence. With the familiar props, cues, and clues of cultural understanding removed, the individual becomes disoriented, afraid of, and alienated from the things that he knows and understands.

The anthropologist George M. Foster (1962:87) described culture shock in extreme terms: "Culture shock is a mental illness, and as is true of much mental illness, the victim usually does not know he is afflicted. He finds that he is irritable, depressed, and probably annoyed by the lack of attention shown him."

It is feasible to think of culture shock as one of four successive stages of acculturation. The first stage is the period of excitement and euphoria over the newness of the surroundings. The second stage—culture shock—emerges as the individual feels the intrusion of more and more cultural differences into his own image of self and security. In this stage the individual relies on and seeks out the support of his fellow countrymen in the second culture, taking solace in complaining about local customs and conditions, seeking escape from his predicament. The third stage is one of gradual, and at first tentative and vacillating, recovery. This stage is typified by what Larson and Smalley (1972) call *culture stress*: some problems of acculturation are solved while other problems continue for some time. But general progress is made, slowly but surely, as the person begins to accept the differences in thinking and feeling that surround him, slowly becoming more empathic with the persons in the second culture. The fourth stage represents near or full recovery, either assimilation or adaptation, acceptance of the new culture and self-confidence in the "new" person that has developed in this culture.

Wallace Lambert's (1967) work on attitudes in second language learning referred often to Durkheim's (1897) concept of *anomie—*

feelings of social uncertainty or dissatisfaction—as a significant aspect of the relationship between language learning and attitude toward the foreign culture. As an individual begins to lose some of the ties of his native culture and adapt to the second culture, he experiences feelings of chagrin or regret, mixed with the fearful anticipation of entering a new group. Anomie might be described as the first symptom of the third stage of acculturation, a feeling of homelessness, where one feels neither bound firmly to his native culture nor fully adapted to the second culture. Lambert's research has supported the view that the strongest dose of anomie is experienced when linguistically a person begins to "master" the foreign language. In Lambert's (1967) study, for example, when English-speaking Canadians became so skilled in French that they began to "think" in French, and even dream in French, feelings of anomie were markedly high. For Lambert's subjects the interaction of anomie and increased skill in the language sometimes led persons to revert or to "regress" back to English—to seek out situations in which they could speak English. Such an urge corresponds to the tentativeness of the third stage of acculturation—periodic reversion to the escape mechanisms acquired in the stage of culture shock. Only until a person is well into the third stage do feelings of anomie decrease as the learner is "over the hump" in the transition from one culture to another.

In keeping with these bleak descriptions of culture shock, Mark Clarke (1976:380) likened second language learning and second culture learning to *schizophrenia*, where "social encounters become inherently threatening, and defense mechanisms are employed to reduce the trauma." Clarke cited Gregory Bateson's (1972:208) description of the "double bind" that foreigners in a new culture experience:

1. ... the individual is involved in an intense relationship; that is, a relationship in which he feels it is vitally important that he discriminate accurately what sort of message is being communicated so that he may respond appropriately.
2. ... the individual is caught in a situation in which the other person in the relationship is expressing two orders of message and one of these denies the other.
3. ... the individual is unable to comment on the messages being expressed to correct his discrimination of what order of message to respond to, i.e., he cannot make a metacommunicative statement.

Clarke then goes on to note that virtually every encounter with people in a foreign culture is an "intense relationship" in which tremendous effort is expended to keep communication from breaking down. For example, "Getting a taxi driver to understand where you want to go; attempting to discover if he has indeed understood you, given that he says he has, but continues to drive in the wrong direction; and searching frantically all the while for the proper phrases to express yourself so that you don't appear stupid or patronizing; all of this combines to give a simple ride across town Kafkaesque proportions which cannot be easily put in perspective by the person who has suffered through them" (p. 380). That such behavior can be compared with schizophrenia is clear from Bateson's (1972:211) description of alternatives commonly adopted by a schizophrenic to defend himself:

1. He might . . . assume that behind every statement there is a concealed meaning which is detrimental to his welfare. . . . If he chooses this alternative, he will be continually searching for meanings behind what people say and behind chance occurrences in the environment, and he will be characteristically suspicious and defiant.

2. He might . . . tend to accept literally everything people say to him; when their tone or gesture or context contradicted what they said he might establish a pattern of laughing off these metacommunicative signals.

3. If he didn't become suspicious of metacommunicative messages or attempt to laugh them off, he might choose to ignore them. Then he would find it necessary to see and hear less and less of what went on around him, and do his utmost to avoid provoking a response in his environment.

The schizophrenic period of culture shock and of language learning is therefore indeed a crucial period during which time the learner will either "sink or swim."

The description I have given of culture shock paints a rather severe picture of an unwitting and helpless victim of an illness, and an illness for which there is no clearcut cure. Peter Adler (1972:14) points out that culture shock, while surely possessing manifestations of crisis, can also be viewed more positively as a profound cross-cultural learning experience, one that leads to "a high degree of self-awareness and personal growth." A *cross-cultural learning experience* can be defined as

a set of situations or circumstances involving intercultural communication in which the individual, as a result of the experiences, becomes aware of his own growth, learning and change. As a result of the culture shock process, the individual has gained new perspective on himself, and has come to understand his own identity in terms significant to himself. The cross-cultural learning experience, additionally, takes place when the individual encounters a different culture and as a result (a) examines the degree to which he is influenced by his own culture, and (b) understands the culturally derived values, attitudes and outlooks of other people. (ibid.)

Teachers of foreign languages would do well to heed Adler's words. While certainly not every learner will find a cross-cultural experience to be totally positive, many do derive positive values from the experience, and for those for whom learning a second culture might otherwise become a negative experience, or an illness, teachers can help that experience to become one of increased cultural awareness and self-awareness for the learner. Howard Nostrand (1966) recommended administration of careful "doses" of culture shock in foreign language classrooms. Thus equipped with self-understanding and a balanced understanding of the differences between two cultures, the learner slowly but empathically steps into the shoes of members of the foreign culture. Nostrand's suggestion is simplistic and un-realistic. Culture shock cannot be prevented with affective vacci-nations. But teachers can play a therapeutic role in helping learners to move through stages of acculturation. If the learner is aided in this process by sensitive and perceptive teachers, he can perhaps more smoothly pass through the second stage and into the third stage of culture learning, and thereby increase his chances for suc-ceeding in both second language learning and second culture learning.

It is exceedingly important that teachers allow the learner to proceed into and through that second stage, through the anomie, and not to force a quick bypass of the second stage. We should not expect the learner to deny the anger, the frustration, the helpless-ness and homelessness he feels. Those are real feelings and they need to be openly expressed. To smother those feelings may delay and actually prevent eventual movement into the third stage. A teacher can enable the learner to understand the source of his anger and frustration, to express those feelings, and then gradually to emerge from those depths to a very powerful and personal form of learning.

Social Distance

The concept of *social distance* has emerged as an affective con-struct to give explanatory power to the place of culture learning in second language learning. Social distance refers to the cognitive and affective proximity of two cultures which come into contact within an individual. "Distance" is obviously used in an abstract sense, to denote dissimilarity between two cultures. On a very superficial level one might observe, for example, that Americans (people from the United States) are culturally similar to Canadians, while Americans and Chinese are, by comparison, relatively dissimilar. We could say that the social distance of the latter case exceeds the former.

John Schumann (1976c:136) described social distance as consisting of the following parameters: "In relation to the TL [target language] group is the 2LL [second language learning] group politically, culturally, technically or economically dominant, non-dominant, or subordinate? Is the integration pattern of the 2LL group assimilation, acculturation, or preservation? What is the 2LL group's degree of enclosure? Is the 2LL group cohesive? What is the size of the 2LL group? Are the cultures of the two groups congruent? What are the attitudes of the two groups toward each other? What is the 2LL group's intended length of residence in the target language area?" Schumann used the above factors (dominance, integration pattern, cohesiveness, congruence, attitude, and length of residence) to describe hypothetically "good" and "bad" language-learning situations, and illustrated each situation with two actual cross-cultural contexts. Two hypothetical "bad" language learning situations were described (p. 139):

1. One of the bad situations would be where the TL group views the 2LL group as dominant and the 2LL group views itself in the same way, where both groups desire preservation and high enclosure for the 2LL group, where the 2LL group is both cohesive and large, where the two cultures are not congruent, where the two groups hold negative attitudes toward each other, and where the 2LL group intends to remain in the TL area only for a short time.

2. The second bad situation has all the characteristics of the first except that in this case, the 2LL group would consider itself subordinate and would also be considered subordinate by the TL group.

The first situation is typical, according to Schumann, of Americans living in Riyadh, Saudi Arabia. The second situation is descriptive of Navajo Indians living in the southwestern part of the United States.

A "good" language learning situation, according to Schumann's model (p. 141),

would be one where the 2LL group is non-dominant in relation to the TL group, where both groups desire assimilation (or at least acculturation) for the 2LL group, where low enclosure is the goal of both groups, where the two cultures are congruent, where the 2LL group is small and non-cohesive, where both groups have positive attitudes towards each other, and where the 2LL group intends to remain in the target language area for a long time. Under such conditions social distance would be minimal and acquisition of the target language would be enhanced.

Schumann cites as a specific example of a "good" language learning situation the case of American Jewish immigrants living in Israel.

Schumann's hypothesis is that the greater the social distance between two cultures, the greater the difficulty the learner will have in learning the second language, and conversely, the smaller the social distance (the greater the social solidarity between two cultures), the better will be the language learning situation.

In later research Schumann (1976a) and colleagues carried out research linking the construct of social distance to the *pidginization* of the interlanguage of a learner. A pidgin is a simplified and reduced form of language used for communication between people with different languages, and is characterized by a lack of inflectional morphology and a tendency to eliminate grammatical transformations. Pidginization was seen to occur as a result of social distance between cultures in the case of the language development of a learner of English as a second language in the United States, a contention supported later by Stauble (1978) in a study of an Italian learner of English.

Perceived Social Distance

One of the difficulties in Schumann's hypothesis of social distance is the measurement of actual social distance. How can one determine *degrees* of social distance? By what means? And how would those means be quantifiable for comparison of relative distances? So far the construct has remained a rather subjectively defined phenomenon which like empathy, self-esteem, and so many other psychological constructs, defies definition even though one can intuitively grasp the sense of what is meant.

William Acton (1979) proposed a solution to the dilemma. Instead of trying to measure *actual* social distance, he devised a measure of *perceived* social distance. His contention was that it is not particularly relevant what the actual distance is between cultures, since it is what the learner perceives that forms his own reality. We have already noted that human beings perceive the cultural environment through the filters and screens of their own world view and then act upon that perception, however "biased" it may be. According to Acton, when a learner encounters a new culture, his acculturation process will be a factor of how he perceives his own culture in relation to the culture of the target language, and vice versa. For example, objectively there may be a relatively large distance between Americans and Saudi Arabians, but an American learning Arabic in Saudi Arabia might for a number of reasons perceive little distance, and in turn act on that perception.

By asking learners to respond to three dimensions of distance, Acton devised a measure of perceived social distance—the Professed Difference in Attitude Questionnaire (PDAQ)—which characterized the "good" or successful language learner (as measured by standard proficiency tests) with remarkable accuracy. Basically the PDAQ asked the learner to quantify what he perceived to be the differences in attitude toward various concepts ("the automobile," "divorce," "socialism," "policemen," for example) on three dimensions: (1) distance (or difference) between himself and his countrymen in general; (2) distance between himself and members of the target culture in general; and (3) distance between his countrymen and members of the target culture. By using a semantic differential technique, three distance scores were computed for each dimension. Acton found that in the case of learners of English who had been in the United States for four months, there is an *optimal* perceived social distance ratio (among the three scores) that typifies the "good" language learner. If a learner perceived himself as either too *close* to or too *distant* from either the target culture or the native culture he fell into the category of "bad" language learners as measured by standard proficiency tests. The implication is that the successful language learner sees himself as maintaining some distance between himself and *both* cultures. Unfortunately, Acton's PDAQ did not *predict* success in language. However, this is no great surprise since we know of no adequate instrument to predict language success or to assess language aptitude. But what the PDAQ did was to describe empirically, in quantifiable terms, a relationship between social distance and second language acquisition.

A Cultural "Critical Period"?

Acton's theory of optimal perceived social distance supports Lambert's (1967) contention that mastery of the foreign language takes place hand in hand with feelings of anomie or homelessness, where the learner has moved away from his native culture but is still not completely assimilated or adjusted in the target culture. More importantly, Acton's model leads us closer to an understanding of culture shock and the relationship of acculturation to language learning by supplying an important piece to a puzzle. If you combine Acton's research with Lambert's a rather interesting hypothesis emerges—namely, that mastery or skillful fluency in a second language (within the second culture) occurs somewhere at the beginning of the third stage of acculturation. The implication of such a hypothesis is that mastery might not effectively occur before that stage, or even more likely, that the learner might never be successful in his mastery of the language if he has proceeded beyond early Stage 3 without accomplishing that linguistic mastery. Stage 3 may provide not only the optimal *distance*, but the optimal cognitive and affective *tension* to produce the necessary *pressure* to acquire the language, yet pressure that is neither too overwhelming (such as that which may be typical of Stage 2 or culture shock) nor too weak (Stage 4). Language mastery at Stage 3, in turn, would appear to be an instrument for progressing psychologically through Stage 3 and finally into Stage 4.

According to my hypothesis, an adult who fails to master a second language in a second culture may for a host of reasons have failed to synchronize linguistic and cultural development. The adult who has achieved nonlinguistic means of coping in the foreign culture will pass through Stage 3 and into Stage 4 with an undue number of *fossilized* forms of language (see Chapter Nine for a discussion of fossilization), never achieving mastery. He has no reason to achieve mastery since he has learned to cope without sophisticated knowledge of the language; he may have acquired a sufficient number of the functions of a second language without acquiring correct forms. On the other hand, the person who has achieved linguistic mastery too early (before Stage 3) may be less likely to achieve healthy acculturation and be unable to cope psychologically even though his linguistic skills are excellent. What I have suggested here might well be termed a culturally based *critical period* that is independent of the age of the learner. A young child, because he has not built up years and years of a culture-bound world view and view of himself, has fewer perceptive filters to readjust, and therefore moves through stages of acculturation more quickly, and of course acquires the language more quickly. He nevertheless may move through the same four stages, just as an adult does. Cases of unsuccessful child second language learning might possibly be attributable to less than optimal synchronization of stages of acculturation and stages of language mastery.

I am suggesting a hypothesis which of course needs further research and refinement. But previous research on sociocultural variables in language learning seems to bear out the hypothesis. Teachers could benefit from a careful assessment of the current cultural stages of learners with due attention to possible optimal periods for language mastery.

LANGUAGE, THOUGHT, AND CULTURE

No discussion about cultural variables in second language acquisition is complete without some treatment of the relationship between language and thought. We saw in the case of first language acquisition that cognitive development and linguistic development go hand in hand, each interacting with and shaping the other. It is commonly observed that the manner in which an idea or "fact" is stated affects the way we conceptualize the idea. Words shape our lives. The advertising world is a prime example of the use of language to shape, persuade, and dissuade. "Weasel words" tend to glorify very ordinary products into those that are "sparkling," "refreshing," or even "scrumpdeliyicious." In the case of food that has been sapped of most of its nutrients by the manufacturing process, we are told that these products are now "enriched" and "fortified." A foreigner in the United States once remarked that in the United States there are no "small" eggs, only "medium," "large," "extra-large," and "jumbo." Euphemisms—or "telling it like it isn't"—abound in American culture where certain thoughts are taboo or certain words connote something less than desirable. We are persuaded by industry, for example, that "receiving waters" are the lakes or rivers into which industrial wastes are dumped and that "assimilative capacity" refers to how much of the waste you can dump into the river before it starts to show. Garbage men are "sanitary engineers"; toilets are "rest rooms"; slums are "substandard dwellings." Even a common word like "family" has for some social scientists been replaced by "a micro-cluster of structured role expectations."

Verbal labels can shape the way we store events for later recall. In a classic study, Carmichael, Hogan, and Walter (1932) found that when subjects were briefly exposed to figures like those in Figure 7-1 and later asked to reproduce them, the reproductions were influenced by the labels assigned to the figures.

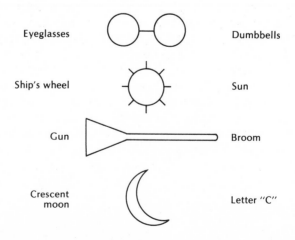

Figure 7-1. Sample stimulus figures used by Carmichael, Hogan, and Walter (1932).

For example, the first drawing tended to be reproduced as something like this:

if the subject had seen the "eyeglasses" label, and on the other hand like this:

if he had seen the "dumbbells" label.

Words are not the only linguistic category affecting thought. The way a sentence is structured will affect nuances of meaning. Elizabeth Loftus (1976) discovered that subtle differences in the structure of questions can affect the answer a person gives. For example, upon viewing a film of an automobile accident subjects were asked questions like "Did you see *the* broken headlight?" in some cases, and in other cases "Did you see *a* broken headlight?" Questions using *the* tended to produce more false recognition of events. That is, the presence of the definite article led subjects to believe that there *was* a broken headlight, whether they saw it or not. Similar results were found for questions like "Did you see some people watching the accident?" vs. "Did you see any people watching the accident?" or even for questions containing a presupposition: "How fast was the car going when it hit the stop sign?" (presupposing both the existence of a stop sign and that the car hit a stop sign, whether the subject actually saw it or not).

On the discourse level of language we are familiar with the persuasiveness of an emotional speech or a well-written novel. How often has a gifted orator swayed opinion and thought? or a powerful editorial moved one to action or change? These are common examples of the influence of language on our cognitive and affective organizations.

Culture is really an integral part of the interaction between language and thought. Cultural patterns, customs, and ways of life are expressed in language; culture-specific world views are reflected in language. Cultures have different ways of dividing the color spectrum, for example, illustrating differing world views on what color is and how to identify color. Gleason (1961:4) notes that the Shona of Rhodesia and the Bassa of Liberia have fewer color categories than speakers of European languages and they break up the spectrum at different points, as Figure 7-2 shows:

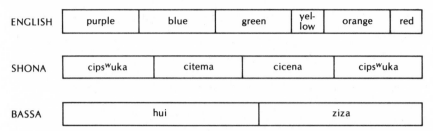

Figure 7-2. Color categories in three cultures.

Of course, the Shona or Bassa are able to perceive and describe other colors, in the same way that an English speaker might describe a "dark bluish green," but the labels which the language provides tend to shape the person's overall cognitive organization of color and to cause varying degrees of color discrimination. Eskimo tribes commonly have as many as seven different words for *snow* to distinguish among different types of snow (falling snow, snow on the ground, fluffy snow, wet snow, etc.), while certain African cultures in the equatorial forests of Zaire have no word at all for snow.

But even more to the point than such geographically conditioned aspects of language are examples from the Hopi language (see Whorf 1956). Hopi does not use verbs in the same way that English does. For example, in English we might say "he is running," but in Hopi we would have to choose from a number of much more precise verbal ideas, depending upon the knowledge of the speaker and the validity of the statement. A different form of the verb expresses: "I know that he is running at this very moment," "I know that he is running at this moment even though I cannot see him," "I remember that I saw him running and I presume he is still running," or "I am told that he is running." Also, *duration* and *time* are expressed differently in Hopi. Time, for example, is not measured or wasted or saved in Hopi. Time is expressed in terms of events, sequences, and development. Plant a seed and it will grow; the span of time for growth is not important. It is the development of events—planting, germination, growth, blossoming, bearing fruit—that are important.

A tantalizing question emerges from such observations. Does language *reflect* a cultural world view or does language actually *shape* the world view? Drawing on the ideas of Wilhelm von Humboldt (1767-1835), who claimed that language shaped a person's *Weltanschauung*, Edward Sapir and Benjamin Whorf proposed a hypothesis that has now been given several alternative labels: the *Sapir-Whorf hypothesis*, the *Whorfian hypothesis*, *linguistic relativity*, or *linguistic determinism*. Whorf (1956:212) sums up the hypothesis:

142

The background linguistic system (in other words, the grammar) of each language is not merely a reproducing instrument for voicing ideas but rather is itself the shaper of ideas, the program and guide for the individual's mental activity, for his analysis of impressions, for his synthesis of his mental stock in trade. Formulation of ideas is not an independent process, strictly rational in the old sense, but is part of a particular grammar and differs, from slightly to greatly, as between different grammars. We dissect nature along lines laid down by our native languages. The categories and types that we isolate from the world of phenomena we do not find there because they stare every observer in the face; on the contrary, the world is presented in a kaleidoscopic flux of impressions which has to be organized by our minds—and this means largely by the linguistic systems in our minds. We cut nature up, organize it into concepts, and ascribe significances as we do, largely because we are parties to an agreement to organize it in this way—an agreement that holds through our speech community and is codified in the patterns of our language. The agreement is, of course, an implicit and unstated one, but its terms are absolutely obligatory; we cannot talk at all except by subscribing to the organization and classification of data which the agreement decrees.

Today the Whorfian hypothesis has few zealous believers. Most linguists have little concern about a debate over whether language shapes thought or thought shapes language. They are more concerned, and rightly so, with the fact that language and culture interact, that world views among cultures differ, and that the language used to express that world view may be relative and specific to that view. Many linguists are more interested in the universality of language and consequently the universality of cognitive and affective experience: what is it that the human race shares in common? Guiora (1976) tested the Whorfian hypothesis for the effect of the gender of nouns between English and Hebrew, and found no support whatever for linguistic relativity. "The import of our findings seems to be that the pattern of our data may suggest the existence of the universality of symbols, at least across these two languages and these two cultures, thus adducing support to the notion of the universality of affective experience" (1976:15).

Ronald Wardhaugh (1976:74) expresses the antithesis of the Whorfian hypothesis even more strongly:

The most valid conclusion to all such studies is that it appears possible to talk about anything in any language provided the speaker is willing to use some degree of circumlocution. Some concepts are more "codable," that is, easier to express, in some languages than in others. The speaker, of course, will not be aware of the circumlocution in the absence of familiarity with another language that uses a more succinct means of expression.

Every natural language provides both a language for talking about every other language, that is, a metalanguage, and an entirely adequate apparatus for making any kinds of observations that need to be made about the world. If such is the case, every natural language must be an extremely rich system which readily allows its speakers to overcome any predispositions that exist.

For second language teachers a knowledge of the commonalities between two languages or of the universal features of language appears to be fruitful for understanding the total language learning process. While we can recognize different world views and different ways of expressing reality depending upon one's world view, we can also recognize through both language and culture some universal properties that bind us all together in one world. The act of learning to *think* in another language may require a considerable degree of mastery of that language, but a second language learner does not have to learn to think, in general, all over again. As in every other human learning experience, the second language learner can make positive use of prior experiences to facilitate the process of learning by retaining that which is valid and valuable for second culture learning and second language learning. It is just the bathwater of interference that needs to be thrown out, not the baby of facilitation.

SUGGESTED READINGS

There are a number of classic references in the field of cultural anthropology which can serve as excellent background material for this chapter. *Hall* (1959) and *Hall* (1966) are both excellent sources written for the layperson. Slightly more technical, but still a very readable source is *Burling* (1970), an introduction to the relationship between language and culture. *Lado* (1957) is dated, but if time permits it can give you an appreciation of a historical perspective in relating linguistics to culture, especially Chapters 1 and 6.

A useful synopsis of the cultural foundations of language learning and teaching can be found in Chapter 4 of *Saville-Troike* (1976). Though her comments are related to learning English as a second language, general principles can be extrapolated for all languages.

You can get some valuable insights from reading one or all of *Oller*'s studies on attitudes (Oller, Hudson, and Liu 1977; Oller, Baca, and Vigil 1978; Chihara and Oller 1978). Those articles provide a picture of the type of instrumentation that is used to measure attitudes and also give more technical information supporting their conclusions on the relationship between attitudes and language learning. *Gardner and Lambert* (1972) is also a good background resource for this chapter and Chapter Six.

A most interesting trilogy of works can be found in *Clarke* (1976), *Schumann* (1976c), and *Acton* (1979).

The notion of a cultural critical period is summarized in *Brown* (1979).

TOPICS AND QUESTIONS FOR STUDY
AND DISCUSSION

1. Think of everyday examples of the subjectivity of perceiving people and behavior through the eyes of your own cultural viewpoint. Refer to eating customs, daily work patterns, family life, marriage customs, politeness patterns, and the like. Does your own pattern somehow seem more reasonable or sensible than that of some other culture with which you are familiar?

2. Consider some of the cultures with which you are familiar and list various stereotypes of those cultures. Share your stereotypes with those of a classmate or friend and compare your perceptions. How might those stereotypes *help* you to understand someone from another culture? How might they *hinder* your understanding?

3. Discuss sensitive cross-cultural differences (religious, political, social, or personal issues) with someone from another culture. Can you empathize (not necessarily sympathize) with those differences? In your discussion, what attitudes were reflected toward your culture? What attitudes do you think you expressed toward the other culture?

4. Try to think of some area of your affective or cognitive self in which you feel some prejudice toward members of another culture or even a subculture (such as people from different parts of your own country). What are the deeply seated causes of that prejudice? Should you overcome that prejudice? How might a person go about eradicating such negative attitudes?

5. Review the distinction between *second* language learning and *foreign* language learning. How might your teaching materials and techniques vary depending upon whether you were teaching a second or a foreign language?

6. If you have ever lived in another country, can you now identify some of the stages of acculturation in your own experience? Describe your feelings. Did you move through all four stages? Did you reach assimilation? Or adaptation? Did you experience *anomie*?

7. Is Clarke pushing matters a little too far in likening culture shock to schizophrenia?

8. Why is Nostrand's suggestion of giving "doses" of culture shock referred to in this chapter as simplistic? Do you agree? Can you think of plausible ways to deal with culture shock in the classroom?

9. Can you think of other "good" and "bad" language learning situations besides those described by Schumann (see pp. 136-37)? What factors make them either good or bad?

10. Summarize the notion of a cultural critical period. In your own experiences or the experiences of those you have known, would you say there is support for the notion of a culturally defined critical period? Have you known people who progressed well into Stage 3 without linguistic mastery? What happened eventually to their language proficiency? Have you known others who mastered a language too *soon*, before going through stages of acculturation? What effect, if any, did that have on eventual cultural adaptation or assimilation?

11. In your second language, find examples that support the contention that language (specific vocabulary items, perhaps) seems to shape the way the speaker of a language views the world. In what way does the Whorfian hypothesis present yet another chicken-or-egg issue?

8

Comparing and Contrasting
Two Languages

Up to this point in the treatment of principles of second language acquisition I have focused essentially on psychological variables, making references to linguistic variables within a psychological framework. The reason for such a focus is that the psychological principles of second language acquisition form the foundation stones for building a comprehensive understanding of the acquisition of the linguistic system—the units and structures of language. Linguistic systems cannot be examined fruitfully without recognition and understanding of the relationship of language to the total human being. The *forms* of language—the sounds, sound systems, grammatical structures, words, and discourse features—are utilized to accomplish certain intended *functions* of communication. We have encountered a good many of those functions of language in our examination of first and second language acquisition, human learning, cognitive strategies and styles, personality variables, and sociocultural dimensions of second language acquisition. We have considered some of the physical, cognitive, and affective factors that come to bear on this most complex process. In this chapter and the two subsequent chapters we will tackle what in common observation is the most *salient* aspect of second language acquisition—the learning of the linguistic system itself. It should be clear, though, that salient language forms are *relevant* only when we perceive their roots in human behavior— verbal behavior whose purpose is communication between and among human beings.

The first of these three chapters on the linguistic system deals with the systematic comparison and contrasting of the native and target (or second) language systems, commonly known as *contrastive analysis*. The next chapter takes up the notion that not only are the native and target languages coming into contact, but the learner himself is imposing a system upon the target language, a system that can be discerned by analysis of the linguistic *errors* that a learner makes, commonly known as *error analysis*. Chapter Ten then examines second language learning from a larger perspective: the stretches of discourse we use for the pragmatic purpose of sending and receiving messages, generally referred to as *discourse analysis*. The latter chapter will bring us full-circle from the consideration of linguistic forms to the ultimate interaction of language with the physical, cognitive, and affective organisms using language.

THE CONTRASTIVE ANALYSIS HYPOTHESIS

During the middle part of this century, when behavioristic psychology and structural linguistics were in their heyday, the language teaching profession began to pay a great deal of heed to the very widely accepted *Contrastive Analysis* hypothesis. This hypothesis, deeply rooted in behaviorism and structuralism, claimed that the principal barrier to second language acquisition is the interference of the first language system with the second language system, and that a scientific, structural analysis of the two languages in question would yield a taxonomy of linguistic contrasts between them which in turn would enable the linguist to predict the difficulties a learner would encounter. It was at that time considered feasible that the tools of structural linguistics would enable a linguist to describe accurately the two languages in question, and to match those two descriptions against each other to determine valid contrasts, or differences, between them. Behaviorism contributed to the notion that human behavior is the sum of its smallest parts and components, and therefore that language learning could be described as the acquisition of all of these discrete units. Moreover, human learning theories highlighted *interfering* elements of learning, concluding that where no interference could be predicted, no difficulty would be experienced since one could *transfer* positively all other items in a language. The logical conclusion from these various psychological and linguistic assumptions was that second language learning basically involved the overcoming of the *differences* between the two linguistic systems— the native and target languages.

Intuitively the Contrastive Analysis hypothesis has appeal in that we commonly observe in second language learners a plethora of errors attributable to the negative transfer of the native language to the target language. It is quite common, for example, to detect certain foreign accents and to be able to infer, from the speech of the learner alone, where the learner comes from. English learners from such native language backgrounds as German, French, Spanish, and Japanese, for example, usually can readily be detected by native English speakers by easily identifiable—stereotypical, if you will—accents that we have grown accustomed to hearing. Such accents can even be represented in the written word. Consider again Mark Twain's *The Innocents Abroad* (1869:111), in which the French-speaking guide introduces himself:

> If ze zhentlemans will to me make ze grande honneur to me rattain in hees serveece, I shall show to him everysing zat is magnifique to look upon in ze beautiful Parree. I speaky ze Angleesh parfaitnaw.

Or William E. Callahan's Juan Castaniegos, a young Mexican in *Afraid of the Dark*, who says: "Help me to leave from thees place. But, Señor Capitán, me, I 'ave to notheeng. Notheeng, Señor Capitán." These excerpts also capture the transfer of vocabulary and grammatical rules from the native language.

Some rather strong claims were made of the Contrastive Analysis hypothesis among language teaching experts and linguists. One of the strongest was made by Robert Lado (1957) in the preface to *Linguistics Across Cultures*: "The plan of the book rests on the assumption that we can predict and describe the patterns that will cause difficulty in learning, and those that will not cause difficulty, by comparing systematically the language and the culture to be learned with the native language and culture of the student" (p. vii). Then, in the first chapter of the book, Lado continues: " . . . in the comparison between native and foreign language lies the key to ease or difficulty in foreign language learning. . . . Those elements that are similar to [the learner's] native language will be simple for him and those elements that are different will be difficult" (pp. 1-2). An equally strong claim was made by Banathy, Trager, and Waddle (1966:37): "The change that has to take place in the language behavior of a foreign language student can be equated with the differences between the structure of the student's native language and culture and that of the target language and culture."

For a number of years materials in foreign languages were prepared on these "fundamental assumptions" about the relationship between two linguistic systems in learning a foreign language. Randal Whitman (1970) noted that contrastive analysis involved four different procedures. The first of these is *description*: the linguist or language teacher, using the tools of formal grammar, explicitly describes the two languages in question. Second, a *selection* is made of certain forms—linguistic items, rules, structures—for contrast, since it is virtually impossible to contrast every possible facet of two languages. Whitman admits that the selection process "reflects the conscious and unconscious assumptions of the investigator" (p. 193) which in turn affect exactly what forms are selected. The third procedure is the *contrast* itself, the mapping of one linguistic system onto the other, and a specification of the relationship of one system to the other which, like selection, "rests on the validity of one's reference points" (p. 196). Finally, one formulates a *prediction* of error or of difficulty on the basis of the first three procedures. That prediction can be arrived at through the formulation of a hierarchy of difficulty or through more subjective applications of psychological and linguistic theory.

It is not difficult to discern from Whitman's outline of procedures the subjectivity of contrastive analysis, something that falls short of a "scientific description" (Fries 1945:9) in the rigorous tradition of behavioristic psychology.

HIERARCHY OF DIFFICULTY

Attempts have been made to formalize the prediction stage of contrastive analysis, to remove some of the subjectivity involved. The best-known attempt was made by Stockwell, Bowen, and Martin (1965), who proposed what they called a *hierarchy of difficulty* by which a teacher or linguist can make a *prediction* of the relative difficulty of a given aspect of the second language. Though the authors devised their hierarchy for English and Spanish, they claimed a universal application of the hierarchy. For phonological systems in contrast, Stockwell and his associates suggested eight possible degrees of difficulty. These degrees were based upon the notions of transfer (positive, negative, and zero) and of optional and obligatory choices of certain phonemes in the two languages in contrast. Let us look, for example, at their explanation of what they define as their fourth degree of difficulty in reference to an English speaker learning Spanish as a second language (pp. 12-13):

> English *Op*, Spanish *Ob*. This correspondence characterizes one of the more difficult problems of Spanish phonology for the English learner. Take, for example, the pronunciation of items like *dado* and *dedo* in isolation. The *d* at the beginning is pronounced differently from the *d* in the middle. The initial *d* is much like the initial *d* of English *den*, *doll*, *door*.

(It is not exactly the same, but the difference is irrelevant for this purpose.) We will write it with the phonetic symbol [d]. The middle *d* of *dado*, *dedo*, on the other hand, is conspicuously different—to the English ear— from the initial *d*. It sounds more nearly like the initial *th* of *then, there, those*. We will write it with the phonetic symbol [đ]. Dado and dedo can now be written phonetically as [dádo], [déđo]. For the Spanish speaker, the pronunciation of [đ], rather than [d], in the middle of these words is obligatory. He will not ordinarily even be aware that he pronounces two quite different sounds for the *d*'s of *dado* and *dedo*. To use the technical terminology introduced earlier, [d] and [đ] are *allophones* of a single phoneme /d/ in Spanish. Among the consonants of Spanish, /d/ exists as one possible optional choice, which may be symbolized:

$$\text{Spanish C} \rightarrow \left\{ \left(\begin{array}{l} /p/ \\ /t/ \\ /k/ \\ /b/ \\ /d/ \\ /g/ \\ \cdot \\ \cdot \\ \cdot \end{array} \right) \text{ in env.} - V \right\}$$

There is then a subsidiary rule about /d/ (illustrated, incompletely, below):

$$/d/ \rightarrow \left\{ \begin{array}{l} [d] \text{ in env.} \left\{ \begin{array}{l} /l/ \\ /n/ \\ \# \end{array} \right\} - \\ [đ] \text{ in env.} \quad V \quad - \end{array} \right\}$$

That is, if /d/ is preceded by silence (a break in utterance continuity symbolized in the formula by #) or an /n/ or /l/, it is pronounced as [d]. If it is preceded by a vowel, it is pronounced as [đ]. The phonetic difference between [d] and [đ] is CONDITIONED by this rule—a rule which merely describes a set of conditions to which Spanish speakers habitually, and unconsciously, conform. Because of this rule, [đ] is for them simply a kind of /d/. But for the English speaker, the conditions are different. For him [d] and [đ] are IN CONTRAST—that is, they belong to different phonemes, /d/ and /đ/. The fact of contrast is proved by pairs such as *dine/thine, dare/there, dough/though*. [d] and [đ] exist as two possible choices among the consonants of English:

$$\text{English C} \rightarrow \left\{ \left(\begin{array}{l} /p/ \\ /t/ \\ /k/ \\ /b/ \\ /d/ \\ /g/ \\ /v/ \\ /đ/ \\ \cdot \\ \cdot \\ \cdot \end{array} \right) \text{ in env.} - V \right\}$$

In English, unlike Spanish, /d/ and /đ/ are in contrast: they are both optional choices, and their distribution cannot be predicted. Predictability is at the heart of the matter: the occurrence of Spanish [d] and [đ] can be predicted by writing merely one symbol, /d/; given this symbol in an environment, it is possible always and infallibly to predict whether it will be pronounced [d] or [đ]. The difference between them is obligatory.

Through a very careful, systematic analysis of the properties of the two languages, and by subjecting this analysis to the hierarchy that Stockwell and his associates devised, one can derive a reasonably complete inventory of phonological difficulties a second language learner will encounter, and that inventory will include prediction of the difficulty—relative to other items in the inventory—of a particular unit of contrast.

Stockwell and his associates also constructed a hierarchy of difficulty for grammatical structures of two languages in contrast. Their grammatical hierarchy included 16 levels of difficulty, based on the same notions used to construct phonological criteria with the added dimensions of "structural correspondence" and "functional/semantic correspondence." The hierarchy that emerges is so complex that it is really inappropriate to summarize here. However, Clifford Prator (1967) captured the essence of this grammatical hierarchy in six categories of difficulty which are more easily explained in the context of this chapter. Moreover, Prator's categories are applicable to both grammatical and phonological features of language. The six categories, in ascending order of difficulty are discussed below. Most of the examples are taken from English and Spanish (a native English speaker learning Spanish as a second language); a few examples illustrate other pairs of contrasting languages.

Level 0—Transfer

No difference or contrast is present between the two languages. The learner can simply transfer (positively) a sound, structure, or lexical item from the native language to the target language. Such transfer is posited to be of no difficulty, hence the label of "level zero." Examples can be found in certain phonemes and their distribution in English and Spanish (cardinal vowels, /s/, /z/, /m/, /n/, structures (say, general word order), or words (mortal, inteligente, arte, americanos).

Level 1—Coalescence

Two items in the native language become coalesced into essentially one item in the target language. This requires that the learner overlook a distinction he has grown accustomed to. For example,

English third-person possessives require gender distinction (*his/her*), and in Spanish they do not (*su*). It is difficult to provide phonological instances of coalescence because of the theoretical difficulty of claiming that two sounds actually "merge." One might, for example, claim that the English-speaking learner of Japanese can overlook the distinction between /r/ and /l/, and simply produce an /r/ in Japanese. But such a contrast can also be argued merely as a case of a phoneme (/l/) that is *absent* (see Level 2) in the target language. A good lexical example of coalescence is found in the case of an English speaker learning French who must overlook the distinction between *teach* and *learn*, and use just the one word *apprendre* in French.

Level 2—Underdifferentiation

An item in the native language is absent in the target language. The learner must avoid that item. English learners of Spanish must "forget," as it were, such items as English *do* as a tense carrier, indefinite determiners (*other*, *certain*), possessive forms of *wh-* words (*whose*), or the use of *some* with mass nouns. A number of phonemes that are present in English are absent in Spanish: several vowels /ɪ/, /æ/, among others), /θ/, /ð/, /ŋ/ and other consonants.

Level 3—Reinterpretation

An item that exists in the native language is given a new shape or distribution. Though it is difficult to argue that Level 3 is distinct from *any* of the other levels, Prator (1967) claimed that in some cases items in the target language are perceived as reinterpreted native language items. The English speaker who learns French, for example, must learn a new distribution for nasalized vowels. Or, when in English we must use a determiner (He's *a* philosopher), in Spanish the determiner is optional (Él es (*un*) filósofo); the learner of Spanish must reinterpret his English system of determiners.

Level 4—Overdifferentiation

A new item entirely, bearing little if any similarity to the native language item, must be learned. For example, in learning Spanish the native English speaker must learn to include determiners in generalized nominals (Man is mortal/*El* hombre es mortal), to use *se* with intransitive verbs for an indefinite subject (*Se* come bién aquí), or, most commonly, to learn Spanish grammatical gender inherent in nouns.

Level 5—Split

One item in the native language becomes two or more in the target language, requiring the learner to make a new distinction. The split is the counterpart of coalescence. Typical of such items in learning Spanish are the learning of the distinction between *ser* and *estar* (to be) and between *tú* and *usted* (you), or even learning the distinction between Spanish indicative and subjunctive moods where in English the indicative alone is appropriate.

Prator's reinterpretation, and Stockwell and his associates' original hierarchy of difficulty, are based on principles of human learning. The first, or "zero," degree of difficulty represents complete one-to-one correspondence and transfer while the fifth degree of difficulty is the height of interference. Prator and Stockwell both claimed that their hierarchy could be applied to virtually any two languages and would thus yield some form of objectivity to the prediction stage of contrastive analysis procedures.

Using the hierarchy of difficulty and the procedures for contrastive analysis described by Whitman, one can make simple predictions about difficulties learners will encounter. Let us look, for example, at the learning of English consonants by a native speaker of Turkish. The *description* and *selection* stages of contrastive analysis are fulfilled in the chart of English and Turkish consonants shown in Figure 8-1.

	ENGLISH							TURKISH						
	bilabial	labio-dental	dental	alveolar	palatal	velar	glottal	bilabial	labio-dental	dental	alveolar	palatal	velar	glottal
Stops	p b			t d		k g		p b		t d			k g	
Fricatives		f v	Θ ð	s z	š ž		h				s z	š ž		h
Affricates					č ǰ							č ǰ		
Nasals	m			n		ŋ		m		n				
Laterals				l						l				
Glides	w			r	y									
Tap										r				

Figure 8-1. English and Turkish consonants.

By superimposing one "map" onto the other, you can engage in the process of *contrasting*—the third of Whitman's procedures—the two systems. The following five statements will suffice for a general contrast:

1. English /t d n l/ are alveolar; the corresponding consonants in Turkish are dental.
2. English has the interdental and labio-dental fricatives /f/, /v/, /θ/, and /ð/, which do not exist in Turkish.
3. English has a phoneme /ŋ/, Turkish does not.
4. English has phonemes, /w/ and /y/, Turkish does not.
5. From an articulatory viewpoint, English /r/ and Turkish /r/ are of quite different natures.

Next, the prediction procedure can be accomplished by subjecting the above contrastive description to a hierarchy of difficulty:

0. Of no difficulty will be consonants that do not appear in the five contrastive statements above. We will assume such consonants bear one-to-one correspondence.
1. No apparent instance of coalescence.
2. Only one instance of absence (a rather unusual fact): Turkish tap /r/ does not appear in English.
3. English consonants /t/ /d/ /n/ and /l/ are alveolar, and the Turkish speaker will have to reshape these consonants from the dental counterparts of his native language.
4. English consonants /θ/ /ð/ /f/ /v/ /ŋ/ /y/ /w/ and /r/ are new to the Turkish speaker.
5. No apparent instance of a split.

The contrastive analysis procedure has identified and contrasted selected features of the two languages and predicted basically three levels of difficulty.

The procedure is not without its shortcomings. For one thing, the process illustrated above is too generalized. Subtle phonetic distinctions between phonemes have been ignored. Phonological environments and allophonic variants of phonemes have been overlooked. The /y/ sound, for example, exists in Turkish, but is not phonemic, and therefore might be placed into category 1, in which various allophones of [y] in Turkish become phonemic /y/ in English.

With attention to such details you might, on the one hand, find it most difficult to use the hierarchy as prescribed, and yet on the other hand find that more than three levels of difficulty can be defined. Surely, for example, the Turkish speaker will find varying degrees of difficulty within Level 4.

Other problems with the model are apparent. It is very difficult, even with six categories, to determine exactly which category a particular contrast fits into. For example, is learning the English /r/ really a case of learning an entirely new item? Phonetically that is the case. But in the underlying structures of the two languages the American English /r/ and the Turkish /r/ have very similar distributions and phonemic value. Moreover, the English learner can indeed substitute the Turkish /r/ in English and be understood. The latter is an argument for placing the /r/ contrast into category 3, rather than 4. Yet intuitively we know that learning the English /r/ may be the most difficult item phonologically for learners from many backgrounds to master. Why, then, isn't the /r/ assigned the fifth degree of difficulty? In such questions lies a hint of some of the subjectivity of "scientific" hierarchies of difficulty. Subjectivity is a factor both in the teacher's or linguist's predictions and assessments and in the learner himself, because he varies and differs from other learners in an unpredictable number of ways.

Fred Eckman (1977) proposed a useful method for determining directionality of difficulty by means of principles of universal grammar. His "markedness differential hypothesis" accounted for the production not only of the areas of difficulty for a second language learner but also the relative degree of difficulty. "Marked" phenomena in a language are those structures which imply the presence of other related structures. For example, the presence of the passive voice with an agent implies the presence of the passive voice without an agent (English or French, for example); however, the presence of a passive without an agent (as in Arabic, Greek, or Persian) does not imply the presence of a passive voice with an agent. English is thus more *marked*, with reference to passives, than Arabic. Eckman showed that in such contrasts, the marked items will be more difficult than unmarked items. Moreover, degrees of markedness correspond to degrees of difficulty.

Eckman gave us a more sophisticated method for predicting difficulty than we had previously from Stockwell. But determining degrees of markedness is still to a large extent a subjective judgment. As is the case with virtually every problem of linguistic analysis, the objectivity of scientific methodology is still elusive.

MODERATING THE CONTRASTIVE
ANALYSIS HYPOTHESIS

The problems touched on above merely scratch the surface of the chaotic state of the Contrastive Analysis hypothesis. The attempt to *predict* difficulty by means of contrastive analysis is what Ronald Wardhaugh (1970) called the *strong version* of the Contrastive Analysis hypothesis, a version that he believed was quite unrealistic and impracticable. Wardhaugh noted (p. 125) that "at the very least, this version demands of linguists that they have available a set of linguistic universals formulated within a comprehensive linguistic theory which deals adequately with syntax, semantics, and phonology." He went on to point out the difficulty (p. 126), already noted, of an adequate procedure, built on sound theory, for actually contrasting the forms of languages: "Does the linguist have available to him an over-all contrastive system within which he can relate the two languages in terms of mergers, splits, zeroes, over-differentiations, under-differentiations, reinterpretations, and so on. ... ?" And so, while many linguists claimed to be using a scientific, empirical, and theoretically justified tool in contrastive analysis, in actuality they were operating more out of mentalistic subjectivity.

Wardhaugh noted, however (p. 126), that contrastive analysis has intuitive appeal, and that teachers and linguists have successfully used "the best linguistic knowledge available . . . in order to account for observed difficulties in second language learning." He termed such observational use of contrastive analysis the *weak version* of the Contrastive Analysis hypothesis. The weak version does not imply the *a priori* prediction of certain fine degrees of difficulty. It recognizes the significance of interference across languages, the fact that such interference does exist and can explain difficulties, but it also recognizes that linguistic difficulties can be more profitably explained *a posteriori*—after the fact. As the learner is learning the language and errors appear, the teacher can utilize his knowledge of the target and native languages to understand sources of error. Clearly, gross predictions can be made by observation and intuition and experience, but a language is made up of hundreds of thousands of items, and it is impossible to predict difficulty beyond some very glaring phonological differences between two languages. In fact, it is really *only* in the phonological component of language that contrastive analysis is mildly successful. In early stages of second language acquisition, learners produce the sounds of a foreign language in fairly consistent patterns, largely because pronunciation is a *psycho-*

motor skill, and with its reliance on muscular coordination, is a factor of more predictable interference. Syntactic, semantic, or lexical interference is far less predictable, since "cognitive coordination" in all its tremendous variability becomes more of a factor than muscular coordination. While one might *expect* a French speaker who is beginning to learn English to say "I am in New York since January," the *prediction* that a learner will make that error is a gamble. But if a learner then makes that error, a contrastive analysis of present-perfect usage in English with its French counterpart will reveal the source of the error.

The most convincing criticism of the strong version of the Contrastive Analysis hypothesis was offered by Whitman himself, who with Kenneth Jackson (Whitman and Jackson 1972) undertook to test empirically the practicability of the Contrastive Analysis hypothesis. The predictions of four separate contrastive analyses (including that of Stockwell, Bowen, and Martin 1965) were applied to a forty-item test of English grammar to determine, *a priori*, the relative difficulty of the test items for speakers of Japanese. The test was administered to 2,500 Japanese learners of English who did not know, of course, the predictions of the contrastive analyses. The results of the test were compared with the predictions. Whitman and Jackson found no support for the predictions of the contrastive analyses so carefully worked out by linguists! They concluded (p. 40) that "contrastive analysis, as represented by the four analyses tested in this project, is inadequate, theoretically and practically, to predict the interference problems of a language learner." While it is of interest to note that the Whitman and Jackson study was performed on *grammar*, which I have already pointed out to be less predictable than phonology, nevertheless the Contrastive Analysis hypothesis—which purported to apply to any aspect of two languages—was found to be inadequate.

While Wardhaugh (1970) called for a "period of quiescence" for the Contrastive Analysis hypothesis, Oller and Ziahosseiny (1970) hinted at a compromise between the strong and weak versions of the hypothesis. They proposed a *moderate* form of the Contrastive Analysis hypothesis on the basis of a rather intriguing study of spelling errors. They found that for learners of English as a second language, English spelling proved to be more difficult for people whose native language used a Roman script (for example, French, Spanish) than for those whose native language used a non-Roman script (Arabic, Japanese). The strong form of the Contrastive Analysis hypothesis would have predicted that the learning of an entirely new writing system (Level 4 in the hierarchy of difficulty) would be more difficult than reinterpreting (Level 3) spelling rules. Oller and Ziahosseiny found the opposite to be true, and reasoned that knowledge of one Romanized system made it more difficult, not less, to acquire another Roman spelling system. They concluded that the strong form was too strong and the weak form too weak, but that a moderate version that centers on the nature of human learning, and not just on the contrast between two languages, has more explanatory power.

That moderate version of the Contrastive Analysis hypothesis was technically defined as follows (p. 186): "The categorization of abstract and concrete patterns according to their perceived similarities and differences is the basis for learning; therefore, wherever patterns are minimally distinct in form or meaning in one or more systems, confusion may result." In other words, the learning of sounds, sequences, and meanings will be the most difficult where the most subtle distinctions are required either between the target language and native language or within the target language itself. In the case of their research on spelling English, there were more *differences* between non-Roman writing and Roman writing, but learners from a non-Roman writing system had to make fewer *subtle* distinctions than did those from the Roman writing system. We have all experienced learning an entirely new game or skill perhaps more easily than one that is somewhat similar to a skill already learned previously. The principle at work is common in human learning: interference can actually be greater when items to be learned are more similar to existing items than when items are entirely new and unrelated to existing items.

Oller and Ziahosseiny's moderate version put the Contrastive Analysis hypothesis into some perspective. They rightly emphasized the generalizing nature of human learning. It is common to overgeneralize to the extent that minimal differences are overlooked; at the same time gross differences—because of their saliency—are often more easily perceived and stored in memory. Greater differences do not always result in greater learning difficulty. Such a perspective underscores the significance of *intra*lingual errors, which are as much a factor in second language learning as *inter*lingual errors. The forms within one language are often perceived to be minimally distinct in comparison to the vast distinctions between the native and target language, yet those intralingual factors can lead to some of the greatest difficulties.

The Contrastive Analysis hypothesis in its strong form was, as Wardhaugh predicted, quietly laid to rest if even with the cautious hope that someday when the tools of linguistic and cultural analysis are perfected, we would then resurrect this messiah that did not deliver the victorious blow as expected. And meanwhile, teachers of foreign languages and researchers in second language acquisition were rightfully dissatisfied with too weak a version of contrastive analysis which only lent an explanation to certain errors after the fact. This state of professional anomie has been somewhat soothed by moderate forms of the Contrastive Analysis hypothesis which have enabled us to get a larger picture of the nature of human learning and to understand a number of factors contributing to learning and forgetting. The next chapter will deal with facets of the learning of a linguistic system that extend beyond and beneath the effect of interference on two languages in contact.

SUGGESTED READINGS

Most of the major references in this chapter provide informative supplementary reading. The time you have to devote to the topic will dictate the extensiveness of your reading. *Lado* (1957) is a classic, but *Wardhaugh* (1970) is a clearly written and highly readable summary of the strong position expressed by Lado and others. *Banathy, Trager, and Waddle* (1966) is a good example of how, in the case of native English-speaking learners of Spanish, a contrastive approach was taken.

Whitman (1970) gave a summary of the procedures of contrastive analysis and *Whitman and Jackson*'s (1972) experimental study of contrastive analysis in action is fascinating.

Thumb through the pages of *Stockwell, Bowen, and Martin* (1965). This is the most comprehensive attempt to apply principles of contrastive analysis to actual language teaching practice. It still stands today as a vital source of information.

Oller and Ziahosseiny (1970) is highly recommended. Some of it is technical but the message is important.

If resources permit, look in your university library for back issues of the journal *Language Learning*. During the period of 1950 to 1969 you will find dozens of contrastive descriptions of parts of languages. You might want to read through one or two of those for an appreciation of both the merits and liabilities of such analyses.

TOPICS AND QUESTIONS FOR STUDY
AND DISCUSSION

1. Try to mimic "typical" accents of a Frenchman or German or Japanese or Latin American trying to speak English. What features do you adopt in your mimicry? Can you identify those features as a product of interference? In

your contact with second language learners try to identify features of speech which are attributable to interference from the native language.

2. Why did the Contrastive Analysis hypothesis receive such widespread attention in the 1950s and 1960s? Refer to linguistic, psychological, and methodological paradigms.

3. Using Whitman's four procedures of contrastive analysis, try to perform a contrastive analysis of a segment of your second language with the corresponding segments in English. The most practical segment might be the consonant systems of the two languages, or the vowel systems. Grammatical systems could be attempted if just one small slice of the total language pie is carefully defined. Use the six categories described by Prator in order to arrive at a hierarchy of difficulty.

4. Why is it that something supposedly "scientific," like the Contrastive Analysis hypothesis, ultimately turns out to be so subjective?

5. Review the *strong* and *weak* versions of the Contrastive Analysis hypothesis. Do you agree with Oller that there should be a moderate version? Or is the weak version as described by Wardhaugh sufficient?

6. What is meant on page 158 by "cognitive coordination"? What are the implications of the variability of cognitive functioning for the *sequencing* of materials in foreign language curricula?

7. Oller's moderate form of the Contrastive Analysis hypothesis claims greater interference where minimal and subtle distinctions are necessary. Do you agree? Can you think of instances in learning other skills and subject matter in which this principle holds true?

9

Error Analysis— The Study of Learners' Interlanguage

The Contrastive Analysis hypothesis stressed the interfering effects of the first language on second language learning, and claimed, in its strong form, that second language learning is primarily, if not exclusively, a process of acquiring whatever items are different from the first language. Such a narrow view of interference ignored the intralingual effects of learning, among other factors. In recent years researchers and teachers have come more and more to understand that second language learning is a creative process of constructing a system in which the learner is consciously testing hypotheses about the target language from a number of possible sources of knowledge: limited knowledge of the target language itself, knowledge about the native language, knowledge about the communicative function of language, knowledge about language in general, and knowledge about life, human beings, and the universe. The learner, in acting upon his environment, constructs what to him is a legitimate system of language in its own right—a structured set of rules which for the time being provide order to the linguistic chaos that confronts him.

By the late 1960s, second language learning began to be examined in much the same way that first language learning had been studied for some time: the learner was looked on not as a producer of malformed, imperfect language replete with mistakes, but as an intelligent and creative being proceeding through logical, systematic stages of acquisition, creatively acting upon his linguistic environment as he encounters its forms and functions in meaningful contexts. By a gradual process of trial and error and hypothesis testing, the learner slowly and tediously succeeds in establishing closer and closer approximations to the system used by native speakers of the language. A number of terms have been coined to describe the perspective which stressed the legitimacy of learners' second language systems. The best known of these terms is *interlanguage* (see Selinker 1972), referring to the separateness of a second language learner's system, a system that has a structurally intermediate status between the native and target languages. Nemser (1971) referred to the same general phenomenon in second language learning but stressed the successive approximation to the target language in his term *approximative system*. Corder (1971:151) used the term *idiosyncratic dialect* to connote the idea that the learner's language is unique to a particular individual, that the rules of the learner's language are peculiar to the language of that individual alone. While each of these designations emphasizes a particular notion, they share the concept that the second language learner is forming his own self-contained linguistic system. This is neither the system of the native language nor the system of the target language, but instead falls between the two; it is a system based upon the best attempt of the learner to provide order and structure to the linguistic stimuli surrounding him. The Interlanguage hypothesis led to a whole new era of second language research and teaching in the early 1970s and represented a significant breakthrough from the shackles of the Contrastive Analysis hypothesis.

This chapter will describe the study of learners' interlanguage systems—approaches to the analysis of the linguistic forms acquired by second language learners. The emphasis here is on the *form* of language, while the next chapter deals more directly with the function of language.

The most obvious approach to analyzing interlanguage is to study the speech of the learners. Production data is publicly observable and is presumably reflective of a learner's underlying competence —production competence, that is. Comprehension of a second language is more difficult to study since it is not directly observable and must be inferred by overt verbal and nonverbal responses, by artificial instruments, or by the intuition of the teacher or researcher. It is also obvious that the study of the speech of learners is the study, largely, of the errors of learners. "Correct" items yield little information about the interlanguage of the learner, only information about the system of the target language which the learner has already acquired. We shall therefore grapple here largely with the significance of errors—error analysis—in the production mode of the learner's interlanguage.

ERROR ANALYSIS

Human learning is fundamentally a process that involves the making of mistakes. Mistakes, misjudgments, miscalculations, and erroneous assumptions form an important aspect of learning virtually any skill or acquiring information. You learn to swim by first jumping into the water and flailing arms and legs until you discover that there is a combination of movements—a structured pattern—that succeeds in keeping you afloat and propelling you through the water. The first mistakes of learning to swim are giant ones, gradually diminishing as you learn from making those mistakes. Learning to swim, to play tennis, to type, or to read all involve a process in which success comes by profiting from mistakes, by using mistakes to obtain feedback from the environment and with that feedback to make new attempts which successively more closely approximate desired goals.

Language learning, in this sense, is like any other human learning. We have already seen in the second chapter that the child learning his first language makes countless "mistakes" from the point of view of adult grammatical language. Many of these mistakes are logical in the limited linguistic system within which the child operates, but by carefully processing feedback from others the child slowly but surely learns to produce what is acceptable speech in his native language. Second language learning is a process that is clearly not unlike first language learning in its trial-and-error nature. Inevitably the learner will make mistakes in the process of acquisition, and indeed will even impede that process if he does not commit errors and then benefit in turn from various forms of feedback on those errors.

Researchers and teachers of second languages soon came to realize that the mistakes a person made in this process of constructing a new system of language needed to be analyzed carefully, for they possibly held in them some of the keys to the understanding of the process of second language acquisition. As Corder (1967:167) noted: "A learner's errors . . . are significant in [that] they provide to the researcher evidence of how language is learned or acquired, what strategies or procedures the learner is employing in the discovery of the language."

In order to analyze learners' errors in a proper perspective, it is crucial to make a distinction between *mistakes* and *errors*, technically two very different phenomena. A mistake refers to a performance error that is either a random guess or a "slip," in that it is a failure to utilize a known system correctly. All people make mistakes, in both native and second language situations. Native speakers are normally capable of recognizing and correcting such "lapses" or mistakes, which are not the result of a deficiency in competence but the result of some sort of breakdown or imperfection in the process of producing speech. These hesitations, slips of the tongue, random ungrammaticalities, and other performance lapses in native-speaker production also occur in second language speech.

Such mistakes must be carefully distinguished from *errors* of a second language learner, idiosyncrasies in the interlanguage of the learner which are direct manifestations of a system within which a learner is operating at the time. Dulay and Burt (1972) referred to errors as "goofs," defined in an earlier work, *The Gooficon* (Burt and Kiparsky 1972:1), as "an error . . . for which no blame is implied." Put in another way, an error is a noticeable deviation from the adult grammar of a native speaker, reflecting the interlanguage competence of the learner. If a learner of English asks, "Does John can sing?" he is probably reflecting a competence level in which all verbs require a pre-posed *do* auxiliary for question formation. He has committed an error, most likely not a mistake, and an error which reveals a portion of his competence in the target language.

Can you tell the difference between an error and a mistake? Not always. If, on one or two occasions, for example, an English learner says "John cans sing," but on other occasions says "John can sing," it is difficult to determine whether "cans" is a mistake or an error. If, however, further examination of the learner's speech reveals such utterances as "John wills go," "John mays come," and so forth, with very few instances of correct third-person singular usage of modal auxiliaries, you might then conclude that "cans," "mays," and other such forms are errors indicating that the learner has not distinguished modals from other verbs, though perhaps—because of the few correct instances—he is on the verge of making the necessary differentiation between the two types of verbs in his systematic conception of the second language. You can thus appreciate the subjectivity of determining the difference between a mistake and an error in learner speech. That undertaking always bears with it the chance of a faulty assumption on the part of a teacher or researcher.

165

The fact that learners do make errors and that these errors can be observed, analyzed, and classified to reveal something of the system operating within the learner, led to a surge of study of learners' errors, called *error analysis*. Error analysis became distinguished from contrastive analysis by its examination of errors attributable to *all* possible sources, not just those which result from negative transfer of the native language. Error analysis easily superseded contrastive analysis, as we discovered that only *some* of the errors a learner makes are attributable to the mother tongue, that learners do not actually make all the errors that contrastive analysis predicted they should, and that learners from disparate language backgrounds tend to make similar errors in learning one target language. Errors—overt manifestations of learners' systems—arise from several possible general sources: interlingual errors of interference from the native language, intralingual errors within the target language, the socio-linguistic context of communication, psycholinguistic or cognitive strategies, and no doubt countless affective variables.

Errors in Error Analysis

There is a danger in too much attention to learners' errors. While errors are indeed revealing of a system at work, the classroom foreign language teacher can become so preoccupied with noticing errors that the correct utterances in the second language go unnoticed. In our observation and analysis of errors—for all that they do reveal about the learner—we must beware of placing too much attention on errors, and not lose sight of the value of positive reinforcement of clear, free communication. While the diminishing of errors is an important criterion for increasing language proficiency, the ultimate goal of second language learning is the attainment of communicative fluency in a language.

Another danger in error analysis is an overstressing of production data. Language is speaking *and* listening, writing *and* reading. The comprehension of language is as important as production. It so happens that production lends itself to analysis and thus becomes the prey of researchers; but comprehension data is equally important in developing an understanding of the process of second language acquisition.

Finally, Jacqueline Schachter (1974) and others (see Kleinmann 1977) have shown in research that error analysis fails to account for the strategy of *avoidance*. A learner who for one reason or another avoids a particular sound, word, structure, or discourse category may be assumed incorrectly to have no difficulty therewith. Schachter found, for example, that it was misleading to draw conclusions about relative-clause errors among certain English learners; native Japanese speakers were largely avoiding that structure and thus not manifesting nearly as many errors as some native Persian speakers. The absence of error therefore does not necessarily reflect nativelike competence since a learner may be avoiding the very structures that pose difficulty for him.

We do well, therefore, in engaging in the analysis of learners' interlanguage errors, to engage in *performance analysis*, a less restrictive concept that places a healthy investigation of errors within the larger perspective of the learner's total performance. While the rest of this chapter emphasizes the significance of error analysis, let us nevertheless remember that production errors are only ultimately significant as a subset of the overall performance and competence of the learner.

PROCEDURES OF ERROR ANALYSIS

One of the common difficulties in understanding the linguistic systems of both first and second language learners is the fact that such systems cannot be directly observed. They must be inferred by means of analyzing production and comprehension data. What makes the task even thornier, however, is the *instability* of learners' systems. Systems are in a constant state of flux as new information flows in and, through the process of subsumption, causes existing structures to be revised. Repeated observations of a learner will often reveal apparently unpredictable or even contradictory data. In undertaking the task of performance analysis, the teacher and researcher are called upon to infer order and logic in this unstable and variable system.

Identifying Errors

The first step in the process of analysis is the identification and description of errors. Corder (1971) provided a model for identifying erroneous or idiosyncratic utterances in a second language. That model is schematized in Figure 9-1. According to Corder's model, any sentence uttered by the learner and subsequently transcribed can be analyzed for idiosyncrasies. A major distinction is made at the outset between *overt* and *covert* errors. Overtly erroneous utterances are those that are unquestionably ungrammatical; covertly erroneous utterances are grammatically well formed but not interpretable within the normal *context* of communication. The model indicates that in both cases if a plausible interpretation can be made of the sentence then one should form a reconstruction of the sentence in

168

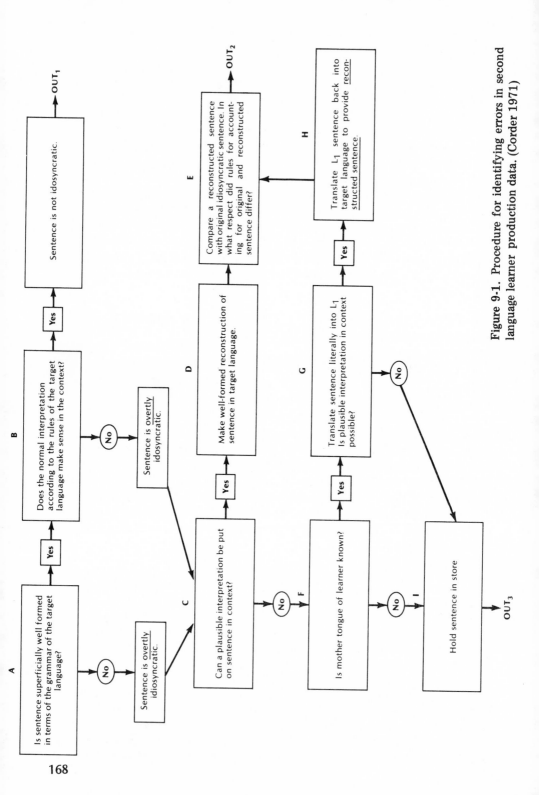

Figure 9-1. Procedure for identifying errors in second language learner production data. (Corder 1971)

A Is sentence superficially well formed in terms of the grammar of the target language?

Yes →

B Does the normal interpretation according to the rules of the target language make sense in the context?

Yes → Sentence is not idosyncratic. → OUT₁

No → Sentence is overtly idiosyncratic.

No → Sentence is overtly idiosyncratic.

C Can a plausible interpretation be put on sentence in context?

Yes →

D Make well-formed reconstruction of sentence in target language. →

E Compare a reconstructed sentence with original idiosyncratic sentence. In what respect did rules for accounting for original and reconstructed sentence differ? → OUT₂

No →

F Translate sentence literally into L₁

G Is plausible interpretation in context possible?

Yes → Is mother tongue of learner known?

Yes →

H Translate L₁ sentence back into target language to provide reconstructed sentence.

No →

I Hold sentence in store → OUT₃

the target language, compare the reconstruction with the original idiosyncratic sentence, and then describe the differences. If the native language of the learner is known, the model indicates using translation as a possible indicator of native language interference as the source of error. In some cases, of course, no plausible interpretation is possible at all, and the researcher is left with no analysis of the error (OUT$_3$).

Consider the following examples of idiosyncratic utterances of learners, and let us allow them to be fed through Corder's procedure for error analysis:

1. Does John can sing?
   A. NO
   C. YES
   D. Can John sing?
   E. Original sentence contained pre-posed *do* auxiliary applicable to most verbs, but not to verbs with modal auxiliaries. OUT$_2$
2. I saw their department.
   A. YES
   B. NO (context was in a conversation about living quarters in Mexico)
   C. NO
   F. YES, Spanish.
   G. Yo vi su departamento. YES
   H. I saw their apartment.
   E. *Departamento* was translated to false cognate *department*. OUT$_2$
3. The different city is another one in the another two.
   A. NO
   C. NO
   F. YES, Spanish.
   G. No plausible translation or interpretation.
   I. No analysis. OUT$_3$

It can be seen that the model is not complicated and represents a procedure that teachers and researchers might intuitively follow. However, once an error is identified, the next step is to describe it adequately, something the above procedure has only begun to accomplish.

Describing Errors

On a rather global level, errors can be described as errors of addition, omission, substitution, and ordering, following standard mathematical categories. In English a *do* auxiliary might be added (Does can he sing?), a definite article omitted (I went to movie), an item substituted (I lost my road), or a word order confused (I to the store went). But such categories are clearly very generalized. Within each category, *levels* of language can be considered: phonology or orthography, lexicon, grammar, and discourse. Often, of course, it is difficult to distinguish different levels of errors. A word with a faulty pronunciation, for example, might hide a syntactic or lexical error. A French learner who says "[ʒɛ ʸ] suis allé à l'école" might be mispronouncing the grammatically correct "je," or correctly pronouncing a grammatically incorrect "j'ai." Nevertheless, the categories can help you to identify where the learner is in terms of his own system.

Is an error apparently random—that is, possibly a mistake? If it is not, there may be evidence from cross-referenced data to indicate that the error is what Corder (1973) calls a *presystematic* error, a stage in which the learner is only vaguely aware that there is some systematic order to a particular class of items. Partial consistency can mask a presystematic error. If a learner at some point said, "John can sing," and on other occasions has been heard to say, "John cans sing," he may be in a presystematic stage with respect to the non-inflectional nature of modals. At this stage the learner is not able to correct his error nor to "explain" it—that is, to paraphrase it or to get his point across in another way.

When the learner has progressed to a *systematic* stage in a particular area of language, he has begun to discern a system, to be more consistent in his patterning, and to exhibit rather consistent errors indicating internalization of rules, albeit "incorrect" rules by native-speaker standards. While there is no standard convention that establishes a certain percentage of correctness to indicate "acquisition" as such, the teacher and researcher are left to judge the systematicity of errors rather subjectively. That subjectivity is always complicated by a common tendency for learners to "backslide"—a form of linguistic regression arising out of the natural spiraling characteristic of human learning. A learner will appear to have acquired a rule or an item, then backslide to an error. A systematic error, in Corder's (1973) conceptualization of the term, usually cannot be corrected by the learner, but he can "explain" his error in the sense of providing, in different wording or structures, alternative linguistic messages that get his point across and let the hearer know what he was driving at. That is, upon making an error and receiving some negative feedback, he can recognize where the error probably was and make another attempt to communicate the idea. The following conversation illustrates the point:

Learner: I lost my road.
Native Speaker: What?

L:	I lost my road.
NS:	You lost your *road*?
L:	Ahh, . . . uh, . . . I lost myself, . . . I got lost . . .
NS:	Oh, you lost your *way*.
L:	Oh, yes, . . . I lost my way.

Or consider the following conversation, which hinges on a syntactic error:

Learner:	John isn't goes to movie with him.
Native Speaker:	You mean . . . he didn't go?
L:	No, uh, . . . today, . . . tonight . . . he will not to go.
NS:	Oh, I see.
L:	How you say . . . John isn't *to go*?
NS:	John isn't *going*.
L:	Yeah, he isn't . . . going to movie tonight.

In each case the learner discerned a problem and was able to explain the error in some sense, even though immediate correction was not made until the native speaker, in each case, provided it. In the second conversation the learner attempted a correction and almost succeeded.

Evidence of a *postsystematic* stage of learning is found when the learner is quite consistent in his speech: when he makes an error he can both explain it *and* correct it. Though errors occur in this stage, they seem to be rather infrequent.

It should be made clear that the above "stages" of systematicity do not describe a learner's total second language system. We cannot say, for example, that a learner is in the presystematic stage, globally. We must refer rather to particular linguistic subsystems. With respect to a verb tense, a person might be in a presystematic stage, while certain preposition usage exhibits systematic errors. Even that conclusion is perhaps too broad, and one would be justified in breaking down the subsystems of language into very detailed units before offering conclusions about systematicity.

It is ultimately important, as was noted earlier, to remember that production errors alone are inadequate measures of overall competence. They happen to be salient features of second language learners' interlanguage and present us with grist for error-analysis mills, but *correct* utterances deserve our attention, and especially in the teaching-learning process, deserve positive reinforcement.

By examining errors in terms of four mathematical categories, four linguistic categories, and three stages, we have available to us some plausible tools for classifying errors. Theoretically an error can be placed into one of forty-eight different cells, as illustrated in Figure 9-2.

SOURCES OF ERROR

Having examined procedures of error analysis used to identify errors in second language learner production data, our final step in the analysis of learner speech is that of determining the *source* of error. Why are certain errors made? What cognitive strategies and styles or even personality variables underlie certain errors? While the answers to these questions are somewhat speculative in that sources must be inferred from available data, in such questions lies the ultimate value of performance analysis in general. By trying to identify sources we can begin to arrive at an understanding of how the learner's cognitive and affective self relates to the linguistic system and to formulate an integrated understanding of the process of second language acquisition.

To enumerate all possible sources of second language errors would be an impossible task, for there are surely hundreds of such sources. What I will do here therefore will be to outline a number of

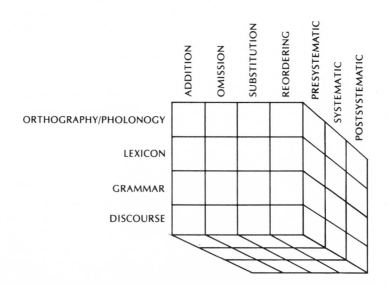

Figure 9-2. Categories of errors.

major sources of learner errors, perhaps overlooking some, but surely touching on factors that are significant in a teacher's understanding of learners' interlanguage systems. Some, if not all, of these sources have been referred to at times as *strategies*. We have already seen that strategies of learning basically hinge on general principles of learning. Strategies for production—discussed here under the rubric of "sources of error"—take varied forms, some related to learning strategies and some to other properties.

Interlingual Transfer

The beginning stages of learning a second language are characterized by a good deal of interlingual transfer (from the native language). In these early stages, before the system of the second language is familiar, the native language is the only linguistic system in previous experience upon which the learner can draw. We have all heard English learners say "sheep" for "ship," or "the book of Jack" instead of "Jack's book"; French learners may say, "Je sais Jean," for "Je connais Jean," and so forth. All these errors are attributable to negative interlingual transfer. While it is not always clear that an error is the result of transfer from the native language, many such errors are detectable in learner speech. Fluent knowledge of a learner's native language of course aids the teacher in detecting and analyzing such errors; however, even familiarity with the language can be of help in pinpointing this common source.

The learning of a *third language* (and subsequent languages) provides an interesting context for research. Depending upon a number of factors including the linguistic and cultural relatedness of the languages and the context of learning, there are varying degrees of interlingual interference from both the first and second language to the third language, especially if the second and third languages are closely related or the learner is attempting a third language shortly after beginning a second language.

Intralingual Transfer

One of the major contributions of error analysis was its recognition of sources of error that extend beyond just interlingual errors in learning a second language. It is now clear that intralingual errors, or intralingual interference—the negative transfer of items within the target language, or, put another way, the incorrect generalization of rules within the target language—is a major factor in second language learning. It has been found (see especially Taylor 1975) that the early stages of language learning are characterized by a predominance of interlingual transfer, but once the learner has begun to acquire parts of the new system, more and more intralingual transfer—generalization within the target language—is manifested. This of course follows logically from the tenets of learning theory. As the learner progresses in the second language, his previous experience and his existing subsumers begin to include structures within the target language itself.

Negative intralingual transfer (overgeneralization) has already been illustrated in such utterances as "Does John can sing?" Other examples abound—utterances like "He goed," "I don't know what time is it," "Il a tombé," "El carro/karo/es caro" (flap r generalized to trill contexts). Once again, the teacher or researcher cannot always be certain of the source of an apparent intralingual error, but repeated systematic observations of a learner's speech data will often remove the ambiguity of a single observation of an error.

The analysis of intralingual errors in a corpus of production data can become quite complex. Consider, for example, Barry Taylor's (1975) analysis of the translations of Spanish sentences into English by a group of native Spanish-speakers. Table 9-1 lists only those classifications of errors in producing auxiliary verb forms in English. A glance at that table reveals dozens of categories, and of course these are limited to the particular data Taylor was analyzing and are therefore not exhaustive within a grammatical category. And these pertain only to errors of overgeneralization, excluding another long list of categories of errors which he found attributable to interlingual transfer. Similarly, Jack C. Richards (1971:185-87) provided a list of typical English intralingual errors in the use of prepositions and articles (see Table 9-2). These are not exhaustive either, but only exemplary of some of the errors one commonly encounters in English learners from disparate native language backgrounds. Both Taylor's and Richards' lists are restricted to English, but clearly their counterparts exist in other languages.

Context of Learning

A third major source of error, though it overlaps both types of transfer, is the context of learning. "Context" refers, for example, to the classroom with its teacher and its materials in the case of school learning, or the social situation in the case of untutored second language learning. In a classroom context the teacher or the textbook can lead the learner to make faulty hypotheses about the language, what Richards (1971) called "false concepts" and what Stenson (1974) termed "induced errors." Students often make errors because of a misleading explanation from the teacher, faulty presentation of a structure or word in a textbook, or even because of a pattern that

Table 9-1.   The Taxonomy of Error Types (from Taylor 1975)

Overgeneralization Errors

  I. Redundant aux insertions
    a. Insertion of *do* in a sentence containing a modal
    b. Two *do*'s in a negative question; 1st: pres tense conjugated
                             2nd: simple + *not*
    c. Two *do*'s in a negative question; 1st: pres tense conjugated
                             2nd: past tense + *not*
    d. Insertion of *do* in a subject-focus Wh-question
    e. Insertion of *be* in a subject-focus Wh-question (with the verb usually in the past participle form)
    f. Insertion of *be* in statements and subject-focus Wh-questions (with the main verb in the simple form)
  II. Aux substitutions
    a. Insertion of *be* instead of *do*
    b. Insertion of *be* instead of *will*
    c. Insertion of *be* instead of *can*
    d. Use of *do + go to* + V instead of *will*
    e. Use of $\left\{ \begin{array}{l} will \\ would \end{array} \right\}$ *go to* + V instead of *will*
    f. Use of *will going to* + V instead of *will*
 IV. Incorrect form of main verb following an auxiliary
    a. Past tense form of verb following a modal
    b. Present tense *-s* on a verb following a modal
    c. *-ing* on a verb following a modal
    d. *are* (for *be*) following *will*
    e. Past tense form of verb following *do*
    f. Present tense *-s* on a verb following *do*
    g. *-ing* on a verb following *do*
    h. Past tense form of verb following *be* (inserted to replace a modal or *do*)
    i. Present tense *-s* on a verb following *be* (inserted to replace a modal or *do*)
 VII. Verb tense errors
      on Aux:
    a. *do*, present instead of past, when the sentence contains an unambiguous adverbial time reference
VIII. Verb number errors
      on Aux:
    a. *do* in singular instead of plural (unnecessary *-s*)
    b. *do* in plural instead of singular (no *-s*)
    c. *do* in singular instead of plural (unnecessary *-s*) when it is in the present tense instead of the past tense
    d. *do* in plural instead of singular (no *-s*) when it is in the present tense instead of the past tense
    e. *do*, in simple form + *not*, inserted before a verb, when the subject is singular and there is a correctly conjugated *do* inserted at the beginning of the question
    f. *be* in singular instead of plural when it has been inserted to replace *do*

Table 9-2. Typical English Intralingual Errors in the Use of Prepositions and Articles (from Richards 1971)

		Errors in the Use of Prepositions
1. *with* instead of	Ø	met with her, married with her
	from	suffering with a cold
	against	fight with tyranny
	of	consist with
	at	laughed with my words
2. *in* instead of	Ø	entered in the room, in the next day
	on	in T.V.
	with	fallen in love in Ophelia
	for	in this purpose
	at	in this time
	to	go in Poland
	by	the time in your watch
3. *at* instead of	Ø	reached at a place, at last year
	by	held him at the left arm
	in	at the evening; interested at it
	to	went at Stratford
	for	at the first time
4. *for* instead of	Ø	serve for God
	in	one bath for seven days
	of	suspected for, the position for Chinese coolies
	from	a distance for one country to another
	since	been here for the 6th of June
5. *on* instead of	Ø	played on the piano for an hour
	in	on many ways, on that place, going on cars
	at	on the end
	with	angry on him
	of	countries on the world
	to	pays attention on it
6. *of* instead of	Ø	aged of 44, drink less of wine
	in	rich of vitamins
	by	book of Hardy
	on	depends of civilisation
	for	a reason of it
7. *to* instead of	Ø	join to them, went to home, reached to the place
	for	an occupation to them
	of	his love to her

176

Table 9-2. (cont'd)

Errors in the Use of Articles	
1. Omission of *the*	
(a) before unique nouns	Sun is very hot
	Himalayas are . . .
(b) before nouns of nationality	Spaniards and Arabs . . .
(c) before nouns made particular in context	At the conclusion of article
	She goes to bazaar every day
	She is mother of that boy
(d) before a noun modified by a participle	Solution given in this article
(e) before superlatives	Richest person
(f) before a noun modified by an *of-phrase*	Institute of Nuclear Physics
2. *the* used instead of Ø	
(a) before proper names	The Shakespeare, the Sunday
(b) before abstract nouns	The friendship, the nature, the science
(c) before nouns behaving like abstract nouns	After the school, after the breakfast
(d) before plural nouns	The complex structures are still developing
(e) before *some*	The some knowledge
3. *a* used instead of *the*	
(a) before superlatives	a worst, a best boy in the class
(b) before unique nouns	a sun becomes red
4. *a* instead of Ø	
(a) before a plural noun qualified by an adjective	a holy places, a human beings, a bad news
(b) before uncountables	a gold, a work
(c) before an adjective	. . . taken as a definite
5. Omission of *a*	
before class nouns defined by adjectives	he was good boy
	he was brave man

was rotely memorized in a drill but not properly contextualized. Two vocabulary items presented contiguously—for example, *point at* and *point out*—might in later recall be confused simply because of the contiguity of presentation. Or a teacher may out of some ignorance provide incorrect information—not an uncommon occurrence—by way of a misleading definition, word, or grammatical generalization. Another manifestation of language learned in classroom contexts is the occasional tendency on the part of learners to give uncontracted and inappropriately formal forms of language. We have all experienced the foreign learner whose "bookish" language gives him away as a classroom language learner.

The social context of language acquisition will produce other types of errors. The sociolinguistic context of natural, untutored language acquisition can give rise to certain dialect acquisition which may itself be a source of error. Corder's term *idiosyncratic dialect* applies especially well here. For example, a Japanese immigrant lived in a predominantly Mexican-American area of a city in the United States, and his interlanguage was a rather interesting blend of Mexican-American English and the standard English to which he was exposed in the university.

Communication Strategies

A fourth major source of learner error can be found in different *communication strategies* employed by the learner to get a message across to a hearer. It is clear that the category of communication strategies overlaps both inter- and intralingual transfer and context of learning; nevertheless, communication strategies form a separate and exceedingly significant source of error, as was pointed out in Chapter Five. A communication strategy is the conscious employment of verbal or nonverbal mechanisms for communicating an idea when precise linguistic forms are for some reason not readily available to the learner at a point in communication. Let us consider some of these strategies.

Avoidance

Avoidance is a common communication strategy that can be broken down into several subcategories and thus distinguished from other types of strategies. The most common type of avoidance strategy is *syntactic* or *lexical* avoidance within a semantic category. When the learner referred to earlier in this chapter could not think of "I lost my *way*," he first avoided the use of "way" with the synonym "road." This was not appropriate in the context and so he *paraphrased* the sentence "I got lost." A French learner who wishes to avoid the use of the subjunctive in the sentence "Il faut que nous partions" may for example commonly use instead the sentence "Il nous faut partir," or, not being sure of the use of *en* in the sentence "J'en ai trois," the learner might simply say "J'ai trois pommes." *Phonological* avoidance is also common, as in the case of a Japanese learner of English who wanted to say "He's a liar," but with the difficulty of the initial /l/ sound in English chose instead to say "He did not speak the truth."

A more direct type of avoidance is *topic* avoidance, in which a whole topic of conversation (say, talking about what happened yesterday if the past tense is unfamiliar) might be avoided entirely. Learners manage to devise ingenious methods of topic avoidance: changing the subject, pretending not to understand (a classical means for avoiding answering a question), simply not responding at all, or noticeably abandoning a message when a thought becomes too difficult to continue expressing.

Prefabricated patterns

Another common communication device is to memorize certain stock phrases or sentences without internalized knowledge of the components of the phrase. "Tourist survival" language is full of prefabricated patterns, most of which can be found in pocket bilingual "phrase" books which list hundreds of stock sentences for various occasions. "How much does this cost?" "Where is the toilet?" "I don't speak English" "I don't understand you" are the sorts of prefabricated patterns that one sometimes learns at the beginning of a language learning experience when the structure of the language is not known. Such phrases are rotely memorized to fit their appropriate context. Prefabricated patterns are sometimes the source of some merriment. In the first few days of Kikongo learning in Africa I tried to say, in Kikongo, "I don't know Kikongo" to those who attempted to converse with me beyond my limits; I was later embarrassed to discover that, in the first few attempts at producing this prefabricated avoidance device, instead of saying "Kizeyi Kikongo ko," I said "Kizolele Kikongo ko" (I don't *like* Kikongo), which brought on reaction ranging from amusement to hostility from Kikongo listeners.

Kenji Hakuta (1974, 1976) reported on prefabricated patterns in the second language development of a Japanese child learning English. He noted that children learning a first language develop certain prefabricated patterns (/ǰu/—"did you"; *gonna*—"going to"; *I dunno*—"I don't know"; /aõwana/—"I don't want to"), and both adults and children do the same in second language learning. Patterns like *can you*, *where's*, *what's*, *let's*, and many other useful phrases are sometimes mastered early in the acquisition process, before the structures are really known. Hakuta (1976:333) notes that prefabricated patterns "enable learners to express functions which they are yet unable to construct from their linguistic system, simply storing them in a sense like large lexical items."

But in the process of storing such items errors are often made, as in the Kikongo example. The errors are due largely to the rote nature of the items, but their roteness is a factor of a lack of knowledge of the structural rules for forming the particular utterance. Errors will also occur in connecting a prefabricated pattern to adjacent forms, such as the English sentence often produced by learners: "I don't know how do you do that," in which possibly even two prefabricated patterns were juxtaposed without the necessary word-order transformation required for indirect questions.

Cognitive and personality styles

One's own personality style or style of thinking can be a source of error, highlighting the idiosyncratic nature of many learner errors. A reflective and conservative style might result in very careful but hesitant production of speech with perhaps fewer errors but errors indicative of the conscious application—or rather, misapplication—of learned rules. Such a person might also commit errors of overformality. A highly empathic personality might attend with much more insight to the deep structure and intended meaning of others' speech and his own speech, thus committing a number of surface structure errors but perhaps errors which do not in general detract from the essence of his intended meaning. A person with high self-esteem may be willing to *risk* more errors, in the interest of communication, since he does not feel as threatened by committing errors as a person with low self-esteem. In answer to "How did you get here?" a broad categorizer might be heard to say "I drove my bicycle" (a broad definition of *drive*), while a narrow categorizer might say "I pedaled my bicycle" in an attempt to be precise. Language errors can thus conceivably be traced to sources in certain personal or cognitive idiosyncrasies. Though such sources may be most difficult to isolate, they are nonetheless a frequent source of error. It should be noted that *discourse* errors (see Chapter Ten) more readily exemplify differences in cognitive and affective styles among learners.

Appeal to authority

A common strategy of communication is a direct appeal to authority. The learner may, if "stuck" for a particular word or phrase, directly ask a native speaker (the authority) for the form ("How do you say_____"). Or he might venture a possible guess and then ask for verification from the native speaker of the correctness of the attempt. He might also choose to look a word or structure up in a bilingual dictionary. The latter case can also produce some rather amusing situations. Once a foreign student of English as a second language, when asked to introduce himself to the class and the teacher, said, "Allow me to introduce myself and tell you some of the . . . " At this point he quickly got out his pocket bilingual dictionary and, finding the word he wanted, continued, " . . . some of the *headlights* of my past."

Language switch

Finally, when all else fails—when appeal, avoidance, transfer, and other strategies are all incapable of producing a meaningful utterance—a learner may resort to language switch. That is, he may simply use his native language whether the hearer knows that native language or not. Sometimes just a word or two are slipped in, in the hope that the hearer will get the gist of what is being communicated. But at other times relatively long stretches of native language discourse emerge from the learner. Surprisingly, the context of communication coupled with some of the universals of nonverbal expression sometimes enable a learner to communicate an idea in his own language to someone unfamiliar with that language. Such marvels of communication are a tribute to the universality of human experience and a balm for those who feel the utter despair of attempting to communicate in a foreign tongue.

ISSUES IN ERROR ANALYSIS

Fossilization

It is common experience to witness in a learner's language various erroneous features which persist despite what is otherwise a fluent command of the language. This phenomenon is ordinarily manifested phonologically in "foreign accents" in the speech of many of those who have learned a second language after adolescence. We also commonly observe syntactic and lexical errors persisting in the speech of those who have otherwise learned the language quite well. The relatively permanent incorporation of incorrect linguistic forms into a person's second language competence has been referred to as *fossilization*. Fossilization has come to connote the internalization of *incorrect* or unnativelike forms of language, but the process of fossilization is really no different from what we commonly call *learning*—the internalization of correct forms.

How do items become fossilized? Until recently there was little attempt to grapple with the cognitive or affective dimensions of fossilization. But now fossilization can be seen as consistent with the laws of human learning. Vigil and Oller (1976) provided a formal account of fossilization as a factor of positive and negative affective and cognitive feedback. They noted that there are two kinds of information transmitted between sources (learners) and audiences (in this case, native speakers): information about the *affective* relationship between source and audience, and *cognitive* information—facts, suppositions, beliefs. Affective information is primarily encoded in terms of kinesic mechanisms—gestures, tone of voice, facial expressions—while cognitive information is usually conveyed by means of linguistic devices—sounds, phrases, structures, discourse. The feedback a learner gets from his audience can be either positive, negative, or neutral. Illustrations of different types of feedback were given by Vigil and Oller (p. 286):

Affective Feedback

Positive: "I like it" (more of the same)
Neutral: "Waiting . . . " (reaction undecided)
Negative: "I don't like it" (try something else)

Cognitive Feedback

Positive: "I understand" (message and direction are clear)
Neutral: "Still processing . . . " (undecided)
Negative: "I don't understand" (message and/or direction are not clear)

Various combinations of the two major types of feedback are possible. For example, an audience can indicate positive affective feedback ("I affirm you and value what you are trying to communicate") but give neutral or even negative cognitive feedback to indicate that the message itself is unclear. Vigil and Oller astutely observe that negative affective feedback, regardless of the degree of cognitive feedback, will likely result in the abortion of future attempts to communicate. This is, of course, consistent with the overriding affective nature of human interaction: where a person is not at least affirmed and his communication valued, there is little reason for communication. So, one of the first requirements for meaningful communication, as has been pointed out in earlier chapters, is an affective affirmation of the other person.

    Vigil and Oller's model thus holds that a positive affective response is imperative to the learner's desire to continue attempts to communicate. Cognitive feedback then determines the degree of internalization. Negative or neutral feedback in the cognitive dimension will, with the prerequisite positive affective feedback, encourage the learner to "try again," to restate, to reformulate, or to draw a different hypothesis about a rule. Positive feedback in the cognitive dimension will result in reinforcement of the forms used and a conclusion on the part of the learner that his speech is well formed. Fossilized items, then, are those *un*grammatical or *in*correct items in the speech of a learner which gain first positive affective feedback ("I like it") then positive cognitive feedback ("I understand"), reinforcing an incorrect form of language. Learners with fossilized items have acquired them through the same positive feedback and reinforcement with which they acquired correct items.

Error Analysis and the Monitor

Stephen Krashen (1976, 1977a, 1977b) has claimed in the "Monitor model" that the adult second language learner has two means for internalizing rules of the target language. The first is *acquisition*, a subconscious and intuitive process of constructing the system of a language, such as that used by the child in acquiring his first language. The other means is *learning*, a conscious representation of rules usually in a deductive or pedagogically oriented context. The *Monitor* is part of *learning*: it is the act of watchdogging one's output to make alterations and corrections of errors as they are perceived. It is of interest to note that fossilization may occur when the Monitor breaks down—that is, when the learner receives positive affective and cognitive feedback, he may be inclined not to monitor his speech. Correction of errors can result from both acquisition and learning, though in pedagogical settings it is often the Monitor which accounts for error correction.

Developmental Sequences and Stages of Acquisition

Are there uniform patterns of acquisition that apply to all second language learners? Are there identifiable stages? developmental sequences of learning? A series of studies conducted by Heidi Dulay and Marina Burt (Dulay and Burt 1972, 1974a, 1974b) supported the notion of an *invariant sequence* of acquisition of eleven morphemes among English learners from varying language backgrounds. This sequence was found to be strikingly similar to the sequence of acquisition for the same morphemes for children acquiring English as their first language. Dulay and Burt claimed that their findings provided evidence of the negligible effect of interference on second language learning. Since then, however, a number of studies (Larsen-Freeman 1976; Rosansky 1976; Andersen 1978) have challenged this notion. The interference of the first language is, after all, an important factor in second language learning for both adults and children. Moreover, eleven morphemes form a very small and almost insignificant proportion of total language upon which to base global judgments. But Dulay and Burt's research suggests that it may be possible, with a great deal of careful research, to identify stages and sequences of acquisition. At present, however, the tremendous variability of language acquisition patterns seems to preclude the dim hope of finding such universals.

Pidginization

Another body of research supports the notion that second-language acquisition has much in common with the *pidginization* of languages. A pidgin, as we discussed earlier, is a mixed language or jargon usually arising out of two languages coming into contact for commercial, political or even social purposes. The vocabulary of at least two languages is incorporated into the pidgin, and simplified grammatical forms are used. John Schumann (1976a) and some of his colleagues have carried out studies to support the notion that the interlanguage of many second language speakers is akin to pidginized forms of language. The implication is that what happens over perhaps several hundred years in pidginization is reproduced to some degree in the short duration of one learner's acquisition of a second language. One would conclude that the learner instinctively attempts to bring two languages—the target and the native—together to form a unique language, an interlanguage, possessing aspects of both languages. It is perhaps only with great persistence that the learner overcomes his pidginization tendency, weeds out interlanguage forms, and adopts the second language exclusively.

Pedagogical Implications of Error Analysis

It is important in a discussion of error analysis and interlanguage to underscore the relevance of such analysis to teaching. Three categories summarize that relevance: correction of error in the classroom, providing grammatical explanations, and designing materials and curricula.

It should be clear that an active second language learner whose Monitor is fully operating and who is perceptive of the cognitive and affective feedback around him will not need a great deal of overt correction of errors if the constructive and meaningful feedback of communicative contexts is present. Some correction, though, is beneficial. The teacher must face a twofold problem: what to correct and how to correct. A decision on what to correct is dependent upon the teacher's perception of the gravity of the error in reference to the effectiveness of the communication act—how much an error interferes with comprehension. Minor errors that do not hinder communication are sometimes best left uncorrected so the learner is free to continue, uninterrupted, with a thought or pattern. The degree of linguistic deviance is also an important criterion. A grossly malformed sentence—though perhaps comprehensible in context—might justifiably be corrected for the sake of shaping linguistic forms. The particular object or goal of the lesson is also important: in a class of modal auxiliaries, for example, one might expect to correct modals and to ignore certain other errors. How to correct requires a merging of affective, cognitive, and linguistic judgment which will not impede communication yet will accomplish a purpose. For example, by requesting a rephrasing or amplification of the message, the teacher can maintain the learner's attention on meaning yet modify incorrect forms.

A knowledge of possible sources of error, of the methods of error analysis, and of the linguistic properties of the second language can help the foreign language teacher to provide a grammatical explanation or correction that is effective in enabling the learner to construct efficient systems of interlanguage. The metamorphosis of those systems is the ultimate adoption of the correct target language system.

Finally, with regard to materials and curricula, it has already been shown that errors cannot be predicted, precisely, for each student of a foreign language. Foreign language materials therefore cannot be grammatically sequenced to meet the needs of all learners. If some day developmental sequences are found to be reasonably predictable, the sequencing of materials could benefit from such ordering. But that day has not arrived yet. Meanwhile, foreign language curricula can benefit from giving teachers maximum flexibility within a program to design extemporaneous lessons around observed learners' errors. Meaningful communication should take priority over grammatical sequencing. Of course, to be successful in a flexible communicative curriculum, teachers need to be properly equipped with the necessary integrated understanding of the process of second language learning.

At least one conclusion that can be drawn from the study of errors in the interlanguage systems of learners is that learners are indeed creatively operating on a second language—constructing, either consciously or subconsciously, a system for understanding and producing utterances in the language. That system should not necessarily be treated as an imperfect system; it is such only insofar as the native speaker compares his own knowledge of the language to that of the learner. It should rather be looked upon as a flexible, dynamic, approximative system, reasonable to a great degree in the mind of the learner, albeit idiosyncratic. The learner is processing language on the basis of knowledge of his own interlanguage, which, as a system lying between two languages, ought not to have the value judgments of either language placed upon it. The teacher's task is to value the learner, to prize his attempts to communicate, and then to provide the optimal cognitive feedback necessary for the system to evolve in successive stages until the learner is communicating meaningfully and unambiguously in the second language.

SUGGESTED READINGS

A great deal of literature on error analysis has appeared in the last decade. Some anthologies are available which almost exclusively deal with topics in error analysis. The best of these are *Oller and Richards* (1973), *Richards* (1974), and *Hatch* (1978b). All three contain pivotal works in second language error analysis.

Corder (1967), *Selinker* (1972), and *Nemser* (1971) wrote important articles which pioneered error analysis efforts.

For an excellent treatment of a major flaw in error analysis, read *Schachter*'s (1974) study of avoidance patterns. *Kleinmann*'s (1977) follow-up article is also of interest.

Corder's (1973) insights into error analysis have been immensely influential. Researchers owe a great debt of gratitude to him for providing both theoretical underpinnings and practical tools for error analysis. Chapter 11 is an excellent summary of his contributions.

If you have not yet sought out a copy of *Taylor*'s (1975) study of errors in native Spanish-speaking learners of English, you might do so. Also, look through *Richards* (1976) for further elaboration on the significance of intralingual errors.

Some rather technical reading is evident in *Vigil and Oller*'s (1976) treatise on the affective and cognitive roots of fossilization, but it is a good mind-stretcher on the topic.

A highly recommended set of articles is found in *Krashen*'s (1977a, 1977b) work on the Monitor model. Both are readable and avoid complex technical references.

TOPICS AND QUESTIONS FOR STUDY
AND DISCUSSION

1. Why must the study of the speech of learners inevitably be the study of the *errors* of learners? How does "performance analysis"—in theory, at least— attempt to overcome negative connotations of error analysis? What are some of those negative connotations or dangers?

2. What is the difference between a mistake and an error? How can a foreign language teacher tell the difference between the two in the speech of learners? Why is it important to distinguish between mistakes and errors?

3. What is Corder's distinction between *overt* and *covert* errors? Give examples in your particular second language.

4. If possible, record a few minutes of the conversation of some second language learner. Then select a few sentences that contain errors and transcribe those sentences. Perform an error analysis of those sentences using Corder's procedures for identifying errors in second language speech. If you wish to record and transcribe even more speech, some insights could be gained from the careful examination of one learner's oral production in a conversation. Certain interlanguage rules might be inferred from cross-referencing the data.

5. The learning of a third language is given passing reference on page 173. Cite a specific example of third language learning. What kinds of interlingual transfer might occur? What other factors are present in the context that would need to be considered?

6. Taylor's and Richards' taxonomies are restricted to subsystems of English. Attempt a listing of typical intralingual errors in a language other than English. Share this list with others and try to arrive at a consensus.

7. Cite some possible prefabricated patterns in a language other than English, typical of learners of that language.

8. What is the minimal distinction between fossilization and learning? Summarize the arguments that explain why learners fossilize certain forms. How do those arguments integrate with the notion of a culturally defined critical period discussed in Chapter Seven? Once an item is presumably fossilized, can it ever be corrected?

9. Krashen's Monitor model distinguishes between conscious learning and subconscious acquisition. Does such a model fall prey to the same weaknesses of the LAD hypothesis discussed in Chapter Two? What, after all, do we mean by "subconscious"? Despite possible weaknesses, the model has intuitive appeal. How can we get learners to do more "acquiring" and less "learning"? What is the optimal mixture of monitoring and acquisition? Does monitoring prevent or encourage fossilization? How does the learn-

ing-acquisition distinction relate to the distinction between field-independent and field-dependent cognitive styles?

10. In your observation of a foreign language class or conversation group, note teacher or native speaker *correction*. How effective were certain corrections? What made them effective or ineffective? Was the teacher able to accomplish some purpose in correction? Was communication impeded?

10

Discourse Analysis—
The Study of the Pragmatic
Functions of Language

In the last chapter we considered the significance of the acquisition of linguistic *forms* of language and the analysis of those forms in the interlanguage of second language learners. The culmination of language learning, however, is not simply in the mastery of the forms of language, but the mastery of forms in order to accomplish the communicative *functions* of language. Mastery of vocabulary and structures results in nothing if the learner cannot *use* those forms for the purpose of transmitting and receiving thoughts, ideas, and feelings between speaker and hearer, or writer and reader. While forms are the manifestation of language, functions are the realization of those forms. The pragmatic purpose of language—the use of signs and symbols for communication—is thus the final and ultimate objective of the second language learner.

The analysis of the functions of language can be referred to as *discourse analysis* to capture the notion that language is more than a sentence-level phenomenon. A single sentence can seldom be fully analyzed without considering its context. We use language in stretches of discourse. We string many sentences together in cohesive units such that sentences bear interrelationships. In speaking a language our discourse is marked by exchanges with another person or several persons, in which a few sentences spoken by one participant are followed and built upon by sentences spoken by another. Both the production and the comprehension of language are a factor of our ability to perceive and process stretches of discourse, to formulate representations of meaning from not just a single sentence but referents in both previous sentences and following sentences. In fact, a single sentence sometimes contains certain presuppositions or entailments which are not overtly manifested in surrounding surface structure, but which are clear from the total context and the understanding of one's cognitive and linguistic environment. So, while linguistic science has traditionally centered on the sentence for the purposes of analysis, recent trends in linguistics have increasingly emphasized the importance of intersentential relations in discourse. In written language, the same intersentential discourse relations hold true as the writer builds a network of ideas or feelings and the reader interprets them.

Without context, without the intersentential and suprasentential relationships of discourse, it would be difficult to communicate unambiguously with one another. Through discourse, we greet, request, agree, persuade, question, command, criticize, and much, much more. The sentence "I didn't like that casserole" could be agreement, disagreement, criticism, argument, complaint, apology, or simply comment if we only considered sentence-level surface structure. The surface structure of a sentence in the context of total discourse, in conjunction with its prosodic features (stress, intonation, and other phonological nuances) and its nonverbal features (gestures, eye contact, body language), determine the actual interpretation of that single sentence. A second language learner not familiar with contextual discourse constraints of English might utter such a sentence or sentences like it with perfect pronunciation and perfect grammar, but fail to achieve the communicative purpose of, say, apologizing to a dinner host or hostess, and instead appear to be impolitely critical or complaining.

Until recently, linguistic research focused on linguistic forms and upon descriptions of the structure of language. But we have seen a shift of interest now to semantic descriptions, to sociolinguistic inquiry, and to language as part of the total communicative conduct of communities. At the present time, according to Dell Hymes (1974: 208), "we are at the threshold [of being] ... distinguished by a concern for the integration of language in sociocultural context and a focus upon the analysis of function."

Second language research has followed the same trend. We now realize that formal approaches that emphasize the speech product of the learner overlook important functions of language. Wagner-Gough (1975), for example, notes that acquisition by a learner of the -ing morpheme of the present progressive tense does not necessarily mean acquisition of varying functions of the morpheme: to indicate present action, action about to occur immediately, future action, or repeated actions. Formal approaches have also tended to shape our conception of the whole process of second language learning. Evelyn Hatch (1978a:404) spoke of the dangers. "In second language learning the basic assumption has been . . . that one first learns how to manipulate structures, that one gradually builds up a repertoire of structures and then, somehow, learns how to put the structures to use in discourse. We would like to consider the possibility that just the reverse happens. One learns how to do conversation, one learns how to interact verbally, and out of this interaction syntactic structures are developed."

It is imperative, then, in the course of understanding the principles of second language learning and teaching, to understand significant variables in linguistic discourse, variables that comprise what has come to be called "communicative competence." This chapter will outline some of those variables in an attempt to provide a global, overall picture of important discourse features of language. The approach here will not be to provide analysis of specific manifestations of discourse in various languages. I will leave that for you to address on your own within your particular language of interest. However, the basic principles of discourse analysis provided here should apply to each individual language.

REGISTERS AND STYLES

We use different styles or *registers* of language depending upon the context in terms of subject matter, our audience, the mode of discourse (speaking or writing), and the formality of the occasion. A register is not a social or regional dialect, but a variety of language used for a specific purpose. Register refers to styles, which vary considerably, within a single language user's idiolect. When you converse informally with a friend, you use a different style than that used in an interview for a job with a prospective employer. Native speakers, as they mature into adulthood, learn to adopt appropriate styles for widely differing contexts. An important difference between a child's and an adult's "fluency" in a native language is the degree to which an adult is able to vary styles for different occasions and persons. The adult second language learner must acquire adaptability of register in order to be able to encode and decode the discourse around him correctly.

Martin Joos (1967) provided one of the most common classifications of speech styles using the criterion of *formality*; this criterion tends to subsume subject matter, the audience, the mode of discourse, and the occasion. Joos recognized five different levels of formality, each implying different forms of speech to fit separate functions: (1) oratorical, or "frozen," (2) deliberative, or formal, (3) consultative, (4) casual, and (5) intimate. An *oratorical* style is used in public speaking before a large audience; wording is carefully planned in advance, intonation is somewhat exaggerated, and numerous rhetorical devices are appropriate. A *deliberative* style is also used in addressing audiences, usually audiences too large to permit effective interchange between speaker and hearers, though the forms are normally not as polished as those in an oratorical style. A typical university classroom lecture is often carried out in a deliberative style. A *consultative* style is typically a dialogue, though formal enough that words are chosen with some care. Business transactions, doctor-patient conversations, and the like are usually consultative in nature. *Casual* conversations are between friends or colleagues or sometimes members of a family; in this context words need not be guarded and social barriers are moderately low. An *intimate* style is one characterized by complete absence of social inhibitions. Talk with family, loved ones, and very close friends, where you tend to reveal your inner self, is usually in an intimate style.

Categories of register can apply to written discourse as well. Most writing is addressed to readers who cannot respond immediately; that is, long stretches of discourse—books, essays, even letters—are read from beginning to end before the reader gives a response. Written style is therefore usually more deliberative with the exception of friendly letters, notes, or literature intended to capture a lower register. Even the latter, however, often carry with them reasonably carefully chosen wording with relatively few performance variables.

Registers are manifested by both verbal and nonverbal features. Differences in register can be conveyed in body language, gestures, eye contact, and the like—all very difficult aspects of "language" for the learner to acquire. We will return to a further discussion of nonverbal features later in this chapter. Verbal aspects of register alone are difficult to learn. Syntax in many languages is characterized by more contractions and other deletions in lower registers. Lexical items vary, too. Bolinger (1975) gave a somewhat tongue-in-cheek illustration of lexical items that have one semantic meaning but represent each of the five registers: *on the ball, smart, intelligent, perceptive,* and *astute*—from intimate to frozen, respectively. He of course recognized other meanings besides those of register which intervene to make the example somewhat overstated. Register distinctions in pronunciation are likely to be most noticeable in the form of hesitations and other misarticulations, phonological deletion rules in lower registers and informal speech, and perhaps a more affected pronunciation in higher registers.

The acquisition of register adaptability for second language learners poses no simple problem. Cross-cultural variation is a primary barrier—that is, understanding cognitively and affectively what levels of formality are appropriate or inappropriate. American culture, for example, tends generally to accept lower registers for given occasions than some other cultures. Some English learners in the United States consequently experience difficulty in gauging appropriate formality distinctions and tend to be overly formal. Japanese students, for example, are often surprised by the level of informality expressed by their American professors. The acquisition of registers thus combines a linguistic and culture-learning process.

COMMUNICATIVE ACTS

Forms of language generally serve specific functions. "How much does that cost?" is usually a form functioning as a question, and "He bought a car" functions as a statement. But linguistic forms are not always unambiguous in their function. "I can't find my umbrella," uttered by a frustrated adult who is late for work on a rainy day may be a frantic request for all in the household to join in a search. A child who says "I want some ice cream" is rarely stating a simple fact or observation but requesting ice cream in his own intimate register. A sign on the street that says "one way" functions to guide traffic in only one direction. A sign in a church parking lot in a busy downtown area was subtle in form but direct in function: "We forgive those who trespass against us, but we also tow them"; that sign functioned effectively to prevent unauthorized cars from parking in the lot.

Communication may be regarded as a combination of *acts*, a series of elements with purpose and intent. Communication is not merely an event, something that happens; it is functional, purposive, and designed to bring about some *effect*—some change, however subtle or unobservable—on the environment of hearers and speakers. Communication is a series of communicative acts or *speech acts*, to use John Austin's (1962) term, which are used systematically to accomplish particular purposes. Austin stressed the importance of consequences of linguistic communication. Researchers have since been led to examine communication in terms of the effect that utterances achieve. That effect has implications for both the production and comprehension of an utterance; both modes of performance serve to bring the communicative act to its ultimate purpose. Second language learners need to understand the purpose of communication, developing an awareness of what the purpose of a communicative act is and how to achieve that purpose through linguistic forms.

Michael Halliday (1973) used the term *functions* to denote the purposive nature of communication, and outlined seven different functions of language:

1. The *instrumental* function serves to manipulate the environment, to cause certain events to happen. Sentences like "This court finds you guilty," "On your mark, get set, go!" or "Don't touch the stove" have an instrumental function; they are communicative acts which bring about a particular condition.

2. The *regulatory* function of language is the control of events. While such control is sometimes difficult to distinguish from the instrumental function, regulatory functions of language are not so much the "unleashing" of certain power, as the maintenance of control. "I pronounce you guilty and sentence you to three years in prison" serves an instrumental function, but the sentence "Upon good behavior, you will be eligible for parole in ten months" serves more of a regulatory function. The regulation of encounters among people—approval, disapproval, behavior control, setting laws and rules, are all regulatory features of language.

3. The *representational* function is the use of language to make statements, convey facts and knowledge, explain, or report—that is, to "represent" reality as one sees it. "The sun is hot," "The president gave a speech last night," or even "The world is flat" all serve representational functions though the last representation may be highly disputed.

4. The *interactional* function of language serves to ensure social maintenance. "Phatic communion," Malinowski's term referring to the communicative contact between and among human beings that simply allows them to establish social contact and to keep channels of communication open, is part of the interactional function of language. Successful interactional communication requires knowledge of slang, jargon, jokes, folklore, cultural mores, politeness and formality expectations, and other keys to social exchange.

5. The *personal* function allows a speaker to express feelings, emotions, personality, "gut-level" reactions. A person's individuality is usually characterized by his use of the personal function of communication. In the personal nature of language, cognition, affect, and culture all interact in ways that have not yet been explored.

6. The *heuristic* function involves language used to acquire knowledge, to learn about the environment. Heuristic functions are often conveyed in the form of questions that will lead to answers. Children typically make

good use of the heuristic function in their incessant "why" questions about the world around them. Inquiry is a heuristic method of eliciting representations of reality from others.

7. The *imaginative* function serves to create imaginary systems or ideas. Telling fairy tales, joking, or writing a novel are all uses of the imaginative function. Using language for the sheer pleasure of using language—as in poetry, tongue twisters, puns—are also instances of imaginative functions. Through the imaginative dimensions of language we are free to go beyond the real world to soar the heights of the beauty of language itself, and through that language to create impossible dreams if we so desire.

These seven different functions of language are neither discrete nor mutually exclusive. A single sentence or conversation might incorporate many different functions simultaneously. Yet it is the understanding of how to use linguistic forms to achieve these functions of language that comprises the crux of second language learning. A learner might acquire correct word order, syntax, and lexical items but not understand how to achieve a desired and intended function through careful selection of words, structure, intonation, nonverbal signals, and astute perception of the context of a particular stretch of discourse.

Halliday's seven functions of language tend to mask the almost infinite variety and complexity of communicative acts. Consider, for example, the list of communicative acts below.

1. Greeting, parting, inviting, accepting
2. Complimenting, congratulating, flattering, seducing, charming, bragging
3. Interrupting
4. Requesting
5. Evading, lying, shifting blame, changing the subject
6. Criticizing, reprimanding, ridiculing, insulting, threatening, warning
7. Complaining
8. Accusing, denying
9. Agreeing, disagreeing, arguing
10. Persuading, insisting, suggesting, reminding, asserting, advising
11. Reporting, evaluating, commenting
12. Commanding, ordering, demanding
13. Questioning, probing
14. Sympathizing
15. Apologizing, making excuses

All of these fall into one or more of Halliday's seven functions, and all of them are common everyday acts whose performance requires a knowledge of language. Subtle differences between communicative acts must be learned. The appropriate contexts for various acts must be discerned. The forms of language used to accomplish the functions must become part of the total linguistic repertoire of the second language learner.

If a learner is attempting to acquire written as well as spoken competence in the language, he must also discern differences in forms and functions between spoken and written discourse. Such differences are both significant and salient. However, we are centering in this chapter, particularly in the next section, on spoken discourse for several reasons. First, it is the most common goal of foreign language classes. Second, the teaching of writing—beyond perfunctory levels of written discourse—is a highly technical task that varies greatly depending upon the goal of written discourse and upon the particular language that is in question. The study of written discourse, or *stylistics*, is best undertaken with a specific language in focus. Third, many of the general principles of discourse analysis apply, as we have already seen, to both spoken and written modes of performance.

RULES OF CONVERSATION

Most of everyday spoken discourse is carried on in the lower or middle registers of language; few occasions provide a second-language user with the opportunity to engage in public speaking or lecturing. Conversation, then, is the most significant locus of the functional use of the rules of discourse. What are the rules that govern our conversations? How do we get someone's attention? How do we initiate topics? terminate topics? avoid topics? How does a person interrupt, correct, or seek clarification? These questions form an area of linguistic competence that every adult native speaker of a language possesses, yet few foreign language curricula traditionally deal with these important aspects of communicative competence. Once again our consideration of conversation rules will be general, since specific languages differ.

Very early in life, children learn the first and essential rule of conversation: *attention getting*. If you wish linguistic production to be functional and to accomplish its intended purpose, you must of course have the attention of the hearer or audience. The attention-getting conventions within each language—both verbal and nonverbal —need to be carefully assimilated by the learner. Without knowledge and use of such conventions the second language learner may be reluctant to participate in conversation because of his own inhibitions, or he may become obnoxious in securing attention in ways that "turn off" his hearer to the topic he wishes to discuss.

Once the speaker has secured the hearer's attention, his task becomes one of *topic nomination*. There are few explicit rules for accomplishing topic nomination in a language. Usually a person will simply embark on an issue by making a statement or a question which leads to a particular topic. H. P. Grice (1971) noted that certain conversational "maxims" enable the speaker to nominate and maintain a topic of conversation: (1) *quantity*: say only as much as is necessary for understanding the communication; (2) *quality*: say only what is true; (3) *relevance*: say only what is relevant; (4) *manner*: be clear. Robin Lakoff (1976) incorporated Grice's maxims into what she defined as rules of communicative competence. (It should be noted, though, that Hymes [1967] was probably the first to coin the now-popular term "communicative competence.")

Once a topic is nominated, participants in a conversation then embark on *topic development*, using conventions of *turn-taking* to accomplish various functions of language. Within topic development one encounters instances of *topic clarification, shifting, avoidance*, and *interruption*. Turn-taking is another of those culturally oriented sets of rules which require an integrated understanding of interchange within the culture. Topic clarification manifests itself in various forms of heuristic functions. In the case of conversations between second language learners and native speakers, topic clarification often involves seeking or giving *repair* (correction) of linguistic forms that contain errors. The learner may ask for repair or the native-speaking hearer may simply provide unsolicited correction. Topic shifting and avoidance may be effected through both verbal and nonverbal signals. Interruptions are a typical feature of all conversations. Language users learn how to interrupt politely—a form of attention getting. Children typically have to be "taught" how and when to interrupt.

Topic termination is an art which even native speakers of a language have difficulty in mastering at times. We commonly experience situations in which a conversation has ensued for some time and neither participant seems to know how to terminate it. Usually, in American English, conversations are terminated by various interactional functions—a glance at a watch, a nicety, or a "Well, I have to be going now." Each language has verbal and nonverbal signals for such termination. It is important for teachers to be acutely aware of the rules of conversation in the second language and to aid learners both to perceive those rules and follow them in their own conversations.

PERSONALITY FACTORS

Personality factors (see Chapter Six) emerge as highly important aspects of carrying on discourse. The *personal* function of language is in some ways the most mysterious of all the functions, the most difficult to analyze, as has been noted again and again in this book. Language and person are inextricably interrelated; one's personality is often the central feature of and embodied in a conversation. And as a participant speaks, comprehends, and provides nonverbal feedback, he reveals his personality.

Along with the previously discussed factors of empathy, self-esteem, and other personality variables, *dominance* is an important factor in conversation analysis. The most assertive and perhaps extroverted personality will usually dominate a conversation. Such dominance can indicate either high self-esteem or it may be a defense of a rather insecure self-concept. Foreign language conversation groups typically consist of some learners who dominate a conversation as a mechanism to mask a vulnerable ego and others who do so brimming with confidence. Still other learners maintain silence either out of shyness or simply to prevent exposing ignorance or error. In general, the *group dynamics* of a conversation are a factor of personality differences and the expression or exposure of certain personalities. Particular mixes of personalities produce certain effects on the conversation.

A careful consideration of personality factors in conversational analysis is important; no single participant should be judged or analyzed apart from the whole context and the total group of persons in a conversation. The degree to which a learner can fully utilize the personal function of his second language in conversation will depend on the total group dynamics and the interaction of personalities in the group. What a person says, how he says it, when he says it, and how he hears others—all these are important considerations in seeking a clear understanding of the effect of personality on conversational discourse.

NONVERBAL DIMENSIONS OF DISCOURSE

We communicate so much information nonverbally in conversations that often the verbal aspect of the conversation is negligible. This is particularly true for interactive language functions in which social contact is of key importance and in which it is not *what* you say that counts but *how* you say it—what you convey with body language, gestures, eye contact, physical distance, and other non-verbal messages. Nonverbal communication, however, is so subtle and subconscious in a native speaker that verbal language seems, by comparison, quite mechanical and systematic. Language becomes distinctly human through its nonverbal dimension, or what Edward Hall (1966) called the "hidden dimension." The expression of culture is so bound up in nonverbal communication that the barriers to culture learning are more nonverbal than verbal. Verbal language requires the use of only one of the five sensory modalities: hearing. But there remain in our communicative repertoire three other senses by which we communicate every day, if we for the moment rule out taste as falling within a communicative category (though messages are indeed sent and received through the taste modality). We will examine each of these.

Visual Modality

Gesture and body language

Every culture and language uses "body language" or kinesics, in unique but clearly interpretable ways. "There was speech in their dumbness, language in their very gesture," wrote Shakespeare in *The Winter's Tale.* All cultures throughout the history of humankind have communicated by body language. Julius Fast's *Body Language* (1970), with its lighthearted but provocative insights on the use of body language in American culture, explained how many messages are communicated as you fold your arms, cross your legs, stand, walk, move your eyes and mouth, and use various gestures. Edward Hall's *The Silent Language* (1959) and *The Hidden Dimension* (1966) in a more comprehensive way opened up the field of nonverbal communication cross-culturally.

But as universal as kinesic communication is, there is tremendous variation cross-culturally and cross-linguistically in the specific interpretation of gestures. Human beings all move their heads, blink their eyes, move their arms and hands, but the significance of these movements varies from society to society. Consider the following categories and how you would express them in American culture:

1. Agreement, "yes"
2. "No!"
3. "Come here"
4. Disinterest, "I don't know"
5. Flirting signals, sexual signals
6. Insults, obscene gestures

There are conventionalized gestural signals to convey these semantic categories. Are those signals the same in another language and culture? Sometimes they are not. And sometimes a gesture that is appropriate in one culture is obscene or insulting in another. Nodding the head, for example, means "yes" among most European language speakers. But in the Eskimo gestural system, head nodding means "no" and head shaking means "yes." Among the Ainu of Japan, "yes" is expressed by bringing the arms to the chest and waving them. The pygmy Negritos of interior Malaya indicate "yes" by thrusting the head sharply forward, but someone from the Punjab of India throws his head sharply backward. A Ceylonese curves his chin gracefully downward in an arc to the left shoulder, whereas a Bengali rocks his head rapidly from one shoulder to the other.

Eye contact

Is eye contact appropriate between two participants in a conversation? When is it permissible not to maintain eye contact? What does eye contact or the absence thereof signal? Cultures differ widely in this particular visual modality of nonverbal communication. In American culture it is permissible, for example, for two participants of unequal status to maintain prolonged eye contact. In fact, an American might interpret lack of eye contact as discourteous lack of attention, while in Japanese culture eye contact might be considered rude. Intercultural interference in this nonverbal category can lead to misunderstanding.

Not only is eye contact itself an important category, but the gestures, as it were, of the eyes are in some instances keys to communication. Eyes can signal interest, boredom, empathy, hostility, attraction, understanding, misunderstanding, and other messages. The nonverbal language of each culture has different ways of signaling such messages. An important aspect of unfettered and unambiguous conversation in a second language is the acquisition of conventions for conveying messages by means of eye signals.

Proxemics

Physical proximity is also a meaningful communicative category. Cultures vary widely in acceptable distances for conversation. Edward Hall (1966) calculated acceptable distances for public, social-consultative, personal, and intimate discourse. He noted, for example, that Americans feel that a certain personal space "bubble" has been violated if a stranger stands closer than 20 to 24 inches away, unless there is restricted space, such as in a subway or an elevator. However, a typical member of a Latin American culture would feel that such a physical distance would be too great.

> The interesting thing is that neither party is specifically aware of what is wrong when the distance is not right. They merely have vague feelings of discomfort or anxiety. As the Latin American approaches the North American backs away; both parties take offense without knowing why. When a North American, having had the problem pointed out to him, permits the Latin American to get close enough, he will immediately notice that the latter seems much more at ease. (Hall 1974:76-77)

Sometimes objects—desks, counters, other furniture—serve to maintain certain physical distances. Such objects tend to establish both the overall register and relationship of participants. Thus, a counter between two people maintains a consultative mood. Similarly, the presence of a desk or a typewriter will set the tone of a conversation. Again, however, different cultures interpret different messages in such objects. In some cultures, objects might enhance a communicative act, but in other cases they impede the communicative process.

Artifacts

The nonverbal messages of clothing and ornamentation are also important aspects of communication. "Clothes make the man," the saying goes, and for both sexes in many cultures clothes often signal a person's sense of self-esteem, socioeconomic class, and general character. Jewelry also conveys certain messages. In a multicultural conversation group such artifacts, along with other nonverbal signals, can be a significant factor in lifting barriers, identifying certain personality characteristics, and setting a general mood.

Kinesthetic Modality

Touching, sometimes referred to as kinesthetics, is another culturally loaded aspect of nonverbal communication. How we touch others and where we touch them is sometimes the most misunderstood aspect of nonverbal communication. Touching in some cultures signals a very personal or intimate register, while for other cultures extensive touching is commonplace. Knowing the limits and conventions is important for clear and unambiguous communication.

Olfactory Modality

Our noses also receive sensory nonverbal messages. The olfactory modality is of course an important one for the animal kingdom, but for the human race, too, different cultures have established different dimensions of olfactory communication. The twentieth century has created in most technological societies a penchant for perfumes, lotions, creams, and powders as acceptable and even necessary; natural human odors, especially perspiration, are thought to be undesirable. In some societies, of course, the smell of human perspiration is quite acceptable and even attractive. Second language and especially second culture learners need to be aware of the accepted mores of other cultures in the olfactory modality.

We cannot underestimate the importance of nonverbal communication in second language learning and in conversational analysis. Communicative competence includes nonverbal competence—knowledge of all the varying nonverbal semantics of the second culture, and an ability both to send and receive nonverbal signals unambiguously.

THE NOTIONAL-FUNCTIONAL SYLLABUS— DISCOURSE ANALYSIS IN THE CLASSROOM

The practical implications of discourse analysis for classroom methods and techniques are abundant and the resources of discourse analysis have only begun to be tapped. As interest has shifted in both linguistics and second language research away from examining just the forms of language to an interest in the functional features of linguistic communication, so also language teaching paradigms have begun to emphasize functional communication, with "communicative competence" one of the bywords of language teaching methodology. Such emphases have placed importance in language curricula on communicative acts and conversational analysis, with grammatical structures assuming a secondary or even at times a subordinate role. Traditional curricula constructed a set of lessons according to a sequence of grammatical structures in such a way that, say, present tense was followed by past tense, then future tense, then modals, and so forth, with lessons on prepositions, articles, and other categories all carefully sequenced in the overall course syllabus. A different type of curriculum, whose aim is primarily to establish the communicative competence of individuals, may present a set of lessons organized around certain functions, acts, or rules of conversation.

The latter type of curriculum has come to be called a *notional syllabus*,* or sometimes a *notional-functional syllabus*. The notional syllabus is an alternative to the former type of curriculum, the *structural syllabus*. The two types of syllabus differ in the way the content of language is conceived and presented. The structural syllabus views language in terms of its *forms*—its grammatical and lexical units; the notional syllabus views language in *functional* terms, as "notions" realized by the formal items of language. A notional syllabus might conceivably organize a curriculum around Michael Halliday's functions of language, in which the units of the curriculum each deal with one or more functions and include forms of language that are used to accomplish a particular functional purpose. In both cases the curriculum is an inventory of language units, though the notional syllabus defines units differently from a structural syllabus.

A typical notional syllabus might, for example, present a unit on "argument"—categories relating to the defense and challenge of information and views. Five subunits might be used: (1) seeking and gathering information, (2) agreeing, (3) disagreeing, (4) denying, and (5) conceding. For each subcategory, the lessons in the foreign language would deal with the expression of the function through various syntactic forms. Structure and vocabulary would not by any means be ignored; rather, they would be taught within the context of certain language functions, and even "sequenced" according to difficulty.

A notional syllabus developed by Imber and Klingler (1976) suggested a curriculum for all four skills (speaking, listening, writing, and reading) consisting of eight basic units, not unlike the categories of communicative acts referred to earlier.

1. Misunderstandings
2. Agreeing, disagreeing, sympathizing, arguing, placating
3. Evading, changing the subject, denying
4. Complimenting, congratulating, flattering, boasting
5. Criticizing, admonishing, insulting, accusing, threatening
6. Reminding, suggesting, advising, persuading, asserting
7. Commenting, questioning, correcting, reporting, analyzing
8. Understandings

Such organization, which interweaves grammatical structures into the syllabus, is a far cry from the traditional text, which takes the student only through sequenced grammatical categories.

Syllabus, in this case, is a term used mainly in the United Kingdom to denote what is commonly referred to as *curriculum* in the United States.

A weakness of the structural syllabus, in its focus on grammar, is its tendency to highlight a grammatical feature to the exclusion of practical application in real situations. While a "situational approach" to a structural syllabus is possible, sometimes the very fact that situations are devised to illustrate grammar, instead of grammar illustrating a notion or function, keys the student artificially into grammatical categories that later impede the communicative process. Notional syllabuses seek to overcome that weakness in their attention to the ultimate purpose of language: functional, pragmatic communication between and among human beings.

Both types of syllabus might claim to provide the necessary components of language in terms of learner needs. On the one hand, the learner may need a basic knowledge of the lexical and grammatical forms of the language on the assumption that this knowledge will provide the essential basis for communication when he is faced with a need to communicate. On the other hand, those who favor the notional syllabus might argue that the learner needs to learn appropriate communicative behavior during the course of studies and that on such a foundation he will more meaningfully acquire the grammar of a language; in essence, the learner cannot simply be left to his own devices in developing an ability to communicate.

Henry Widdowson (1978) noted that while the notional syllabus claims to develop communicative competence within the actual design of the syllabus itself, such is not necessarily the case, since the notional syllabus still presents language as an inventory of units— notional rather than structural units, but still isolates. "Communicative competence is not a compilation of items in memory but a set of strategies or creative procedures for realizing the value of linguistic elements in contexts of use, an ability to make sense as a participant in discourse, whether spoken or written, by the skillful deployment of shared knowledge of code resources and rules of language use" (p. 2). The notional syllabus deals with the components of discourse, but may not deal with discourse itself.

The notional syllabus should not be viewed by language teachers as a panacea, the last word. Nor, however, are notional syllabuses merely "structural lamb served up as notional-functional mutton" (Campbell 1978:18). What notional syllabuses do give us is, first of all, an organization of language content by functional categories. Second, they provide a means of developing structural categories within a general consideration of the functions of language. We have not arrived at a final solution with the notional-functional syllabus, but we have rather begun an avenue of exploration which we should continue with the full awareness that communication in a foreign language is something so complex that it will probably never be reduced to a simple formula or a neatly packaged syllabus. Communication is qualitative and infinite; a syllabus is quantitative and finite.

We have seen in this chapter alone that discourse is such an intricate web of psychological, sociocultural, physical, and linguistic features that it is easy to get entangled in but one part of that web. And it is probably impossible in the near future to describe the whole of human discourse in such a way that language teachers are provided with ready solutions to the teaching of a foreign language. But some of the features of human communication are becoming clearer, and I believe we are moving in positive and creative directions. The language teacher and researcher can be a part of that creative event by fashioning an integrated and cohesive understanding of how learners acquire the ability to manipulate the discourse features of a second language.

SUGGESTED READINGS

Joos' (1967) classic treatise on the "five clocks" or five styles used in human communication will give you a more technical understanding of the meaning and uses of the registers summarized in the chapter. If it is difficult to locate Joos, registers and styles are usually discussed in such introductory linguistics books as *Bolinger* 1975: 358-63).

Halliday's (1973) book on the functions of language is an important one. It may be too long and too technical to read now, but certain parts of it might be skimmed. *R. Lakoff* (1976) also provided a technical treatment of language and society; if you have some background in linguistics her article will be understandable.

One of the best introductions to discourse analysis in second language acquisition is offered by *Hatch* (1978a), in which she explained and provided numerous examples of specific discourse features in second language conversation. A number of studies on discourse analysis are available in *Henning* (1977) and in *Hatch* (1978b).

If you have never read either of *Hall*'s (1959, 1966) books, at least read the latter in the near future for your own pleasure. Also *Fast*'s (1970) humorous but informative paperback makes enjoyable armchair reading.

Read *Savignon* (1972:8-15) for an overview of the notion of communicative competence.

Four excellent brief commentaries on the notional-functional syllabus are contained in *Blatchford and Schachter* (1978): articles by Finocchiaro, Rutherford, Campbell, and Widdowson. These make an ideal summary of issues surrounding the notional-functional syllabus.

TOPICS AND QUESTIONS FOR STUDY
AND DISCUSSION

1. Hatch contended that in second language learning "one learns how to do conversation" first, and then builds up a repertoire of structures. This suggests that learning may be in some sense a deductive process: one learns linguistic "wholes" and then learns "parts." Do you agree with Hatch? What are the classroom implications of her contention?

2. Review once again the distinction between the *form* and the *function* of language. Why is an analysis of second language acquisition incomplete if it includes only forms and not functions? In what way does Skinner's theory account for both form and function in language?

3. Give examples of language in each of the five registers. How many registers are appropriate to teach in a foreign language class? What are some surface linguistic manifestations of differences in register? nonverbal manifestations? How do registers vary cross-culturally?

4. Give examples in your second language of Halliday's seven functions. Do you detect some overlap in assigning function to certain sentences?

5. Select one or two of the communicative acts listed on page 195 and develop either a lesson (for a foreign language class) or a topic of conversation (for a conversation group) around each communicative act. How effective is such an approach?

6. Try to think of a number of linguistic differences between spoken and written language in your second language. What implications for teaching do those differences hold?

7. In a conversation group or a conversation period in a class, take note of the use of the various *rules of conversation* described in this chapter. If a tape recording of the conversation is available you might engage in a mini-discourse analysis of the conversation. Note personality dynamics, nonverbal features of the conversation, and the discourse itself. Can you learn something about the second language learning process through such an exercise? or about a particular learner?

8. In your own native language discourse over the next day or two, notice how people get attention, change topics, clarify topics, terminate topics, take turns, avoid topics, and interrupt. What are some major differences between your own native language conversation and second language discourse?

9. Attempt a concise definition of communicative competence. Do existing foreign language programs with which you are familiar strive for the goal of communicative competence? Is the goal achieved?

10. Compare nonverbal expressions in your own native culture with those of a second culture. How might such expressions interfere with second language communication? How might they facilitate communication?

11. What is wrong with "structural lamb served up as notional mutton"? How does the notional-functional syllabus help us to reach communicative competence in the classroom? What are the limitations of the notional-functional syllabus?

11

Foundations
of Measurement
and Research

The principal theme running through this book has been the importance of theory building in teaching foreign languages. The assumption is that the best teacher is the teacher who devises classroom methods and techniques that derive from a comprehensive knowledge of the total process of language learning, of what is happening within the learner and within the teacher and in the interaction between the two. All of this knowledge, however, remains somewhat abstract in the mind of the teacher unless it can be empirically tested in the real world. It is one thing to have a thorough grasp of the principles of foreign language learning and teaching and another to creatively formulate specific hypotheses about language learning in particular contexts and to garner empirical support for those hypotheses.

That support can be gathered by means of careful measurement of the language competence of learners in given situations. That is, your theory of second language acquisition can be put into practice every day in the classroom, but you will never know how valid your theory is unless you systematically measure the success of your learners—the success of your theory-in-practice. It is to that end that this chapter takes up general considerations of what it is that you, the teacher, need to know about *language testing*, first in respect to classroom learning and teaching, and then to the broader framework of *research* on language learning. The first portion of the chapter concentrates on theoretical foundations of language testing, with a view to presenting basic concepts of testing, on the assumption that subsequent training and experience in classroom methodology can then focus on practical implications and applications. The second section aims to introduce you to the idea that "research"—seeking support for hypotheses about language learning or teaching—is not something that needs to be feared, but an everyday process through which you can creatively enrich your understanding of how people learn foreign languages.

LANGUAGE TESTING

Whether we realize it or not, we test every day in virtually every cognitive effort we make. When we read a book, listen to the news on TV, or prepare a meal, we are testing hypotheses and making judgments. Anytime we "try" something—a new recipe, a different tennis racquet, a new pair of shoes—we are testing. We are formulating a judgment about something on the basis of a sample of behavior. The foreign language learner is testing his newly acquired forms of language almost every time he speaks. He devises hypotheses about how the language forms are structured and how certain functions are expressed in forms. On the basis of the feedback he receives, he makes judgments and decisions. Language teachers also test, informally and intuitively, in every contact with learners. As a learner speaks or writes or indicates either aural or reading comprehension, the teacher makes a judgment about the performance and from that judgment infers certain competence on the part of the learner. Classroom-oriented informal testing is an everyday and very common activity in which teachers engage almost intuitively.

What Is a Test?

A test, in plain, ordinary words, is a method of measuring a person's ability or knowledge in a given area. The definition captures the essential components of a test. A test is first *a method*. There is a set of techniques, procedures, test items, which constitute an instrument of some sort. And that method generally requires some performance or activity on the part of either the testee or the tester, or both. The method may be quite intuitive and informal, as in the case of judging offhand someone's authenticity of pronunciation. Or it may be quite explicit and structured, as in a multiple-choice technique in which the tester or the teacher can objectively discern correct responses.

Next, a test has the purpose of *measuring*. Some measurements are rather broad and inexact, while others are quantified in mathematically precise terms. The difference between formal and informal testing exists to a great degree in the nature of the quantification of data. Informal tests, the everyday intuitive judging that we do as laypersons or teachers, are difficult to quantify. Judgments are rendered in rather global terms. For example, it is common to speak of a "good" tennis player, "fair" performance by an actor in a play, or a "poor" reader. In formal testing, in which carefully planned techniques of assessment are used, quantification is important, especially for comparison either within an individual (say, at the beginning and the end of a course) or across individuals.

A test measures *a person's* ability or knowledge. Care must be taken in any test to understand who the *testee* is. What is the previous experience of the testee—his entry behavior? Is the test appropriate for the testee? How are scores to be interpreted for individuals?

Also being measured in a test is *ability or knowledge*—that is, competence. A test samples performance but infers certain competence. A driving test for a driver's license is a test requiring a sample of performance, but that performance is used by the tester to infer someone's general competence to drive a car. A language test samples language behavior and infers general ability in a language. A test of reading comprehension may consist of some questions following one or two paragraphs, a tiny sample of a second language learner's total reading behavior. From the results of that test the examiner infers a certain level of general reading ability.

Finally, a test measures *a given area*. In the case of a proficiency test, even though the actual performance on the test involves only a sampling of skills, that *area* is overall proficiency in a language— general competence in all skills of a language. Other tests may have more specific criteria. A test of pronunciation might well be a test only of a particular phonemic minimal pair in a language. One of the biggest obstacles to overcome in constructing adequate tests is to measure the *criterion* and not inadvertently something else.

Practicality, Reliability, and Validity

The foregoing discussion implicitly dealt with the three requirements of a "good" test: practicality, reliability, and validity. If these three axiomatic criteria are carefully met, a test should then be administerable within given constraints, be dependable, and actually measure what it intends to measure.

Practicality

A test ought to be practical—within the means of financial limitations, time constraints, ease of administration, and scoring and interpretation. A test that is prohibitively expensive is impractical. A test of language proficiency that takes a student ten hours to complete is also impractical. A test that requires individual one-to-one proctoring is impractical for a group of 500 people and only a handful of examiners. A test that takes a few minutes for a student to take and several hours for the examiner to correct is impractical for a large number of testees and one examiner if results are expected within a short time. A test that can be scored only by computer is impractical if the test takes place a thousand miles away from the nearest computer. The value and quality of a test are dependent upon such nitty-gritty, practical considerations.

Reliability

A reliable test is a test that is consistent and dependable. Sources of unreliability may lie in the test itself or in the scoring of the test, known respectively as test reliability and rater (or scorer) reliability. If you give the same test to the same subject or matched subjects on two different occasions, the test itself should yield similar results; it should have *test reliability*. A test of skating ability, for example, should be reasonably consistent from one day to the next. However, if one skating test is conducted on bumpy ice and another on smooth ice, the reliability of the test—of one aspect of the test, at least—is suspect. I once witnessed the administration of a test of aural comprehension in which a tape recorder played items for comprehension, but because of street noise outside the testing room, some students in the room were prevented from hearing the tape accurately. That was a clear case of unreliability. Sometimes a test yields unreliable results because of factors beyond the control of the test writer, such as illness, a "bad day," or no sleep the night before.

Scorer reliability is the consistency of scoring by two or more scorers. If very subjective techniques are employed in the scoring of a test, one would not expect to find high scorer reliability. A test of authenticity of pronunciation in which the scorer is to assign a number between 1 and 5 might be unreliable if the scoring directions are not clear. If scoring directions are clear and specific as to the exact details the judge should attend to, then such scoring can become reasonably consistent and dependable. It is very difficult to establish scorer reliability in a composition test in which a student is asked to write an essay on a certain topic. Very few guidelines exist for rating a person's writing proficiency, and scorers usually assign a mark on the basis of relatively subjective reactions.

Validity

By far the most complex criterion of a good test is validity, the degree to which the test actually measures what it is intended to measure. A valid test of reading ability is one that actually measures reading ability and not 20/20 vision, previous knowledge in a subject, or some other variable of questionable relevance. To measure writing ability, one might conceivably ask students to write as many words as they can in 15 minutes, then simply *count* the words for the final score. Such a test would be practical and reliable; the test would be easy to administer, and the scoring quite dependable. But it would hardly constitute a valid test of writing ability unless some consideration were given to the communication and organization of ideas, among other factors. Some have felt that standard language proficiency tests are not valid measures of overall proficiency in view of the ultimate goal of the communicative competence of the language learner. There is good reasoning behind such criticism; however, it has been found consistently that standard proficiency test scores correlate positively with other measures of "success"—academic success, conversation ability, and other tests of language ability.

In the face of such arguments, how does one establish the validity of a test? Statistical correlation with other related measures is a standard method. But ultimately, validity can only be established by observation and theoretical justification. There is no final, absolute, and objective measure of validity. In fact, several kinds of validity can be considered.

Criterion validity is validity in its basic, classical sense of measuring what a test sets out to measure. Does the test accurately and sufficiently measure the testee for the particular purpose of the test? Does it enable the tester to reach his *criterion*? A driving test is normally used to predict driving ability and one could assume that an actual test behind the wheel has high criterion validity. However, in many localities a paper-and-pencil test of road signs and driving regulations is a sufficient criterion for *renewal* of a driver's license. Does such a test contain criterion validity? Observational studies seem to bear out the contention that no subsequent driving test is needed, but it is doubtful that the written test actually predicts the quality of driving ability. It is more likely that simply previous experience in driving is the best predictor of good driving ability. The paper-and-pencil license-renewal test probably has little criterion validity for predicting good driving; what it does measure is knowledge of various regulations, which is only a small part of total driving ability.

In tests of language, criterion validity is supported most convincingly by subsequent personal observation of teachers and peers. The criterion validity of a high score on the final exam of a foreign language course will be substantiated by "actual" proficiency in the language (if the claim is that a high score is indicative of high proficiency). A classroom test designed to assess mastery of a point of grammar in communicative use will have criterion validity if test scores correlate either with observed subsequent behavior or with other communicative measures of the grammar point in question.

Content validity is demonstrated by showing how well the content of the test samples the class of situations, the universe of subject matter, about which conclusions are to be drawn. Does the test actually involve the testee in a sample of the behavior that is being measured? A definition of the achievement that is being measured usually enables one to determine content validity. If "proficiency" is defined as ability to read test questions and to pick out correct answers in multiple-choice items, then a standard proficiency test has content validity. However, if by "proficiency" we mean communicative oral use of the language, then such tests have little content validity, even though their criterion validity—which is of more ultimate importance—is relatively good.

Aside from highly specialized and sophisticated testing instruments, there are few cases of tests which do not have content validity but somehow have criterion validity. In most human situations we are best tested in something when we are required to perform a sampling of the criterion behavior. But, by a process of empirical validation and careful test development, there are some tests without content validity which accurately measure criterion behavior. Language proficiency tests fall into this category. Projective personality tests are better examples. The Thematic Apperception Test, or the Rorschach "inkblot" tests, have little content validity, yet they have been shown to be accurate in assessing certain types of deviant personality behavior. Other well-known psychological tests have little content validity. The Micro-Momentary Expression test (MME) is a test of empathy which requires subjects to detect facial changes in a participant in a conversation. The more facial changes a testee detects, the more empathic he is said to be. Such a test has little content validity, especially if the astute detection of facial changes might be argued to require field independence which has been shown to correlate negatively with empathy! A test of field independence as a prediction of language success in the classroom is another example of a test with potentially good criterion validity but poor content validity in that the ability to detect an embedded geometric figure bears little direct resemblance to the ability to speak and hear a language.

Content validity is not essential for ultimate (criterion) validity, but when there is little or questionable content validity in a test, it becomes very important to establish *construct validity*. Construct validity is the degree to which certain explanatory or theoretical constructs account for performance on a test. When a test has content validity, one can account for performance and for the interpretation of that performance on the grounds that the test actually sampled the criterion behavior. When a test does not have content validity, the achievement of criterion validity can be supported by the various underlying theoretical constructs that went into the construction of the test. For example, the theoretical argument justifying the MME test as a valid test of empathy is that the empathic person will attend to facial changes in his effort to empathize and understand the deepest levels of meaning within a speaker. A test of field independence for predicting language success can be argued to be valid for predicting classroom success by an appeal to theoretical constructs discussed in Chapter Five, in which it was noted that field independence may be a key style for success in all educational contexts, not excluding language classes.

An increasingly popular type of test being used in foreign-language contexts is the *cloze* test, in which a reading passage has been "mutilated" by the deletion of every sixth or seventh word, and the testee is required to supply words that fit into the context of the passage. A substantial amount of testing research has shown that cloze tests correlate well with tests of global proficiency, and some (Oller 1976, for example) have claimed that the cloze test is as good a predictor of overall proficiency as traditional tests. In this case there is, on the surface, only minor content validity, but according to theoretical constructs underlying the claim, the ability to supply appropriate words in the blanks requires a number of abilities which lie at the very heart of competence in a language: knowledge of vocabulary, grammatical structure, discourse structure, "expectancy" grammar, and reading ability, to name some. It is argued that the person who can accurately complete a cloze test has tapped all these abilities, and that few people who have such abilities do not have global fluency and proficiency in a language.

We have seen that validity is a complex concept, yet crucial to the understanding of what constitutes a "good" test. If in your language teaching you can attend to the practicality, reliability, and validity of tests of language, whether those tests are classroom tests related to a part of a lesson or final exams, or proficiency tests, then you are well on the way to making accurate and viable judgments about the competence of the learners with whom you are working.

Kinds of Tests

There are many kinds of tests, each with a specific purpose, a particular criterion to be measured. The purpose of this chapter is not to expound on the many varieties of tests, nor to instruct you on how exactly to devise even a few varieties. However, in examining the general underlying principles of language testing, it is appropriate and necessary to devote a few brief words to outlining some categories of language tests. Your training as a teacher of a particular language should then involve the more specific matters of test construction and interpretation for that language.

If your aim in a test is to tap global competence in a language, then you are, in conventional terminology, testing *proficiency*. A proficiency test is not intended to be limited to any one course, curriculum, or single skill in the language. Proficiency tests typically consist of standardized, multiple-choice items on grammar, vocabulary, reading comprehension, aural comprehension, and sometimes writing proficiency. Proficiency tests need not, however, be defined in such limited terms. Cloze tests, for example, may after all prove to be valid tests of proficiency.

A language *aptitude* test is designed to measure a person's capacity or general ability to learn a foreign language and to be successful in that undertaking. Aptitude tests are considered to be independent of a particular foreign language, predicting success in the acquisition of any foreign language. Two standardized aptitude tests have been popular in the United States—the Modern Language Aptitude Test (Carroll and Sapon 1958) and the Pimsleur Language Aptitude Battery (Pimsleur 1966). Both of these are English language tests, and require students to perform such tasks as learning numbers, listening, detecting spelling clues and grammatical patterns, and memorizing. While they claim to measure global aptitude, it seems more appropriate to say that they predict success in a typical foreign language classroom—which may be somewhat removed from actual *language* aptitude.

A *diagnostic* test is designed to diagnose a particular aspect of a particular language. A diagnostic test in pronunciation might have the purpose of determining which particular phonological features of the language pose difficulty for a learner. Prator's (1972) Diagnostic

Passage, for example, is a short written passage which a student of English as a second language reads orally; the teacher or tester then examines a tape recording of that reading against a very detailed checklist of pronunciation errors. The checklist serves to diagnose certain problems in pronunciation. Some proficiency and achievement tests can serve as diagnostic tests by isolating and analyzing certain sets of items within the test. An achievement test on a particular module in a curriculum might include a number of items on modal auxiliaries; these particular items could serve to diagnose difficulty on modals.

A *placement* test is often a combination of proficiency, diagnostic, and/or achievement tests whose purpose it is to place a student in a particular level or section. A placement test typically includes a sampling of material to be covered in the curriculum (that is, it has content validity), and thereby places the student into a level or type of class. Some placement tests, however, use global measures. Sometimes cloze tests or dictations serve as excellent global placement tests. They are practical, reliable, and have construct validity: the skills a person uses to perform well on them are skills of overall proficiency.

Finally, an *achievement* test is related directly to classroom lessons, units, or even a total curriculum. Achievement tests are limited to particular material covered in the lessons within a particular time frame.

The importance of these five different kinds of language tests lies in the fact that different tests serve different purposes. In order to select tests adequately and to interpret their results accurately, teachers need to be aware of the ultimate purpose of the testing context.

Within each category of test above there is a vast variety of different possible techniques and procedures. These range from objective to subjective techniques, open-ended to structured, multiple-choice to fill-in-the-blank, written to oral. Moreover, language has been viewed traditionally as consisting of four separate skills; therefore language tests have attempted to measure differential ability in speaking, listening, reading, and writing. It is not uncommon to be quite proficient in reading a foreign language but not in speaking, or of course, for aural comprehension to outstrip speaking ability.

Beyond such considerations, tests of each of the modes of performance can be focused on a continuum of linguistic units, from smaller to larger: phonology and orthography, words, sentences, and discourse. In interpreting a test it is important to note which linguistic units are being tested. Oral production tests can be tests of overall conversational fluency or pronunciation of a particular subset of phonology, and can take the form of structured responses, free responses, or imitation. Similarly, listening-comprehension tests can concentrate on a particular feature of language or on overall listening for general meaning. Tests of reading can cover the range of language units and can aim to test comprehension of long or short passages, single sentences, or even phrases and words. Writing tests can take on an open-ended form with free composition, or be structured to elicit anything from correct spelling to discourse-level competence.

DISCRETE POINT VS. INTEGRATIVE TESTING

One of the key issues in language testing during the last decade has been the question of whether language should be tested by *discrete points* or by *integrative* tests. Traditionally, language tests have been constructed on the assumption that language can be broken down into its component parts and those component parts duly tested. Such a rationale is derived from the structural linguistic and behavioral psychological theories which claimed that behavior is in essense the sum of its parts. In this case the "parts" are the four skills and the hierarchical units of language. So, for example, it is claimed that a typical proficiency test with its sets of multiple-choice questions divided into grammar, vocabulary, reading, and the like, with some items attending to smaller units and others to larger units, can measure these discrete points of language and by adequate sampling of these units can achieve criterion validity. Such a rationale is not unreasonable if one considers types of testing theory in which certain constructs are measured by the breaking down of their componential parts.

John Oller (1976) illustrated these discrete points of language (see Figure 11-1). Each of the smallest cells represents one possible "point" of language that can be tested.

But the discrete-point approach met with some criticism, particularly in view of more recent trends toward viewing the units of language and its communicative nature and purpose, and away from viewing language as the arithmetic sum of all its parts. The criticism came largely from John Oller (1976), who argued that language competence is a unified set of interacting abilities which cannot be separated apart and tested adequately. The claim is, in short, that communicative competence is so global and requires such

Input–Output MODE / Sensory-Motor MODALITY	Receptive			Productive		
Auditory / Articulatory	Listening			Speaking		
	Phono-ology	Struc-ture	Vocab-ulary	Phono-ology	Struc-ture	Vocab-ulary
Visual/ Manual	Reading			Writing		
	Graph-ology	Struc-ture	Vocab-ulary	Graph-ology	Struc-ture	Vocab-ulary

Figure 11-1. Discrete points of language. (Oller 1976:150)

integration (hence the term "integrative" testing) for its *pragmatic* (some refer to "pragmatic" testing) use in the real world that it cannot be captured in additive tests of grammar or reading or vocabulary and other discrete points of language. Oller and others therefore proposed that such tests as cloze tests are more adequate measures of proficiency since they "successfully invoke the use of the internalized grammar of the learner" (Oller 1976:151). Oller and his colleagues have amassed a good deal of research data in support of their claim. The cloze test, as explained earlier, is a reading selection in which every *n*th (where *n* usually ranges from 5 to 8) word has been deleted and the testee is asked to supply in the blanks words that are semantically and syntactically appropriate to the sense of the surrounding language and the selection as a whole. (One form of cloze testing requires the testee to supply the *exact word* that has been deleted; *appropriate-word* scoring seems to be more psychologically reassuring for the testee. Both types of scoring, however, differentiate testees equally well.)

Oller's hypothesis is not abstract, theoretical speculation; it warrants the special attention of the foreign language teacher. We are, after all, ultimately concerned with criterion validity in testing, and if an integrative test reaches that criterion *practically* and *reliably*, then traditional proficiency tests are of little value. But let us not be too quick to jump on the integrative testing bandwagon. John Upshur (1976:169) points out that "at issue . . . is whether competence is only a single factor, independent of input-output mode and sensory-motor modality, and of certain hypothetical dimensions of knowledge: phonology, graphology, structure and vocabulary." While certainly the recent direction of linguistic study has been toward viewing language as an integrated and pragmatic skill, we cannot be certain that a test like a cloze test meets the criterion of predicting or assessing a unified and integrated underlying linguistic competence. We do well, then, to be cautious in selecting or constructing tests of language. There is probably nothing "wrong" with the more traditional tests of discrete points of language, especially in achievement and other classroom-oriented testing in which certain discrete points are important.

In view of Widdowson's comment that the notional syllabus is merely a shift from syntactically based language structure to discourse-based structure, we might do well to test the "discrete points" of second language discourse, or the various specific categories of language functioning. We are a long way from discovering adequate integrative tests that tap the totality of language competence. A step in a positive direction would be to concentrate on tests of communicative competence. To do that of course requires first the discovery of a good definition of communicative competence. We are getting closer to that at the present time.

The first part of this chapter has not attempted in any way to provide a do-it-yourself testing manual for teachers. In keeping with the theme of the book itself, the chapter has so far presented principles of testing, some issues in laying the groundwork for an understanding of what a "good" test is, an inkling of the varieties of foreign language tests, and one of the key theoretical issues in language testing, which is ultimately linked to the key to formulating a theory of language acquisition—forming an integrated understanding of second language acquisition in communicative, meaningful contexts.

THE FOREIGN LANGUAGE TEACHER
AS RESEARCHER

"Research" is a scary word for most people. Research is something teachers are usually just as happy leaving in someone else's hands. Research usually involves a lot of statistics (which many people detest), experimental design (for which many are not trained), and interpretation of ambiguous results (which is tedious and often discouraging). But research need not be scary, for we all engage in research in one way or another: particularly when we seek explicit answers to carefully framed questions Every successful teacher of a foreign language, whether he realizes it or not, is researching ideas all the time, and through that research is getting answers to questions which ultimately help him to become a better teacher and to continue to grow in the understanding of the teaching-learning process. It is to that end that this section attempts to outline how the foreign language teacher can be a researcher—and ask questions which he might otherwise be afraid to ask.

"Research" is a set of conventions for asking questions, looking for answers to those questions, and supporting those answers; it is a process of gathering evidence to support certain assumptions. Labovitz and Hagedorn (1971) note that there are three common, everyday sources of evidence: authority, intuition, and logic. These three sources are used by both laypersons and professionals in all disciplines to support arguments and assumptions. A fourth source of evidence that has taken on a great deal of importance in our scientific, technological society is known as the "scientific method," or controlled observation and analysis under carefully defined conditions. It is this kind of evidence that the "research" is called upon to produce, for it is here that objectivity is perhaps best achieved. Much of the current evidence in second language acquisition falls into the first three categories. Intuition has long been a source of support for many conclusions about second language acquisition and for the feasibility of teaching methods. "Authorities," often in contradiction with each other, are also cited as supportive evidence. And although language is often illogical, logic is a common form of evidence for second language assumptions. We have only just begun to stockpile some empirical, scientific evidence in second language acquisition, partly because of the overwhelming difficulty of controlling variables.

During the 1960s linguists and psychologists began to compile empirical data on the child's first language acquisition, as we learned in Chapters Two and Three. Reacting to the earlier notion that the child's semigrammatical utterances are "incorrect" forms of adult grammar, researchers looked at the child's first language learning as a "natural" process, and treated the child's speech as legitimate manifestations of an internalized linguistic system. Such an approach to language analysis has now been adopted by second language researchers. In Chapter Nine we saw that the adult second language learner may have much in his interlanguage performance that is the result of an equally legitimate self-constructed system. But such second language research is in its infancy, and with an overwhelming phenomenon to examine, the few researchers presently working in the field are only scratching the surface. On the other hand, there are thousands of capable language teachers who have daily exposure to second language learners; much could be gained by the research of teachers, however minuscule the individual contributions. From the discussion here a set of guidelines should emerge which will help the classroom teacher to engage in such research.

Types of Research

There are several common types of research relating to language teaching. Each type involves different goals and thus uses different approaches and designs.

The language acquisition process

Little normative information is available on the actual process of second language acquisition in children and adults. Recently, however, researchers began to study second language acquisition independently of classroom methodology in an effort to discover what linguistic or psychological factors all second language learners share in common. Some examples of this research are Dulay and Burt's (1972, 1974a, 1974b) studies mentioned in earlier chapters, which took the view that the child or adult systematically approaches the second language task and which attempted to describe some linguistic features of such a system. Another example of this kind of research is found in studies of "good" language learners where a researcher attempts to discover the psychological correlates of successful language learning. In each case data are gathered under relatively controlled circumstances and examined using established procedures of analysis. The key to the success of such studies lies in the construction and repeated try-out of instruments for eliciting responses and in an unbiased method of analyzing the elicited responses.

Small-scale intervention

A second type of research involves some form of pedagogical "intervention" in the second language learning process, in a study of the effect of a particular treatment upon a subject or group of subjects. The scope of such an investigation is normally restricted to a small sample and a rather limited technique. The advantage of the small-scale study is that experimental controls can be exercised to a great extent. But it is difficult to control all the relevant variables, and so generalizations must be made with due caution. This kind of research is imperative, however, if we are to discover optimal forms of teaching methodology for second language pedagogy.

Large-scale methodology

A third type of research may be described as involving a long-range study over several weeks, months, or even years, with a very large sample of subjects, and usually a treatment involving a total curriculum or generalized method. While this level of research is theoretically useful, a carefully controlled situation yielding clearly definable results is virtually impossible. Two examples of large-scale research are the Scherer and Wertheimer (1964) study and the Pennsylvania study (Smith 1970), both of which suffered from the uncontrolled variables of a large sample and an extended treatment. At this level, a subjective, observational study—one that relies a good deal on intuition and on analysis by one or more "authorities"—is more realistic.

Research Procedures

Most second language research falls into the above three categories, and it is helpful for you to understand, before the fact, how your own research can be categorized. Some guidelines for the teacher are now suggested for conducting an actual research study in the second language classroom.

Asking the right questions

In the problems which language teachers encounter every day, countless questions come to mind related to the language learning process. But the principal difficulty in engaging in meaningful research is asking the "right" questions, questions that will lead to the formulation of a plausible research hypothesis. The first criterion for asking such questions is somewhat obvious; the questions should reflect a legitimate, significant, and relevant problem. If, for example, you asked if tall people learned foreign languages better than short people, it is doubtful that a case could be made for the significance or relevance of the question. But this criterion rarely causes difficulty, for in a task as complex as language learning almost any question could conceivably be relevant.

A second and much more complicated criterion is that research questions should have specificity: to whom does the question refer and under what set of conditions does the question apply? Consider the following typical questions which have been asked with respect to the teaching of reading in a second language: (1) Is there a relationship between first language reading ability and second language reading ability? (2) Should reading classes make use of lists of phoneme-grapheme correspondences? (3) How useful is reading aloud in class? The three questions satisfy the first but not the second criterion: the questions simply cannot be answered in such broad terms. In order to fulfill the criterion of specificity, the questions should first refer to a population of learners. For example, one might specify learners of a particular language or family of languages (the Roman/non-Roman alphabet distinction alone is of interest). Also, the general ability or educational level of the learner should be considered along with the learner's particular goals in learning a second language. Questions 1 to 3 are also too global in their lack of implicit specific conditions under which they apply. Questions 2 and 3 particularly require the context of "when," "where," and "how"— in what kind of class? at what level? under what constraints? Question 2, for example, might be limited to a particular language and to an intermediate level.

Formulating researchable "ideas"

In order to find answers to such questions as those posed in the last paragraph, the researcher must use his ingenuity to devise potential answers to the questions, and then creatively test those answers empirically. The next logical step in the research process, then, is the formulation of an "idea"—a means of gaining an answer to a question. Suppose question 1 above had been more clearly specified to read:

(4) In the case of Japanese-speaking learners of English as a second language preparing for an academic career in an English-speaking country and university, is there a positive correlation between the learners' ability to read in their native language (Japanese) and their degree of success in learning to read English?

The first step in the formulation of an idea would be to construct operational definitions of "success" and "ability," in which the developmental nature of the acquisition of second language reading skills would have to be carefully considered. Some ideas on valid instruments that measure such skills would then have to be explored. In this particular instance the task is far from easy; however, it is not impossible if the researcher vigorously maintains the all-important factor of objectivity. Many experiments fail because of too much subjectivity—too much "intuitive" judgment by the experimenter.

Constructing a research hypothesis and design

Once a specific, legitimate question has been stated and some "ideas" have been fully explored, you are then ready to construct a research hypothesis and a design within which the hypothesis can be tested. The task up to this point has been quite exploratory in nature. Now a more definitive process begins, but if the first stages have been fully explored, the present stage becomes a lengthy but logical step for which a great deal of preparatory work has been completed.

A hypothesis is simply a formal prediction that is tested by means of an experimental design. A logical hypothesis for question 4 would be that "the learners' first language reading ability and second language reading success will correlate positively." A design to test a hypothesis should have as one of its key goals the elimination and/ or control of variables which might contaminate or otherwise render conclusions invalid. Four aspects of experimental design are discussed here in connection with question 4.

(a) Subjects. Now it is necessary to define a specific population and to select a reasonable sample of that population. Populations are typically defined in terms of age, sex, language proficiency level, native language background, educational background, and perhaps occupation. It is difficult, in classroom research, to define a homogeneous population because students in the class often lack the homogeneity of an ideal experimental situation, and of course the more homogeneous a sample, the more likelihood of supporting a hypothesis, since subject variables are minimized. However, teachers ought not to refrain from conducting research using their classroom students as subjects; the heterogeneity that does exist can just be recognized as a set of uncontrolled variables that could limit the implications to be drawn from the study.

(b) Experimenter. Classroom research usually implies that the teacher is the experimenter. Several precautions must be taken in such a case. Whatever the form of the actual treatment, whether the teacher "teaches" something or administers a relatively objective test, the potential teacher bias must always be recognized; if possible, the administrator of the treatment ought to be someone other than the teacher.

(c) Materials and procedures. The conditions under which the actual "treatment" is administered require careful definition so that contamination from time, prelearning, postlearning, and treatment variables is minimized. Explicit, well-designed materials are essential for effective research. The most important research criterion here is *replicability*. All materials, whether a test, a technique, or a program, should be replicable: another researcher must be able to repeat the experiment exactly. Otherwise, there is some kind of bias present and it will not be possible to generalize beyond the individual experiment itself. Replicability can best be achieved by absolute clarity and objectivity in the treatment. In the case of question 4 above, a

valid test of reading ability in the native language needs to be selected and administered under controlled conditions. This would then be followed by a series of tests to determine reading "success" in English; current standard tests of second-language reading proficiency might fulfill the replicability criterion, even though validity could pose a problem.

(d) Analysis of results. A person need not be a statistician or professional researcher in order to gather the data necessary for a successful research study and to effectively analyze those data. "Statistics" is a term that often discourages and frightens would-be researchers. Statistics, in the formal sense of the term as it relates to the theory of experimental design, are not always necessary in order to present useful data. Often a report of raw scores, averages, and/or percentages is sufficient to support a study. If the design of a study is *clear* and *logical*, then with the help of a consultant, an appropriate statistical test can be found which will test the significance of the data.

Drawing implications

The most important aspect of any research study is its capability of being generalized: on the basis of the results, what do we now "know" that extends beyond the subjects and materials of the particular study? One danger in drawing implications is to be too liberal and careless in assuming that what is true for some subjects at one point in time is true for a large population over time. Since no study is free from uncontrolled variables, the researcher should exercise caution in drawing conclusions that are too broad. However, in exercising due caution, one should not be reluctant to draw some conclusions. Nor should the researcher lose sight of the conviction that creative research is indeed possible if he can think critically and follow a few basic rules. Such research is urgently needed at this time, when too many questions about second language acquisition remain unanswered.

Practical Implications

The foregoing discussion may cause some confusion about exactly how to carry out meaningful research in the classroom. Some practical examples—beyond the one question touched on already—should help to clear up what may still be muddy waters.

Following the classification of types of research discussed earlier in the chapter, what are some research possibilities? In attempting to discover something about the process of language acquisition, "natural" language data can be gathered by the novice researcher without undue difficulty. A tape recorder and a subsequent transcription of speech will yield analyzable data. With some linguistic training a teacher can, as field linguists have done for years, examine recorded conversations for evidence of systematic rules of interlanguage. With the help of the procedures for error analysis set forth in Chapter Nine, it is possible to draw some conclusions about a learner or group of learners, as long as there is a sufficient amount of carefully recorded data. One must, of course, beware of the possible artificiality of recorded conversations. As Tarone (1979) aptly warns, the presence of a microphone alone makes "spontaneous" speech virtually impossible.

A limited amount of information on the process of second language acquisition can be obtained by the use of structured tests. Existing published tests like the Bilingual Syntax Measure (Dulay, Burt, and Hernández 1975) or the Ilyin Oral Interview (Ilyin 1973) have been used to elicit oral production data which can be analyzed according to the instructions of the test manual. Free compositions form another source of production data that can be analyzed linguistically. A translation exercise will often yield certain predicted interlingual or intralingual interference, as Taylor (1975) showed. In fact, Taylor's study is an excellent example of both the use of the techniques of error analysis and the wealth of data that can be extracted from elicited translations.

Analyzing language data is much like solving a cryptogram. There are no strict conventional procedures. The researcher must simply spend hours or days sifting through the data to find evidence of systematicity. Yet such evidence is available even to an inexperienced researcher.

The more daring teacher might also endeavor to carry out some research in the psychological processes of language acquisition. The sample question regarding native and second language reading ability, referred to earlier, is an example of one kind of psychological question that can be asked. Careful testing of native and second language reading ability would yield some data in support of an answer to the question. The relationship of second language success to empathy, field independence, or self-esteem is another set of issues that could be explored by means of existing psychological tests and language proficiency measures (see Naiman, Fröhlich, and Stern 1975; Heyde 1979). A simple correlation of results of a personality measure with results of a proficiency test could reveal something about the possible relationship between the two variables.

The second type of research mentioned earlier in this chapter referred to small-scale intervention. Teachers are in fact engaging in this type of research every time they try out a new method, technique, or procedure. You are "intervening" in the language learning process when you direct, guide, or even assist a language learner. Research on the success of various types of intervention is most difficult to carry out. An observational level of research is perhaps practical for inexperienced researchers. You can try out a new procedure and intuitively but systematically *observe* its relative merits. Or you can ask a fellow teacher to experiment with the new technique and get that person's response. Above all, it is important to determine as carefully as possible the effects of the intervention on the learners themselves. While statistical comparisons at this level are useless because of the many possible contaminating variables, careful, intelligent observations can be good indicators.

Without training in research methodology, you should not even attempt experimental designs to test teaching techniques. Nor should large-scale measures of teaching methodology—the third category of research—be attempted. Such endeavors are best left to "experts," those trained in research procedures. Nevertheless, the foreign language teacher can, within constraints suggested here, be a researcher. You can be creatively involved in the systematic elicitation and analysis of data in the quest for the best ways to teach a foreign language.

SUGGESTED READINGS

Two suggested references in the area of foreign language testing: *Harris* (1969) devoted substantial portions of his book to giving theoretical groundwork for testing as well as offering practical material on testing English as a second language; *Valette* (1967) outlines almost every imaginable kind of test for the classroom teacher.

Sometimes the best way to understand how different kinds of tests vary is to examine them yourself. If proficiency or placement tests are available in your library or nearest language institute, you will find it profitable to look them over.

Oller's (1976) defense of integrative testing, followed by *Upshur*'s (1976) response to Oller, together provide a more complete description of the controversy than this chapter offered.

TOPICS AND QUESTIONS FOR STUDY
AND DISCUSSION

1. Give examples of informal tests that you can perform every day in a classroom or conversation group (questions, giving directions, etc.). Do they fit the definition of a test?

2. Examine a readily available standardized or classroom test of language. Analyze it to discover what the *method* of *measurement* is, for *whom* the test is intended, what *competence* it purports to measure, and exactly what it *actually* measures.

3. For the same test, assess its practicality, reliability, and various forms of validity. On the basis of your evaluation, is it a "good" test?

4. Distinguish the three types of validity. If content validity is absent, why does construct validity assume greater importance? Explain the statement (p. 212): "There is no final, absolute, and objective measure of validity." Why does validity ultimately go back to the rather subjective opinion of testers and theorists?

5. What is a cloze test? Do you think cloze tests are valid measures of language proficiency?

6. What is language aptitude? Can it be sufficiently measured? If possible, examine the Modern Language Aptitude Test. Does it really test language aptitude? On the basis of the multiplicity of variables at play in the process of second language acquisition, what other factors would *you* include in a test of aptitude?

7. Why is oral production perhaps the most difficult of the traditional four skills to test? How would you test oral production?

8. Relate the discrete-point/integrative testing controversy to other poles of thinking: structural linguistics vs. discourse analysis, behaviorism vs. cognitivism, form vs. function.

9. In taking stock of what you "know" about second language learning, consider how you have gained that knowledge. By intuition, authority, and/or logic? Or by experimentation? Is there anything really "wrong" with the first three forms of evidence? What are the advantages and disadvantages of seeking experimental evidence?

10. Try to find a solid experimental study in second language acquisition. Taylor's (1975) study would be an excellent example which you may have already read. Identify in his study the various steps in researching a problem and forming conclusions.

11. If possible, carry out your own research study on a very limited problem within the context of a conversation group or foreign language class. Proceed through the suggested steps in carrying out the research. Were you able to achieve results? Could you draw any conclusions that could be generalized?

12

From Theory
to Practice

When we approach any complex task in human experience we tend to form hypotheses—definitions, theories—relating to the task, and we then test our hypotheses through empirical observation and intuitive analysis. A tremendous amount of observation and analysis is necessary before a strong and valid theory can be constructed, especially in the case of the set of experiences that make up the process of learning a second language. A full theory of second language acquisition has yet to be constructed, though a good deal of research, particularly in the past decade, has begun to dictate the general framework of a theory. We are in the process of theory building at the present time, but are much in need of further observation and feedback in order to continue to press toward the goal of a viable, integrated theory of second language acquisition.

The principal purpose of this book is to encourage teachers and teacher trainees to develop an integrated understanding of the principles underlying the learning and teaching of foreign languages. That purpose has necessarily involved theoretical considerations. A theory, as I noted in the first chapter, is an extended definition. We have examined essential components of an extended definition of second language acquisition. That is, we have attempted to answer the perplexing question "What is second language acquisition?" And we have seen that second language acquisition is, among other things, not totally unlike first language acquisition, is a subset of general human learning, involves cognitive variations, is closely related to one's personhood, is interwoven with second culture learning, involves interference, the creation of new linguistic systems, and the learning of discourse and communicative functions of language. All of these categories and the nearly infinite number of subcategories subsumed under them form the basis for structuring an integrated definition—a theory—of second language acquisition.

That theory remains abstract and relatively useless if it is simply a theory without practical, day-to-day ramifications for teaching behavior. It is sometimes pleasantly intriguing to concoct theoretical systems and networks and to subject them to argument and debate. In fact, it is necessary to engage in such argument in order to come to grips with integrating all the factors that are at play in the act of acquiring a second language. But theories do not become good theories unless they are tested in practice, and theories are of little use to anyone without pragmatic applications. For the teacher of a foreign language, a theory of second language acquisition becomes valuable insofar as that theory has applications, or at least implications, for certain practices in the classroom.

This final chapter puts before you some of the important considerations for moving from theory to practice. In the first section of the chapter the general problem of application of theory is addressed. The application of theory is explicated from the point of view of the discipline of *linguistics* for two reasons: linguistics serves as an example of the application of a disciplinary perspective, and it presents unique problems of application not found in psychology and pedagogy—the other two major disciplines contributing to language learning theory. The second section follows with examples of theories put into practice in the form of major teaching approaches and methodologies. The final section is much more personal in first coming to grips with precisely what kind of unified theory is implied in the pages of this book, then in leading you to the development of your own personalized rationale for language teaching—your own integrated theory of second language acquisition.

APPLIED LINGUISTICS

A theory of second language acquisition emerges out of a number of disciplines. Linguistics, psychology, and pedagogy have been the major sources of theory over the years, with sociology, anthropology, and other disciplinary perspectives coming to bear. It has never been clear exactly how such disciplines ought to be applied to such practical matters as second language teaching, or whether applied aspects are really separate from theoretical aspects. Where does theory end and application begin?

In the case of the discipline of linguistics, theory and application are difficult to tease apart. There is little agreement on what, exactly, the term *applied linguistics* means. Applied linguistics has been considered a subset of linguistics for several decades, and has generally been interpreted to mean the applications of linguistic principles or theories to certain more or less "practical" matters. Second language teaching and the teaching of reading, composition, and language arts in the native language are typical areas of practical application. In the British tradition, "applied linguistics" is quite often considered synonymous with language teaching; however, the applications of linguistics certainly extend well beyond pedagogical concerns. But the term remains disturbingly vague.

One of the difficulties in understanding the limits and scope of applied linguistics lies in the deliberate distinction between "theoretical" or "pure" linguistics on the one hand and "applied" linguistics on the other. It is a distinction every linguist is aware of, and one that has caused considerable controversy and argument. Claims have even been made that there can be no such thing as applied linguistics. But efforts to separate linguistics and applied linguistics have proved to be generally unfruitful and opinionated rather than informed.

A possible way to understand what applied linguistics is or is not is to return here to the subject of the very first chapter, where the term *language* was defined. We saw in Chapter One that a simple definition of language suggested many issues and concerns within linguistics, all of which relate directly to the central goal of linguistic study: discovering what language is. However, among the concerns listed were a number that are typically grouped into "applied" rather than "theoretical" linguistics. Is it possible to draw a line of demarcation which separates the applied from the theoretical? In studies of phonetics, nonverbal communication, semantics, dialectology, first language acquisition, the psychology of language, and second language acquisition, there is much that is theoretical—that is, much that bears on seeking an extended definition of language. Some might argue that the devising of explicit and formal accounts of linguistic systems is surely theoretical; however, semantics, speaker-hearer interaction, and communication systems are important in any consideration of the nature of the linguistic system. Perhaps, then, every question about language—from devising lessons on the subjunctive in French to formulating universal syntactic rules—is theoretical in that the answers to those questions both derive from and contribute to an understanding of just what language is.

Must we conclude, therefore, that there is really no such thing as applied linguistics? This is indeed too simplistic and too easy a solution. Every discipline has its theoretical and its applied aspects. The theoretical and applied areas simply must not be thought of as necessarily mutually exclusive. An area of inquiry may evidence certain applications of theory to practice and at the same time contribute to a better theoretical understanding of the particular phenomenon.

Reacting to the common British usage of the term *applied linguistics*, Corder (1973:10) pointed out that "whilst applied linguistics and language teaching may be closely associated, they are not one and the same activity." He then offered a definition of applied linguistics which distinguished rather clearly between application and theory:

> The application of linguistic knowledge to some object—or applied linguistics, as its name implies—is an activity. It is not a theoretical study. It makes use of findings of theoretical studies. The applied linguist is a consumer, or user, not a producer, of theories.

Corder's view could be misleading, however, if you were to presume that applied and theoretical linguistics are mutually exclusive. Consumers, by virtue of the fact that they are testing and confirming hypotheses generated by theory, provide reinforcement and feedback to theorists.

Many important components of a theory have arisen from such "consumer" feedback. In first language acquisition, for example, researchers discovered that the purely svntactic, rational linguistic theories of the 1960s held explanatory power for only a small portion of the actual data. Neither the semantic/cognitive aspect of language nor the social aspect could be accounted for adequately. Partly as a result of the "demands" of first language researchers, and partly through other forces, theoretical linguists quickly began to focus on the semantic component of language, which brought a renewed interest in psycholinguistic topics in general. Along with this focus has emerged a revived interest in the social aspects of language, formerly considered to be irrelevant to theoretical linguistics. Psycholinguistics and sociolinguistics, once very clearly considered to be "applied" areas, now just as clearly overlap both the applied and theoretical domains.

The purity of so-called pure linguistics is rapidly becoming impossible to maintain, as Robin Lakoff (1976:222) notes:

Linguistics is heading in the direction of practicality. There will be in the ensuing years an ever-greater emphasis on application of theoretical discoveries; and application will be considered as valuable in its own right as pure theoretical contributions to knowledge have been. In fact, it will be increasingly recognized that theory severed from applications is suspect, that data generated in the rocking chair, tested at the blackboard, and described in learned jargon are probably ridden with errors and inaccuracies.

Historical Perspectives

While applied linguistics, or applied psychology or applied sociology, has never been adequately defined as an entity separate from its theoretical counterparts, nevertheless applications of theory have formed the stepping stones of progress in foreign language teaching. A glance through the past few decades of history turns up some rather interesting relationships between theoretical paradigms and language teaching methods and techniques.

In the middle of the century, with structural linguistics and behavioral psychology acting as theoretical paradigms for research and practice, language teachers were not only strongly influenced by theory but also were able to make direct applications of theory in the classroom. A linguistic paradigm such as that devised by Charles C. Fries in his renowned *The Structure of English* (1952) made a perfect marriage with language teaching. Fries proposed a *slot-filler* grammar in which English sentences fell into fundamental *patterns*, each pattern with designated slots, defined by the position and relationship to other slots in the pattern. These slots could be filled by certain parts of speech consisting of four form-classes and fifteen types of function words. The four form-classes were much like what we understand as nouns, verbs, adjectives, and adverbs, while the fifteen function word-classes included what we recognize as articles, auxiliary verbs, negative markers (*not*), conjunctions, prepositions, and others.

The knowledge of prescribed patterns and their defined slots and fillers armed the teacher with "instant" pattern-practice models. A pattern described in the first line could account for the sentence in the second line:

Group A	Class 1	Group G	Group C	Class 2	Group A	Class 1	Class 4
The	boys	do	not	do	their	work	promptly.

Dozens of sentences could be constructed which follow the same pattern by substitution of different fillers in the slots. A language teacher could have students practice that pattern by simply substituting different Class 1, 2, and 4 fillers. A linguistic theory such as Fries' was clearly applicable to language teaching in a most direct way. It was made particularly applicable because of prevailing psychological theory which claimed that language, like any other aspect of human behavior, was something that could be broken into component parts and practiced repeatedly by the learner for ultimate mastery. Thus arose the rather common drilling technique known as *pattern practice.*

During the 1950s and early 1960s such direct applications enjoyed considerable prestige. Theory and practice were united. But the decade of the 1960s saw a revolution in linguistic theory. The advent of generative linguistics brought with it a new way of looking at language, and at the same time cognitive psychology similarly turned the attention of those studying human behavior away from programs of mechanistic conditioning. Transformational grammar at first promised to be as applicable and relevant to the classroom as structural grammar had been; teachers had grown to expect such relevance and to grasp longingly at new theories in the hope that they would provide the clue to successful language teaching. But alas, it was not to be, for after much tilting at windmills, language teachers discovered that the new grammar would bring no such final solution. No less a giant than Noam Chomsky (1966:37) said in the most frequently-quoted statement in the language teaching profession: "I am, frankly, rather skeptical about the significance, for the teaching of languages, of such insights and understanding as have been attained in linguistics and psychology. . . . It is difficult to believe that either linguistics or psychology has achieved a level of theoretical understanding that might enable it to support a 'technology' of language teaching." Of course, such a statement was symptomatic of a general skepticism within many disciplines toward direct and final answers for practitioners. The early 1970s abounded with articles and statements by both theorists and practitioners bemoaning the "irrelevance" of generative models of linguistics for language teaching.

The difficulty of the "new grammar" was experienced not only by foreign language teachers but also by language arts teachers around the country. New theories, new terms, new ways of analyzing English, met with partial success. The frustration of the new grammar was delightfully illustrated in the following letter written by the mother of a third-grade Los Angeles child to his language arts teacher:

Dear Mrs. Klein,

Eric's homework will be late.

I have gone through three dictionary's to find, if nothing else, a definition for the word "determiner." Sounds easy doesn't it?! I mean this is for third grade English. Well, no luck.

So, I called my sister, she's in her second year of college—no luck.

Then I called my brother-in-law who teaches English and courses at U.C.L.A. He has a masters degree and doctors degree!

None of us know what a determiner is! This doesn't make any sense at all. You are hearing from a mother who is loosing her marbles.

Eric doesn't know what it is. Jon (he's in fifth grade) doesn't know. Michael (he's in sixth grade) says it has something to do with the word "the," but he isn't sure.

I went to see my grandmother in the hospital this evening. She knows everything. Almost, but not determiner. My husband doesn't know, and by golly neither do I!

I was going to intrude on you this evening, but do you know how many Klein's there are in the phone book?

Does this give you any idea of our evening?

If this is a simple part of speech I'll cut my throat. I have a terrible idea that it is.

When I stop to think about this, it's almost funny.

So please excuse Eric for not turning in his homework today.

> Most Sincerely,
> Eric's Mother

It is important to note that generative linguistics did not necessarily "fail" in its task. Transformational grammar never purported to be directly applicable in the classroom. It is a logical, mathematical model of language, the goal of which is to account for linguistic competence. Its applicability was not an issue among generative grammarians themselves. Robert Krohn (1970) expressed balanced judgment when he noted that linguistic theory could not *justify* language teaching methods but it could provide general *insight* to the teacher on the nature of language. Similarly, Bernard Spolsky (1970) distinguished between *applications* of linguistics which suggested a one-way relationship between linguistics and language teaching, and *implications* of linguistic theory—a two-way relationship involving feedback from practice to theory and theory to practice. Those insights and implications, from which we are still benefiting today, were momentous. Without generative linguistics we would not have the formal and fundamental distinction between deep and

surface structures of language, explicit models capturing the creativity
of language, ways of formalizing the relatedness of sentences, and
rule-writing conventions for describing language data.

Psychological Reality

While transformational grammar may not have provided the
relevance that language practitioners were looking for, there have
been some other theoretical perspectives within generative linguistics
which have come closer to psychological reality. Psychological
reality—the degree to which a theory accurately accounts for actual
behavior—is an important criterion for language teachers. Grammarians, in their search for explanatory adequacy of theories, have
at times opted for simplicity but ignored human behavioral reality.
Martin Braine noted (1965:491): "If there is a possibility that the
simpler of two possible grammatical solutions might require the more
complex acquisition theory, then the domain over which simplicity is
taken cannot be restricted to grammar alone and must include
acquisition theory—otherwise the grammarian merely purchases
simplicity at the psychologist's expense."

A linguistic theory that is "psychologically real" contains rules
which, as described, represent or at least approximate actual cognitive
processes and categories through which human beings operate. That
is to say, grammatical structures are psychologically real if they
describe or directly relate to mental processing, storage, and recall.
For example, in transformational grammar, we could ask if a sentence
in the passive voice is indeed processed and stored in some kind of
"active" form with a "passive" node attached. Or if the number of
transformations involved in deriving a particular surface structure
correlates with the "complexity" of the sentence when compared
with other sentences. So, for example, one could ask whether the
sentence

1. Bill doesn't have a home.

is more "complex" cognitively than

2. Bill has a home.

If a negative transformation makes sentence 1 more complex than
sentence 2, then we have to decide whether, cognitively, sentence 1
is really any more complex than

3. Bill is homeless.

In this light, grammatical complexity is seen as rather difficult to define.

Actually, both structural and transformational grammar seem to provide rather ill-conceived notions of "grammar." Structuralists gave us detailed methods for analyzing surface features of languages, but offered little insight into teaching the underlying structures of language which are necessary to account for creativity in second language acquisition. Transformational grammar provides explicit formal systems accounting for the generative, creative nature of language, but those systems are so far removed from reality that the language teacher is left confused and bewildered. From the point of view of meaningful learning, discussed in Chapter Four, one of the main problems with transformational grammar is that the syntactic component is the base component of language, where semantic rules are "interpretive" rules, operating on the syntax. The criterion of psychological reality calls for a complete reversal of this notion, with the semantic or cognitive component as the base, at the deepest level of language. A meaningful theory of language must give grammar a cognitive base. In this perspective, it is easy to see how transformational grammar "failed" in foreign language teaching.

A cognitive or semantic base—and thus a greater degree of psychological reality—is suggested by recent *generative semantic* theories of language. *Case grammar* falls into this category of grammatical description. Nilsen (1971) described some of the potential uses of case grammar in teaching English as a foreign language, showing that it can lead to structurally based lessons that are at the same time situational and meaningful. Consider the following sentences:

> The city is noisy.
> The rush hour is noisy.
> The motor is noisy.

To describe "the city," "the rush hour," and "the motor" all as subject noun-phrases is probably farther from reality than to differentiate the three by describing them, respectively, as a "locative," a "temporal," and an "instrument." Similarly, "John" and "Bill" are an "experiencer" and an "agent," respectively, in the following sentences:

> John has a new car.
> Bill ate the bananas.

Semantic organization is the base and forms the deep structure; syntax then emerges from this semantic base.

This of course does not mean that among traditional, structural, and transformational grammars there have been no rules that are "real." For centuries English grammarians have spoken of the distinction between present perfect and past tenses, quite "real" in the sense that human beings conceptualize many items not only in terms of chronological order but also with the present moment as a focal point of reference. The grammatical description reflects this phenomenon. But, in contrast, if words like "might," "can," and "will" are called "auxiliaries" or "helping verbs" we may have wandered far from reality in that the cognitive categories of potentiality, capability, and futurity are major categories by which we analyze and classify the world and ourselves. So if you say:

He might be able to go to the game tonight.

in terms of cognitive reality you are speaking of "potentiality + capability + futurity + agent + locomotion + locative + time." It would be hard to argue that what you "really" thought in your mind was something like "pronoun + auxiliary + verb + adjective + infinitive + prepositional phrase + adverb," or even "noun-phrase + verb-phrase."

With a semantically or cognitively based grammar, furthermore, such sentences as the following—structurally diverse by some standards—could be categorized as semantically similar:

I saw a boy who had red hair.
I saw a boy and he had red hair.
I saw a red-headed boy.
The boy I saw was a red-head.
A red-headed boy was seen by me.

They all involve, in various permutations of categories, and in varying degree of emphasis, "agent + visual perception + object + attribute." The concept of the notional-functional syllabus explained in Chapter Ten is closely related to principles of case grammar: several syntactic renditions of one semantic idea are generated, allowing the learner to focus on meaning.

Pedagogical and Scientific Grammars

A resolution to the difficulty of reconciling theory and practice can be found in the concept of pedagogical and scientific grammars. A pedagogical grammar is a grammatical description of a language specifically designed as an aid to teaching that language. Transformational grammar was never designed to be a pedagogical grammar. A good model of a pedagogical grammar can be found in Robert Krohn's *English Sentence Structure* (1971), in which major grammatical categories of English are presented in simply stated rules and accompanied by exercises tailored for the learner. Most grammar textbooks used in foreign language classes are pedagogical grammars. A scientific grammar (sometimes called an *analytical grammar*) attempts to account formally and logically for the structure of a language without reference to pedagogy, sequencing, levels of difficulty, or ease of explanation.

Few scientific grammars are suitable for pedagogy. Fries' *Structure of English* (1952) was an exception. Even the traditional grammars of Jespersen (1933) and others were more scientific in nature; they were of interest to the grammarian, but not very helpful for the language student. Transformational grammar—a scientific grammar—was valuable to language teachers for its implications, not its applications. Its purpose was scientific, analytical, and formal. More recent generative models of language, however, present a different face. Case grammar, generative semantic models of language, and formal accounts of linguistic discourse are all attending much more meticulously to language in its communicative contexts and language as it is actually used in human interaction. Such grammars are therefore much more relevant to language learning and language teaching because they are less abstract than previous generative grammars. Specific analysis of discourse and of the functions of language lends itself to language textbooks and classroom materials (see, for example, Leech and Svartvik 1975). So perhaps the relevance of the scientific grammars of the mid-century is now returning in the form of communicative grammars in the last part of the century. The dilemma of putting theory into practice may resolve itself as theoretical grammars get away from "data generated in the rocking chair" and attend more faithfully to the real world.

LANGUAGE TEACHING METHODS

An appropriate way to encounter theories in practice is to examine major language teaching approaches and methods of the twentieth century. Every language teaching method has as its foundation certain theoretical underpinnings. And these foundations almost always combine more than one discipline, for, as we have seen, language teaching is not just linguistics or just psychology, but involves both, along with pedagogical, sociological, and other interdisciplinary considerations. A review of language-teaching methods could become quite an exhaustive undertaking, so only a brief overview is presented here with the intent of illustrating how, in methodology, theory is either successfully or unsuccessfully applied to practice.

A look back across nearly a century of language teaching reveals a cyclical history. The "changing winds and shifting sands" (Marckwardt 1972:5) of language teaching methods manifest a new paradigm (see Kuhn 1970) every quarter of a century or so, with each new paradigm a break from the old but taking with it positive aspects of previous paradigms. These changing methodologies are very much theories in practice. Methods, however, are difficult to define. They manifest themselves in such varieties at times that the term *approach* may be more accurately descriptive of these general moods. An approach is a general and theoretical view of how language ought to be taught, while a method includes a developed procedure for teaching. The Audiolingual Method, for example, would be better termed an approach because there is such variation within the so-called method and because it is derived from a specific set of theoretical assumptions. I nevertheless refer below to a number of "methods"—since that is the traditional nomenclature—keeping in mind the fuzzy line of distinction between method and approach.

The Direct Method

Before 1900 little attention was given to the teaching of modern foreign languages in educational institutions. Language teaching was limited largely to the classical languages for scholarly or religious purposes, and involved little oral-aural work for communicative purposes. But the turn of the century saw the first concerted and widespread interest in teaching foreign languages for speaking purposes. A popular method of this time was the Direct Method, in which classes were conducted orally and directly in the foreign language without translation. The attempt was to be as "natural" as possible in the classroom, with no grammar and deductive thinking, and with a concentration on communicative practice.

The rationale behind such a method was that a person should learn to speak a foreign language not by the usual classical method of memorization, translation, and learning of grammar rules but by the same mechanisms a child uses to learn his native language. The theoretical impetus for the Direct Method dates as far back as 1880, when François Gouin began to question seriously the unsuccessful academic routine of the classical method. Gouin himself, after an agonizing and unsuccessful year of trying to learn German by means of one self-devised "method" after another, discovered that his own 3-year-old nephew learned a language in a matter of a few months, and decided that the child ultimately held the secret to learning a language. What resulted was the Gouin Series Method (see Gouin 1880), which formed the first language teaching "revolution" of sorts in modern history. Unfortunately though, Gouin was a man ahead of his time and many of his Piaget-like assertions were lost in an array of doubts about the proper place of modern language teaching in the academy. It was not until the turn of the century that the spirit of Gouin's assertions gained a foothold in the form of the Direct Method; this method persists in various forms today, especially in Berlitz language schools.

The Grammar-Translation Method

Soon after World War I there was a return, principally in the United States, to a somewhat "beefed-up" version of the Classical Method, called the Grammar-Translation Method. In 1924 a long-term investigation was conducted to study the success of modern foreign language teaching in the United States. The results of that study were released in a number of publications which reported that the paucity of class time spent in foreign language study in high schools and universities precluded the opportunity for students to acquire even a minimal proficiency in a foreign language, especially in all four skills. It was recommended therefore that schools and universities concentrate on reading foreign languages as a reasonably attainable goal in most curricula. It was with this philosophical bent that the Grammar-Translation Method came to dominate foreign language teaching. This method stressed reading ability, the study of grammar as an aid to reading comprehension, and a great deal of both written and oral translation. Spontaneous oral work was de-emphasized; pronunciation was important only for classroom intelligibility.

The Grammar-Translation Method is still used today in various forms. In many cases the method is adapted to include some oral work, but maintains its identity in the emphasis on reading, translation, and grammatical rules. The theoretical underpinnings of the Grammar-Translation Method were more pedagogical than linguistic or psychological. Economy of time and resources in educational institutions were of high priority and the method appeared to accomplish necessary educational objectives. Though no real linguistic and psychological foundations were put forth to justify the various translation and grammar activities, it was simply concluded that these were the essence of learning to read a foreign language.

At that time little knowledge of general reading skills was available, and even less knowledge of foreign language reading skills.

The Audiolingual Method

Around the middle of the century the unique advances of both linguistics and psychology had a profound and lasting effect on language teaching methodology. Structural linguistics had provided tools for dissecting language into its smallest parts and for contrasting two languages "scientifically," and behavioral psychology had provided a model for teaching virtually any behavior by operant conditioning. The two theoretical stances merged perfectly to give language teachers a method firmly grounded in theory: the Audiolingual Method (ALM). The ALM, also known by such names as the Oral-Aural Approach, and the Mim-Mem (mimicry-memorization) Method, was in one sense a return to the Direct Method. Oral-aural activity was emphasized, and translation was forbidden in most versions of the ALM. Conversation centered around topical dialogues, with a great deal of drilling activity and emphasis on pronunciation. The ALM is now familiar to many who have attempted to learn foreign languages in an educational setting.

For many years the ALM enjoyed widespread acceptance. It seemed that the last word in language teaching had been delivered from on high. But it was not to be. Beginning with Wilga Rivers' classic criticism, *The Psychologist and Foreign Language Teacher* (1964), linguists, psychologists, and language teachers hammered away at the shortcomings of the method. Generative linguistics had shown that language could not be neatly dissected into linear and discrete units, that language was a hierarchical structure in which all the bits and pieces do not add up to a single whole. Cognitive psychology had begun to show that aspects of human behavior, especially linguistic behavior, could not be drummed into an individual by rote repetition. And language teachers were discovering that the ALM actually was not working! People were not learning the communicative functions of language. Though learners were acquiring reasonably good pronunciation and were able to produce language in memorized chunks, the meaningful functions of language, if they were learned at all, were learned perhaps in spite of the ALM.

The 1970s brought with it an age of skepticism, restlessness, and dissatisfaction. As criticism of the ALM mounted and more and more teachers sought alternative methods and approaches, there seemed to be no one method that emerged to prominence. But there was in language teaching a revolution in the making. In some circles the importance once again of deductive and analytical approaches to language teaching was stressed in what came to be called Cognitive Code-Learning, which itself was not a method, but rather a vaguely defined approach. Many teachers and theorists were recognizing the crucial importance of meaningful communication in language teaching and devised a number of methods and techniques for presenting language in contexts, generally referred to as Situational Approaches. Meanwhile remnants of the Grammar-Translation Method and Direct Method were being used in various modifications and versions. So the third quarter of the twentieth century was a period when language teaching methodology went from a well-accepted method strongly rooted in both linguistic and psychological theory to times of uncertainty and searching.

Interpersonal Approaches

In the last quarter of the century we are still searching for the ultimate method, though we understand more clearly that there will be no such panacea in teaching a behavior as complex as a second language. The revolution in language teaching that was building in the early 1970s is here, though it is not a revolution that came with flashing swords and sudden coups. It is a quiet revolution that has come about gradually. A number of characteristics can be cited which describe this revolution.

First, the revolution is cautiously eclectic. No single method suffices to answer all the needs of all learners at all times. We are wary of jumping onto bandwagons. But there is no magic about eclecticism. It is easy to claim to be an eclectic, and dip haphazardly into every attractive aspect of every conceivable method or approach, and then jumble everything together. It is quite another task to practice "enlightened" eclecticism—that is, to engage in an intelligent use of selected approaches built upon and guided by an integrated and broadly based theory of second language acquisition. Second, the revolution does not look to the traditional disciplines— linguistics, psychology, education—for direct applications, but rather for insights into language, human behavior, and pedagogy which undergird language teaching practices. Third, the tremendous variation among learners is being recognized. Human beings do not behave, each one like the other, consistently and uniformly. Every person is unique, and language classes can celebrate that uniqueness. Fourth, for the first time in history there is a substantial and growing body of research that has provided comprehensive insight into the process of second language acquisition. This research is characterized by a rigorous empirical approach coupled with cautious rationalism. Finally, and perhaps most importantly, the learning and teaching of language have become personal encounters. The affective domain has come to take primary importance as we recognize in human communication the building of interpersonal relationships through social interchange. Stevick (1974) noted that in previous paradigms methods have first provided means, then goals, then data flow, and finally personal relationships. This order, which, according to Stevick, makes for *defensive* learning, is now being reversed so that we start with personal relationships. We have become human; we are teaching persons.

The interpersonal approaches of this period are being supported by linguistic research into the nature of human discourse and communicative interaction. Studies of human cognition along with psychological research on transactional analysis, self-esteem, and interpersonal communication all have direct relevance to language teaching approaches. Sociocultural findings on the cultural foundations of language are particularly important because the learning of a second culture is so often a part of the learning of a second language. And new insights in the field of education are opening the way for creative methods of teaching which break the barriers of the traditional classroom.

This interdisciplinary coming of age in the language-teaching profession has brought with it some new methods. Community Language Learning—as we saw in Chapter Six—is a method in which students and teacher form a client-counselor relationship and in nondefensive openness struggle with the forms of language inductively but always with the security of acceptance by both counselor and other clients. The Silent Way capitalizes on the motivation of students to communicate with each other with little prodding or direction from the teacher. Suggestopedia, used for teaching many different skills besides language, relies on the significance of the subconscious cognition of human beings and promotes learning through relaxation and indirect acquisition of forms. The Total Physical Response connects physical activity directly with meaningful language use. There are other approaches, methods, and techniques—too many to enumerate—that are characteristic of the current period. And new methods will surface as language teachers continue the quest for optimal means of teaching the meaningful and communicative functions of language.

No, we have not "arrived" yet. There is no panacea, no final word. The development of the profession of language teaching can be compared to the development of a human being. The child in his innocence often sees the world in discrete categories with few "shades of gray," and tends to be quite defensive in his protection of that perception. As the child becomes an adult he acquires more knowledge, to be sure, but more importantly he learns that there are few ultimate, final answers. And he learns to be secure within the uncertainty of knowledge, confident in his ability to make intelligent perceptions, but affectively and cognitively able to accept alternative viewpoints, even views that may seriously shake his foundations. The language teaching profession has been through its stage of childhood and adolescence, its grasping at a method here and a technique there, and its wild claims of final, clearcut answers. It now stands in young adulthood, secure in its general understanding of the language-acquisition process. But language teachers are prepared to face the complexity and unpredictability of human behavior and ready to convert momentary failures into new ventures in the search for better and better ways to enable second language learners to communicate effectively.

PUTTING YOUR THEORY INTO PRACTICE

At the beginning of this chapter I noted that the language teacher needs to develop an integrated understanding of the process of second language acquisition, but that such an understanding is of no use whatever if there is little or no relevance in *practice* of that understanding. We can develop great networks of theory for giving explanatory adequacy to our understanding of the process, and expound on this theory eloquently, but there comes a time, either in the classroom or in the researcher's laboratory, when that theory must be tested.

No one can serve that theory to you on a silver platter. You must develop it yourself and learn to apply it in your own experience. If you do not, you will never develop your own personal uniqueness in creative interaction with learners. But to do so requires concentrated awareness, insight, and practice, practice, practice. Putting your theory into practice implies two things: that you have a theory and that you have an opportunity to practice. Let us look at those two implications.

Toward a Unified Theory
of Second Language Acquisition

To say that second language learning is a complex process is at this point almost trite. The pages of this volume all bear testimony to that truth. But complexity means that there are so many separate but interrelated factors within one intricate entity that it is exceedingly difficult to bring order and simplicity into that entity. "Models" of second language learning—attempts to provide order—have a-bounded in the literature. Most of these models are oversimplified. A model that claims, erroneously of course, that second language acquisition is just like first language acquisition is too simple. A model that highlights "creative construction" as the antithesis to an interference model ignores vast domains of the total process. Even a model that singles out the differences between acquisition and monitoring touches on only one facet. To say that language learning is simply a matter of motivation, or of meaningful learning, or even of interpersonal communication, is to simplify the process ridiculously.

Roger Brown (1966:326) expressed the behavioral scientist's frustration in constructing adequate models:

> Psychologists find it exciting when a complex mental phenomenon—something intelligent and slippery—seems about to be captured by a mechanical model. We yearn to see the model succeed. But when, at the last minute, the phenomenon proves too much for the model and darts off on some uncapturable tangent there is something in us that rejoices at the defeat.

While we may indeed rejoice at our many defeats, we must nevertheless pursue the task of model building. That process begins with establishing a framework. A framework to capture the essence of the process of second language acquisition will itself be complex. Some recent attempts have been made to capture the multifaceted interaction of second language variables. A few of these attempts will be summarily referred to here, often only by way of a diagram, just to give you a picture of the variety of possibilities for models of second language acquisition (and not to probe the meaning of models in depth).

Barry Taylor (1974) noted that a theory of second language acquisition needed to blend several important components: the critical period hypothesis, the nature of learning strategies, the influence of the native language, and affective variables. His very general discussion, though, was only a beginning. John Schumann (1976b) presented a schematic representation of the second language learning process (see Figure 12-1) in which three components interacted to give us a "global look" at the second language learner. One must of course give credit to Schumann's lengthy verbal exposition of the schematic representation, but even Schumann would readily admit that his diagram and its explanation hardly comprised a full-blown theory. Merrill Swain (1977) built upon Schumann's

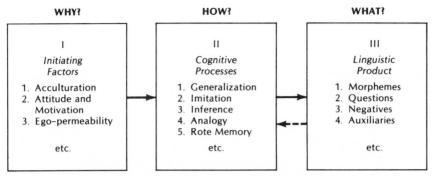

WHY?	HOW?	WHAT?
I	II	III
Initiating	*Cognitive*	*Linguistic*
Factors	*Processes*	*Product*
1. Acculturation	1. Generalization	1. Morphemes
2. Attitude and	2. Imitation	2. Questions
Motivation	3. Inference	3. Negatives
3. Ego-permeability	4. Analogy	4. Auxiliaries
	5. Rote Memory	
etc.	etc.	etc.

Figure 12-1. Schematic representation of the second
language learning process. (Schumann 1976b:15)

diagram by including four components and defining the components further, and engaging in a comprehensive explanation of each of the components (see Figure 12-2). Carlos Yorio (1976) provided not so much a "model" of second language acquisition as a classification of a multiplicity of learner variables at play in the second language learning process. His taxonomy (see Figure 12-3) illustrates the tremendous difficulty of classifying learners and learning contexts. Yet another attempt to capture the relationships of aspects of the second language learning/teaching process was made by Peter Strevens (1977), who saw second language teaching as being derived from social and even political factors—an observation deserving careful attention (see Figure 12-4). Finally, Ellen Bialystok (1978) devised a model of second language acquisition in still other terms (see Figure 12-5). A glance at these models—even without further elucidation— illustrates many possible means of conceptualizing the process of second language acquisition.

The presentation of the bits and pieces of theory in this book has reflected my own theoretical bias. Though flowcharts, diagrams, and outlines do not adequately capture the complexity and variability of interrelating components, it is evident that the chapter topics and discussions are themselves a verbal outline of a theory of second language acquisition. That theory might be summarized as follows:

1. A theory of second language acquisition includes an understanding, in general, of what language is, what learning is, and for classroom contexts, what teaching is.
2. Knowledge of the child's learning of his first language provides essential insights to an understanding of second language acquisition.
3. However, a number of important differences between adult and child learning and between first and second language acquisition must be carefully accounted for.

247

248

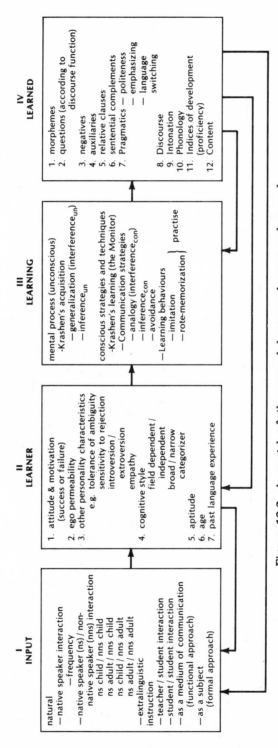

Figure 12-2. A model of the second language learner and second language learning. (Swain 1977:16)

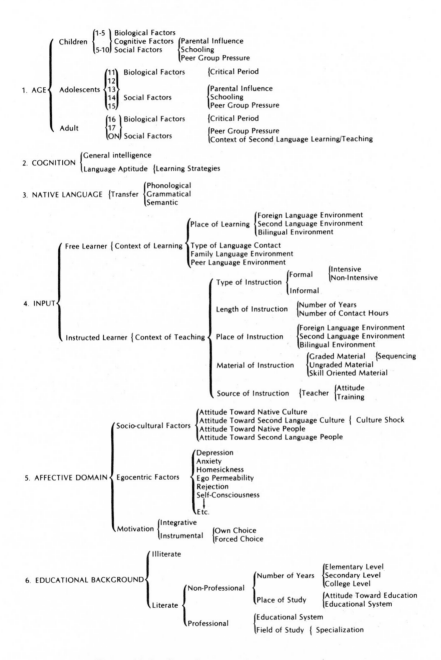

Figure 12-3. Classification of learner variables.
(Yorio 1976:61)

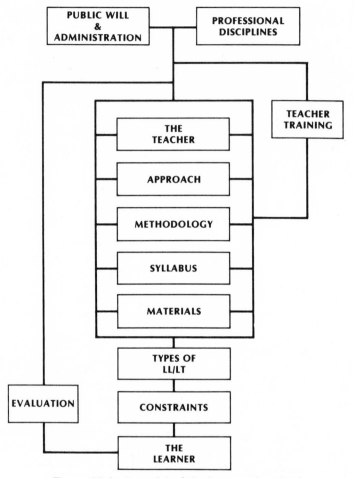

Figure 12-4. A model of the language learning/
language teaching process. (Strevens 1977:276)

4. Second language learning is a part of and adheres to general principles of human learning.

5. There is tremendous cognitive variation from learner to learner in style and strategies.

6. One's personality, the way a person views himself and reveals himself in communication, will affect both the quantity and quality of second language learning.

7. Learning a second culture in all its ramifications is often very much a part of learning a second language.

8. The linguistic contrasts between the native and target language are important—but not exclusively important—aspects of learning the linguistic system.

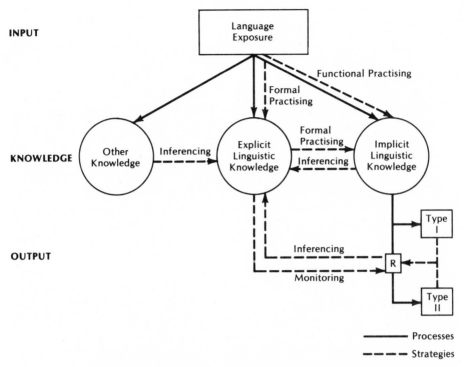

INPUT

KNOWLEDGE

OUTPUT

———— Processes
– – – – Strategies

Figure 12-5. Model of second language learning.
(Bialystok 1978:71)

9. Language learning, as a creative process of forming a system, inevitably involves the making of errors which are really necessary aspects of the learning process, and from which the teacher and learner can gain further insight into perfecting knowledge of the target language.

10. Human communicative discourse is the locus of the function of language, and without a knowledge of discourse a language learner will never achieve communicative competence.

11. One's theory is viable only if one is able—informally, if not formally—to devise hypotheses about the teaching/learning process and test these hypotheses with actual learners with a view to formulating an integrated understanding of second language acquisition. Certain principles of testing and research are thus germane to a theory of second language acquisition.

12. Finally, a theory of second language acquisition is of value in that it has practical application in the real world.

However vague and general those twelve statements are, they constitute a framework for a theory of second language acquisition. That framework has had substance built into it in the course of each chapter of the book. The interrelationships within that framework have been dealt with. One cannot, for example, engage in contrastive analysis and draw implications from it without knowledge of the place

251

of interference in human learning in general. In comparing and contrasting first and second language acquisition it is impossible to ignore affective and cultural variables and differences between adult and child cognition. Determining the source of a second language learner's error inevitably involves consideration of cognitive strategies and styles, group dynamics, and even the validity of data-gathering procedures. No single component of this "theory" is sufficient alone: the interaction and interdependence of the other components is necessary.

What has been presented here is an extended definition of how people learn second languages. But definitions are never exhaustive and theories are never complete, never without loopholes or without new terrain to explore. So while the framework has been presented here and some substance to that framework has been provided, a good share of the task of forming an integrated theory of second language acquisition is left to individuals—to you, whose understanding of the process of second language acquisition will become your own self-constructed theory. That theory, it is hoped, will have solid grounding in principles of language learning and teaching that are broadly conceived from an interdisciplinary perspective.

Practice Makes Perfect

Good theories distinguish themselves from bad theories by their adequacy for explaining phenomena in the real world. The theory of gravity is good because it works. The theory of relativity is good because it is useful and captures the essence of truth for a large number of events. But a theory never becomes good without testing and verification among the set of the events it purports to define. So a theory of second language acquisition, to be good, must work. It must be tested and modified and retested and remodified over and over again, until it approaches adequacy. It is incumbent upon you, the theorist, to engage in the trial-and-error process of theory building. By acting upon your *own* theory of second language acquisition, your understanding of that process will always be dynamic, alive, and relevant.

Devising your own theory has decided advantages. How valuable is it for a would-be foreign language teacher to gobble up, in a few easy steps, 101 techniques for teaching a foreign language, and armed with that meager arsenal, face the mighty challenges of language teaching? Unfortunately, some teacher-training programs have believed it feasible to equip future teachers only with the necessary mechanical skills—a cookbook of foreign language teaching recipes—to the exclusion of true understanding. What has happened in those cases is that the teacher very quickly runs out of techniques, or very soon encounters an institution and a curriculum and a group of learners that do not fit the prescribed formulas he was given in his training program, and he is at a loss to know where to turn. His well has run dry, and with no foreign language teachers' "Dear Abby" to turn to, he flounders in frustration. The successful teacher-training program, along with solid practice in selected techniques and procedures, equips the trainee with a comprehensive understanding of the teaching/learning process. This understanding enables the teacher to assess the uniqueness of every learning context he faces, to make informed choices among options, and to continue to refine both his theory and his practice in the context of classroom feedback.

The subject matter of this book will mean very little unless you engage in the day-by-day practice of continually seeking further understanding of second language acquisition within meaningful communicative contexts and among valued human beings. Through such efforts we can collectively advance our knowledge of how people learn second languages and slowly perfect a viable theory. Practice makes perfect. Or, almost perfect.

SUGGESTED READINGS

For an informative survey of applied linguistics in twelve different subfields, consult *Wardhaugh and Brown* (1976). The scope of the book will give a good overview of topics in applied linguistics.

Look at *Fries'* (1952) classic on English grammar, especially Chapters 5, 6, and 7. You will readily discern how such grammars were immediately applicable to language teaching.

Three articles which treat the "irrelevance" of transformational grammar are *Lamendella* (1969), *Krohn* (1970), and *Spolsky* (1970). The latter two are both readable and constructive in offering hope beyond their criticisms.

Nilsen's (1971) description of the uses of case grammar in the teaching of English as a second language is informative reading and aimed at an audience of language teachers without formal training in linguistics.

Leech and Svartvik's (1975) communicative grammar of English is an excellent example of the relevance of discourse grammars for language teaching.

Diller (1971) summarized a number of language teaching methods, and gave a delightful accent of François Gouin's frustrating experiences learning a language, and the resulting Series Method.

By all means thumb through *Rivers'* (1964) classic in the field. You will discover convincing arguments against audiolingual techniques.

For some quite technical reading you could consult the five sources referred to at the end of the chapter which outline models or theories of second language acquisition. Schumann (1976b), Swain (1977), Yorio (1976), and Strevens (1977) are aimed at a nontechnical audience. Bialystok's (1978) article is considerably more technical.

TOPICS AND QUESTIONS FOR STUDY
AND DISCUSSION

1. How would you distinguish between theoretical and applied linguistics, if at all? Every discipline has theoretical and applied aspects. What would similar distinctions be in psychology, sociology, anthropology, or other related disciplines?

2. Explain how you think "consumer feedback" has helped to formulate a theory of second language acquisition.

3. What does R. Lakoff mean by "data generated in the rocking chair"?

4. Can you think of examples in your second language which illustrate Braine's caution against "purchasing simplicity at the psychologist's expense"? In what way did transformational grammar "purchase simplicity" at the expense of foreign language and language arts teachers? Are there some rules you have used or encountered which oversimplify or gloss over grammatical details which the learner must eventually contend with?

5. What is the difference between a scientific and a pedagogical grammar? Can you find instances of each?

6. Review each of the major language teaching methods described in this chapter. Specify ways in which each method successfully or unsuccessfully applied theory to practice. If possible, try to observe various methods being used to teach foreign languages. Assess the effectiveness of the methods for particular groups of learners and their goals.

7. Review the five characteristics of the current language teaching revolution. Do you find evidence of these characteristics in classes you have taken or observed? What other characteristics are present? If we are on the verge of discovering a brand-new language teaching method, what do you think that method will be like?

8. Go back to your definitions of language, learning, and teaching which you formulated at the beginning of the book. How might you revise those definitions now?

9. If possible, try to state *your* theory of second language acquisition (this could involve many pages of explanation and/or diagrams). How does your theory compare with the theory implied in the content of this book? What particular emphases would you give? priorities? hierarchies? Can your understanding of second language learning be represented in some kind of diagram or flowchart? Share your thoughts with classmates or colleagues. Above all else, in your language teaching experience, don't let your theory stagnate. Keep it alive and dynamic.

Bibliography

Acton, William. (1979) Second language learning and perception of difference in attitude. Unpublished doctoral dissertation, University of Michigan.

Adler, Peter S. (1972) Culture shock and the cross-cultural learning experience. *Readings in Intercultural Education*, Vol. 2. Pittsburgh: Intercultural Communication Network.

Andersen, Roger W. (1978) An implicational model for second language research. *Language Learning*, 28:221-282.

Anderson, Richard C., and Ausubel, David (editors). (1965) *Readings in the Psychology of Cognition*. New York: Holt, Rinehart & Winston.

Augustine, St. (1838) *Confessions*. trans, Edward B. Pusey. Oxford: J.C. Parker Co.

Austin, John L. (1962) *How to Do Things with Words*. Cambridge, Mass.: Harvard University Press.

Ausubel, David A. (1963) Cognitive structure and the facilitation of meaningful verbal learning. *Journal of Teacher Education*, 14:217-221.

Ausubel, David (1964) Adults vs. children in second language learning: Psychological considerations. *Modern Language Journal*, 48:420-424.

Ausubel, David. (1965) Introduction to Part One. In Andersen and Ausubel.

Ausubel, David. (1968) *Educational Psychology—A Cognitive View*. Holt, Rinehart & Winston.

Banathy, Bela, Trager, Edith C., and Waddle, Carl D. (1966) The use of contrastive data in foreign language course development. In Albert Valdman (editor), *Trends in Language Teaching*. New York: McGraw-Hill Book Co.

256

Bandura, Albert, and Walters, Richard H. (1963) *Social Learning and Personality Development*. New York: Holt, Rinehart & Winston.

Bar Adon, A., and Leopold, Werner F. (editors). (1971) *Child Language: A Book of Readings*. Englewood Cliffs, N.J.: Prentice-Hall, Inc.

Bateson, Gregory. (1972) *Steps to an Ecology of Mind*. New York: Ballantine Books.

Bellugi, Ursula, and Brown, Roger (editors). (1964) *The Acquisition of Language*. Monographs of the Society for Research in Child Development 29 (Serial No. 92).

Berko, Jean. (1958) The child's learning of English morphology. *Word*, 14: 150-177.

Bialystok, Ellen. (1978) A theoretical model of second language learning. *Language Learning*, 28:69-83.

Bierce, Ambrose. (1967) *The Devil's Dictionary*. New York: Doubleday, Inc.

Blatchford, Charles H., and Schachter, Jacqueline (editors). (1978) *On TESOL 78: EFL Policies, Programs, Practices*. Washington, D.C.: TESOL.

Bloom, Lois. (1971) Why not pivot grammar? *Journal of Speech and Hearing Disorders*, 36:40-50.

Bloom, Lois. (1976) Language development. In Wardhaugh and Brown.

Bloom, Lois (editor). (1978) *Readings in Language Development*. New York: John Wiley & Sons.

Bolinger, Dwight. (1975) *Aspects of Language*, 2nd ed. New York: Harcourt Brace Jovanovich, Inc.

Braine, Martin D. S. (1965) On the basis of phrase structure: A reply to Bever, Fodor, and Weksel. *Psychological Review*, 72:483-492.

Brodkey, Dean, and Shore, Howard. (1976) Student personality and success in an English language program. *Language Learning*, 26:153-159.

Brown, H. Douglas. (1970) English relativization and sentence comprehension in child language. Unpublished doctoral dissertation, University of California at Los Angeles.

Brown, H. Douglas. (1971) Children's comprehension of relativized English sentences. *Child Development*, 42:1923-1936.

Brown, H. Douglas. (1972) Cognitive pruning and second language acquisition. *Modern Language Journal*, 56:218-222.

Brown, H. Douglas. (1973) Affective variables in second language acquisition. *Language Learning*, 23:231-244.

Brown, H. Douglas (1977a) Cognitive and affective characteristics of good language learners. In Henning.

Brown, H. Douglas. (1977b) Some limitations of C-L/CLL models of second language teaching. *TESOL Quarterly*, 11:365-372.

Brown, H. Douglas. (1979) A socioculturally determined critical period for second language acquisition. Paper delivered at the TESOL Convention, Boston, Mass.

Brown, Roger. (1966) The "tip of the tongue" phenomenon. *Journal of Verbal Learning and Verbal Behavior*, 5:325-337.

Brown, Roger. (1973) *A First Language: The Early Stages.* Cambridge, Mass.: Harvard University Press.

Brown, Roger, and Bellugi, Ursula. (1964) Three processes in the child's acquisition of syntax. *Harvard Educational Review*, 34:133-151.

Brown, Roger, and Hanlon, C. (1970) Derivational complexity and order of acquisition in child speech. In J. Hayes (editor), *Cognition and the Development of Language.* New York: John Wiley & Sons.

Bruner, Jerome S. (1966) *Toward a Theory of Instruction.* New York: W. W. Norton & Co.

Bruner, Jerome S., Olver, Rose, and Greenfield, P. (editors). (1966) *Studies in Cognitive Growth.* New York: John Wiley & Sons.

Burling, Robbins. (1970) *Man's Many Voices.* New York: Holt, Rinehart & Winston.

Burt, Marina K., and Kiparsky, Carol. (1972) *The Gooficon: A Repair Manual for English.* Rowley, Mass.: Newbury House Publishers.

Campbell, Russell. (1978) Notional-functional syllabuses 1978: Part I. In Blatchford and Schachter.

Carmichael, L., Hogan, H. P., and Walter, A. A. (1932) An experimental study of the effect of language on visually perceived form. *Journal of Experimental Psychology* 15:73-86.

Carroll, John B. and Sapon, Stanley M. (1958) *Modern Language Aptitude Test.* New York: The Psychological Corporation.

Carroll, Lewis. (1872) *Through the Looking Glass.* Boston: Lee & Shapard.

Chastain, Kenneth D. (1970) Behavioristic and cognitive approaches in programmed instruction. *Language Learning*, 20:223-235.

Chihara, Tetsuro, and Oller, John W. (1978) Attitudes and attained proficiency in EFL: A sociolinguistic study of adult Japanese speakers. *Language Learning*, 28:55-68.

Chomsky, Noam. (1959) A review of B. F. Skinner's *Verbal Behavior. Language*, 35:26-58.

Chomsky, Noam. (1964) Current issues in linguistic theory. In Jerry A. Fodor and Jerrold J. Katz (editors), *The Structure of Language.* Englewood Cliffs, N.J.: Prentice-Hall, Inc.

Chomsky, Noam. (1965) *Aspects of the Theory of Syntax.* Cambridge, Mass.: M.I.T. Press.

Chomsky, Noam. (1966) Linguistic theory. In Robert C. Mead, Jr. (editor), *Reports of the Working Committee.* New York: Northeast Conference on the Teaching of Foreign Language.

Clark, Herbert H., and Clark, Eve V. (1977) *Psychology and Language: An Introduction to Psycholinguistics.* New York: Harcourt Brace Jovanovich, Inc.

Clarke, Mark. (1976) Second language acquisition as a clash of consciousness. *Language Learning*, 26:377-390.

Condon, E. C. (1973) Introduction to culture and general problems of cultural interference in communication. *Introduction to Cross Cultural Communication*, No. 1. New Jersey: Rutgers University.

Cook, Vivian. (1969) The analogy between first and second language learning. *IRAL*, 7:207-216.

Cook, Vivian. (1973) Comparison of language development in native children and foreign adults. *IRAL*, 11:13-28.

Coopersmith, Stanely. (1967) *The Antecedents of Self-Esteem*. San Francisco: W. H. Freeman & Co.

Corder, S. Pit. (1967) The significance of learners' errors. *IRAL*, 5:161-170.

Corder, S. Pit. (1971) Idiosyncratic dialects and error analysis. *IRAL*, 9:147-159.

Corder, S. Pit. (1973) *Introducing Applied Linguistics*. Harmondsworth: Penguin Books.

Curran, Charles A. (1972) *Counseling-Learning: A Whole-Person Model for Education*. New York: Grune & Stratton.

Curran, Charles A. (1976) *Counseling-Learning in Second Languages*. Apple River, Ill.: Apple River Press.

Curtiss, Susan. (1977) *Genie: A Psycholinguistic Study of a Modern-Day "Wild Child."* New York: Academic Press.

DeVito, Joseph A. (1971) *Psycholinguistics*. Indianapolis: The Bobbs-Merrill Co., Inc.

Dewey, John. (1910) *How We Think*. Boston: D. C. Heath.

Diller, Karl C. (1971) *Generative Grammar, Structural Linguistics, and Language Teaching*. Rowley, Mass.: Newbury House Publishers.

Dollard, J., Doob, L. W., Miller, N. E., Mowrer, O. H., and Sears, R. R. (1939) *Frustration and Aggression*. New Haven, Conn.: Yale University Press.

Donne, John. (1975) *Devotions upon Emergent Occasions*. Edited with commentary by Anthony Raspa. Montreal: McGill-Queen's University Press.

Doron, Sandra. (1973) Reflectivity-impulsivity and their influence on reading for inference for adult students of ESL. Unpublished manuscript, University of Michigan.

Drach, K. (1969) The language of the parent: A pilot study. In *The Structure of Linguistic Input to Children*, Working Paper No. 14. Language Behavior Research Laboratory, University of California, Berkeley.

Dulay, Heidi C., and Burt, Marina K. (1972) Goofing: An indicator of children's second language learning strategies. *Language Learning*, 22:235-252.

Dulay, Heidi C., and Burt, Marina K. (1974a) Errors and strategies in child second language acquisition. *TESOL Quarterly*, 8:129-136.

Dulay, Heidi C., and Burt, Marina K. (1974b) Natural sequences in child second language acquisition. *Language Learning*, 24:37-53.

Dulay, Heidi C., and Burt, Marina K. (1976) Creative construction in second language learning and teaching. *Language Learning*, Special Issue No. 4. 65-79.

Dulay, Heidi C., Burt, Marina K., and Hernandez-Ch., Eduardo. (1975) *Bilingual Syntax Measure*. New York: Harcourt Brace Jovanovich, Inc.

Durkheim, Emile. (1897) *Le suicide*. Paris: F. Alcan.

Eckman, Fred R. (1977) Markedness and the contrastive analysis hypothesis. *Language Learning*, 27:315-330.

Ervin-Tripp, Susan. (1974) Is second language learning like the first? *TESOL Quarterly*, 8:111-127.

Ewing, David. (1977) Discovering your problem-solving style. *Psychology Today*, 11:69-73.

Fast, Julius. (1970) *Body Language*. New York: M. Evans Co.

Fersh, Seymour (editor). (1974) *Learning About People and Cultures*. Evanston, Ill.: McDougal, Littel & Co.

Finocchiaro, Mary. (1964) *English as a Second Lanaguage: From Theory to Practice*. New York: Simon & Schuster.

Foster, George M. (1962) *Traditional Cultures*. New York: Harper & Row.

Freud, Sigmund. (1920) *A General Introduction to Psychoanalysis*. New York: Liveright.

Fries, Charles C. (1945) *Teaching and Learning English as a Foregin Language*. Ann Arbor: University of Michigan Press.

Fries, Charles C. (1952) *The Structure of English*. New York: Harcourt Brace Jovanovich, Inc.

Gage, Nathan L. (1964) The theories of teaching. In N. L. Gage (editor), *Handbook of Research on Teaching*. Chicago: Rand McNally & Co.

Gagné, Robert M. (1965) *The Conditions of Learning*. New York: Holt, Rinehart & Winston.

Gardner, Robert, and Lambert, Wallace E. (1972) *Attitudes and Motivation in Second Language Learning*. Rowley, Mass.: Newbury House Publishers.

Geschwind, Norman. (1970) The organization of language and the brain. *Science*, 170:940-944.

Gleason, Henry A. (1961) *An Introduction to Descriptive Linguistics*, rev. ed. New York: Holt, Rinehart & Winston.

Goodman, Kenneth S. (1970) Reading: a psycholinguistic guessing game. In H. Singer and R. B. Ruddell (editors), *Theoretical Models and Processes of Reading*. Newark, Del.: International Reading Association.

Gouin, François. (1880) *L'art d'enseigner et d'étudier les langues*. Paris: Librairie Fischbacher.

Greenberg, Joseph H. (editor). (1963) *Universals of Language*. Cambridge, Mass.: M.I.T. Press.

Greenberg, Joseph H. (1966) *Language Universals*. The Hague: Mouton Publishers.

Grice, H. P. (1967) Logic and conversation. Unpublished manuscript, University of California, Berkeley.

Guidelines for the Preparation of Teachers of English to Speakers of Other Languages in the United States. (1975) Washington, D.C.: TESOL.

Guiora, Alexander Z. (1976) Are symbols universal? A psycholinguistic perspective. Paper presented at the Major Conference of the Department of Psychiatry, University of Michigan, March 3.

Guiora, Alexander Z., Beit-Hallami, Benjamin, Brannon, Robert C. L., Dull, Cecilia Y., and Scovel, Thomas. (1972a) The effects of experimentally induced changes in ego states on pronunciation ability in second language: An exploratory study. *Comprehensive Psychiatry*, 13.

Guiora, Alexander Z., Brannon, Robert C. L., and Dull, Cecilia Y. (1972b) Empathy and second language learning. *Language Learning*, 22:111-130.

Hakuta, Kenji. (1974) Prefabricated patterns and the emergence of structure in second language acquisition. *Language Learning*, 24:287-297.

Hakuta, Kenji. (1976) A case study of a Japanese child learning English as a second language. *Language Learning*, 26:326-351.

Hall, Edward. (1959) *The Silent Language.* New York: Doubleday & Co.

Hall, Edward. (1966) *The Hidden Dimension.* New York: Doubleday & Co.

Hall, Edward. (1974) Making sense without words. In Seymour Fersh (editor), *Learning About Peoples and Cultures.* Evanston, Ill.: McDougal, Littel & Co.

Halliday, Michael. (1973) *Explorations in the Functions of Language.* London: Edward Arnold.

Hansen-Bede, Lynne. (1975) A child's creation of a second language. *Working Papers on Bilingualism,* 6:103-126.

Harris, David P. (1969) *Testing English as a Second Language.* New York: McGraw-Hill Book Co.

Hatch, Evelyn. (1978a) Discourse analysis and second language acquisition. In Evelyn Hatch (editor), *Second Language Acquisition.* Rowley, Mass.: Newbury House Publishers.

Hatch, Evelyn (editor). (1978b) *Second Language Acquisition.* Rowley, Mass.: Newbury House Publishers.

Henning, Carol A. (editor). (1977) *Proceedings of the Los Angeles Second Language Research Forum.* Los Angeles: University of California at Los Angeles.

Heyde, Adelaide. (1979) The relationship between self-esteem and the oral production of a second language. Unpublished doctoral dissertation, University of Michigan.

Hilgard, Ernest. (1963) Motivation in learning theory. In S. Koch (editor), *Psychology: A Study of Science,* Vol. 5. New York: McGraw-Hill Book Co.

Hill, Jane. (1970) Foreign accents, language acquisition, and cerebral dominance revisited. *Language Learning*, 20:237-248.

Hill, Joseph. (1972) *The Educational Sciences*. Detroit: Oakland Community College.

Hogan, Robert. (1969) Development of an empathy scale. *Journal of Consulting and Clinical Psychology*, 33:307-316.

Holzman, P. S., and Gardner, R. W. (1960). Leveling-sharpening and memory reorganization. *Journal of Abnormal Social Psychology*, 61:176-180.

Hymes, Dell. (1967) On communicative competence. Unpublished manuscript, University of Pennsylvania.

Hymes, Dell. (1974) *Foundations in Sociolinguistics: An Ethnographic Approach*. Philadelphia: University of Pennsylvania Press.

Ilyin, Donna. (1972) *Ilyin Oral Interview*. Rowley, Mass.: Newbury House Publishers.

Imber, Brenda, and Klinger, Larry. (1976) A communicative ESL curriculum. Unpublished manuscript, University of Michigan.

Jakobovits, Leon. (1968) Implications of recent psycholinguistic developments for the teaching of a second language. *Language Learning*, 18:89-109.

James, William. (1890) *The Principles of Psychology*, Vol. 1. New York: Henry Holt and Co. (Dover Publications 1950).

Jenkins, James, and Palermo, David. (1964) Mediation processes and the acquisition of linguistic structure. In Bellugi and Brown.

Jespersen, Otto. (1904). *How to Teach a Foreign Lanugage*, trans. Sophia Yhlen-Olsen Bertelsen. London: Allen & Unwin.

Jesperson, Otto. (1933) *Essentials of English Grammar*. London: Allen & Unwin.

Joos, Martin. (1967) *The Five Clocks*. New York: Harcourt Brace and World, Inc.

Kachru, Braj B. (1965) The Indianness in Indian English. *Word*, 21:391-410.

Kachru, Braj B. (1976) Models of English for the third world: White man's linguistic burden or language pragmatics? *TESOL Quarterly*, 10:221-239.

Kachru, Braj B. (1977) New Englishes and old models. *English Language Forum*, July.

Kagan, Jerome. (1965) Reflection-impulsivity and reading ability in primary grade children. *Child Development*, 36:609-628.

Kagan, Jerome, Pearson, L., and Welch, Lois. (1966) Conceptual impulsivity and inductive reasoning. *Child Development* 37:583-594.

Kimble, Gregory A., and Garmezy, Norman. (1963) *Principles of General Psychology*, 2nd ed. New York: The Ronald Press Co.

Kleinmann, Howard. (1977) Avoidance behavior in adult second language acquisition. *Language Learning*, 27:93-107.

Krashen, Stephen. (1973) Lateralization, language learning, and the critical period: Some new evidence. *Language Learning*, 23:63-74.

Krashen, Stephen. (1976) Formal and informal linguistic environments in language acquisition and language learning. *TESOL Quarterly*, 10:157-168.

Krashen, Stephen. (1977a) The monitor model for adult second language performance. In M. Burt, H. Dulay, and M. Finocchiaro (editors), *Viewpoints on English as Second Lanugage*. New York: Regents.

Krashen, Stephen. (1977b) Some issues relating to the monitor model. In H. Douglas Brown et al. (editors), *On TESOL 77*. Washington, D. C.: TESOL.

Krathwohl, David R., Bloom, Benjamin, and Masia, Bertram B. (1964) *Taxonomy of Educational Objectives*, Handbook H: Affective Domain. New York: David McKay Co.

Krohn, Robert. (1970) The role of linguistics in TEFL methodology. *Language Learning*, 20:103-108.

Krohn, Robert. (1971) *English Sentence Structure*. Ann Arbor: University of Michigan Press.

Kuhn, Thomas. (1970) *The Structure of Scientific Revolutions*. Chicago: University of Chicago Press.

Labov, William. (1970) The study of language in its social context. *Studium Generale*, 23:30-87.

Labovitz, S., and Hagedorn, R. (1971) *Introduction to Social Research*. New York: McGraw-Hill Book Co.

Lado, Robert. (1957) *Linguistics Across Cultures*. Ann Arbor: University of Michigan Press.

LaForge, Paul. (1971) Community language learning: A pilot study. *Language Learning*, 21:45-61.

Lakoff, Robin. (1976) Language and society. In Wardhaugh and Brown.

Lambert, Wallace E. (1963) Psychological approaches to the study of language. *Modern Language Journal*, 47:51-62, 114-121.

Lambert, Wallace E. (1967) A social psychology of bilingualism. *The Journal of Social Issues*, 23:91-109.

Lambert, Wallace E. (1972) *Language, Psychology, and Culture: Essays by Wallace E. Lambert*. Stanford, Calif.: Stanford University Press.

Lamendella, John. (1969) On the irrelevance of transformational grammar to second language pedagogy. *Language Learning*, 19:255-270.

Landes, James. (1975) Speech addressed to children: Issues and characteristics of parental input. *Language Learning*, 25:355-379.

Langacker, Ronald W. (1973) *Language and Its Structure*, 2nd ed. New York: Harcourt Brace Jovanovich, Inc.

Larsen-Freeman, Diane. (1976) An explanation for the morpheme acquisition order of second language learners. *Language Learning*, 26:125-134.

Larson, Donald N., and Smalley, William A. (1972) *Becoming Bilingual: A Guide to Language Learning*. New Canaan, Conn.: Practical Anthropology.

Leech, Gregory, and Svartvik, Jan. (1975) *A Communicative Grammar of English*. London: Longman Group, Ltd.

Lenneberg, Eric H. (1964) The capacity for language acquisition. In Jerry A. Fodor and Jerrold J. Katz, (editors), *The Structure of Language: Readings in the Philosophy of Language.* Englewood Cliffs, N. J.: Prentice-Hall, Inc.

Lenneberg, Eric H. (1967) *The Biological Foundations of Language.* New York: John Wiley & Sons.

Leopold, Werner F. (1949) *Speech Development of a Bilingual Child: A Linguist's Record,* Vols. 1, 2, 3, 4. Evanston, Ill.: Northwestern University Press.

Leopold, Werner F. (1954) A child's learning of two languages. *Georgetown University Round Table on Language and Linguistics,* 7:19-30.

Loftus, Elizabeth F. (1976) Language memories in the judicial system. Paper presented at the NWAVE Conference, Georgetown University.

Lukmani, Yasmeen. (1972) Motivation to learn and language proficiency. *Language Learning,* 22:261-274.

MacCorquodale, Kenneth. (1970) On Chomsky's review of Skinner's *Verbal Behavior. Journal of the Experimental Analysis of Behavior,* 13:83-99.

Maclay, Howard, and Osgood, Charles E. (1959) Hesitation phenomena in spontaneous English speech. *Word,* 15:19-44.

Macnamara, John. (1973) The cognitive strategies of language learning. In Oller and Richards.

Macnamara, John. (1975) Comparison between first and second language learning. *Working Papers on Bilingualism,* 7:71-94.

Malinowski, Bronislaw. (1923) The problem of meaning in primitive languages. In Charles K. Ogden and I. A. Richards (editors), *The Meaning of Meaning.* London: Kegan Paul.

Marckwardt, Albert D. (1972) Changing winds and shifting sands. *MST English Quarterly,* 21:3-11.

Maslow, Abraham H. (1970) *Motivation and Personality,* 2nd ed. New York: Harper & Row.

McNeill, David. (1966) Developmental psycholinguistics. In Frank Smith and George A. Miller (editors), *The Genesis of Language: A Psycholinguistic Approach.* Cambridge, Mass.: M.I.T. Press.

McNeill, David. (1968) On the theories of language acquisition. In T. R. Dixon and D. L. Horton (editors), *Verbal Behavior and General Behavior Theory.* Englewood Cliffs, N.J.: Prentice-Hall, Inc.

Menyuk, Paula. (1971) *The Acquisition and Development of Language.* Englewood Cliffs, N.J.: Prentice-Hall, Inc.

Milhollan, Frank and Forisha, B.E. (1972) *From Skinner to Rogers: Contrasting Approaches to Education.* Lincoln, Neb.: Professional Educators Publications, Inc.

Miller, George A. (1956) The magical number seven, plus or minus two: Some limits on our capacity for processing information. *Psychological Review* 63:81-97.

Miller, W. R. (1963) The acquisition of formal features of language. *American Journal of Orthopsychiatry*, 34:862-867.

Milon, J. (1974) The development of negation in English by a second language learner. *TESOL Quarterly*, 8:137-143.

Murdock, George Peter. (1961) The cross-cultural survey. In Frank W. Moore (editor), *Readings in Cross Cultures*. New Haven, Conn.: HRAF Press.

Naiman, Neil, Fröhlich, Maria, and Stern, H. H. (1975) *The Good Language Learner*. Toronto: Ontario Institute for Studies in Education.

Natalicio, D. S., and Natalicio, L. F. S. (1971) A comparative study of English pluralization by native and non-native English speakers. *Child Development*, 42:1302-1306.

Nelson, Robert, and Jakobovits, Leon A. (1970) Motivation in foreign language learning. In Joseph Tursi (editor), *Foreign Languages and the "New" Student, Reports of the Working Committees*. New York: Northeast Conference on the Teaching of Foreign Languages.

Nemser, W. (1971) Approximative systems of foreign language learners. *IRAL*, 9:115-123.

New Standard Encyclopedia. (1940) ed. Frank Vizetelly. New York: Funk & Wagnalls.

Nilsen, Don L. F. (1971) The use of case grammar in teaching English as a foreign language. *TESOL Quarterly*, 5:293-300.

Nostrand, Howard L. (1966) Describing and teaching the sociocultural context of a foreign language and literature. In Albert Valdman (editor), *Trends in Language Teaching*. New York: McGraw-Hill Book Co.

Oller, John W. (1976) A program for language testing research. *Language Learning*, Special Issue No. 4:141-165.

Oller, John W., Baca, Lori L., and Vigil, Alfredo. (1978) Attitudes and attained proficiency in ESL: A sociolinguistic study of Mexican-Americans in the Southwest. *TESOL Quarterly*, 11:173-183.

Oller, John W., Hudson A., and Liu, Phyllis F. (1977) Attitudes and attained proficiency in ESL: A sociolinguistic study of native speakers of Chinese in the United States. *Language Learning*, 27: 1-27.

Oller, John W., and Richards, Jack C. (editors). (1973) *Focus on the Learner: Pragmatic Perspectives for the Language Teacher*. Rowley, Mass.: Newbury House Publishers.

Oller, John W., and Ziahosseiny, Seid M. (1970) The contrastive analysis hypothesis and spelling errors. *Language Learning*, 20:183-189.

Osgood. Charles E. (1953) *Method and Theory in Experimental Psychology*. 'ork: Oxford University Press.

rles E. (1957) A behavioristic analysis of perception and language as cognitive phenomena. In *Contemporary Approaches to Cognition.* Cambridge, Mass.: Harvard University Press.

Pei, Mario. (1966) *Glossary of Linguistic Terminology.* New York: Anchor Books.

Pike, Kenneth. (1967) *Language in Relation to a Unified Theory of the Structure of Human Beahvior.* The Hague: Mouton Publishers.

Pimsleur, Paul. (1966) *Pimsleur Language Aptitude Battery.* New York: Harcourt, Brace & World.

Prator, Clifford. (1967) "Hierarchy of Difficulty." Unpublished classroom lecture, University of California at Los Angeles.

Prator, Clifford H. (1972) *Diagnostic Passage, Manual of American English Pronunciation.* New York: Holt, Rinehart & Winston.

Random House Dictionary of the English Language. (1966) New York: Random House.

Ravem, Roar. (1968) Language acquisition in a second language environment. *IRAL,* 6:175-185.

Richards, Jack C. (1971) A non-contrastive approach to error analysis. *English Language Teaching,* 25:204-219.

Richards, Jack C. (editor). (1974) *Error Analysis: Perspectives on Second Language Acquisition.* London: Longman Group Ltd.

Richards, Jack C. (1975) Simplification: A strategy in the adult acquisitiion of a foreign language: An example from Indonesian/Malay. *Language Learning,* 25:115-126.

Richards, Jack C. (1976) Second language learning. In Wardhaugh and Brown.

Rivers, Wilga M. (1964) *The Psychologist and the Foreign Language Teacher.* Chicago: University of Chicago Press.

Rogers, Carl. (1951) *Client Centered Therapy.* Boston: Houghton Mifflin Company.

Rosansky, Ellen J. (1975) The critical period for the acquisition of language: Some cognitive developmental considerations. *Working Papers on Bilingualism,* 6:92-102.

Rosansky, Ellen J. (1976) Methods and morphemes in second language acquisition research. *Language Learning,* 26:409-425.

Saussure, Ferdinand de. (1916) *Cours de linguistique générale. (Course in General Linguistics,* trans. Wade Baskin. New York: McGraw-Hill Book Co., 1959.)

Savignon, Sandra. (1972) *Communicative Competence: An Experiment in Foreign Language Teaching.* Philadelphia: The Center for Curriculum Development, Inc.

Saville-Troike, Muriel. (1976) *Foundations for Teaching English as a Second Language.* Englewood Cliffs, N.J.: Prentice-Hall, Inc.

Schachter, Jacqueline. (1974) An error in error analysis. *Language Learning,* 24:205-214.

Scherer, G. A. C., and Wertheimer, M. (1964) *A Psycholinguistic Experiment in Foreign Language Teaching.* New York: McGraw-Hill Book Co.

Schumann, John H. (1975) Affective factors and the problem of age in second language acquisition. *Language Learning,* 25:209-235.

Schumann, John H. (1976a) Second language acquisition: The pidginization hypothesis. *Language Learning,* 26:391-408.

Schumann, John H. (1976b) Second language acquisition research: Getting a more global look at the learner. *Language Learning,* Special Issue No. 4:15-28.

Schumann, John H. (1976c) Social distance as a factor in second language acquisition. *Language Learning,* 26:135-143.

Scovel, Thomas. (1969) Foreign accents, language acquisition, and cerebral dominance. *Language Learning,* 19:245-254.

Selinker, Larry. (1972) Interlanguage. *IRAL,* 10:201-231.

Skinner, B. F. (1938) *Behavior of Organisms: An Experimental Analysis.* New York: Appleton-Century-Crofts.

Skinner, B. F. (1953) *Science and Human Behavior.* New York: Macmillan Co.

Skinner, B. F. (1957) *Verbal Behavior.* New York: Appleton-Century-Crofts.

Skinner, B. F. (1968) *The Technology of Teaching.* New York: Appleton-Century-Crofts.

Slobin, Dan I. (1971) *Psycholinguistics.* Glenview, Ill.: Scott, Foresman & Co.

Smith, Frank. (1975) *Comprehension and Learning: A Conceptual Framework for Teachers.* New York: Holt, Rinehart & Winston.

Smith, Philip D. (1970) *A Comparison of the Cognitive and Audiolingual Approaches to Foreign Language Instruction.* Philadelphia: Center for Curriculum Development.

Sorenson, Arthur. (1967) Multilingualism in the Northwest Amazon. *American Anthropologist,* 69:670-684.

Spolsky, Bernard. (1969) Attitudinal aspects of second language learning. *Language Learning,* 19:271-283.

Spolsky, Bernard. (1970) Linguistics and language pedagogy—Applications or implications. *Monograph on Languages and Linguistics,* 22 (Report of the 20th Annual Round Table Meeting, Georgetown University).

Stauble, Ann-Marie E. (1978) The process of decreolization: A model for second language development. *Language Learning,* 28:29-54.

Stenson, Nancy. (1974) Induced errors. In John Schumann and Nancy Stenson (editors), *New Frontiers of Second Language Learning.* Rowley, Mass.: Newbury House Publishers.

Stern, H. H. (1970) *Perspectives on Second Language Teaching.* Toronto: Ontario Institute for Studies in Education.

Stevick, Earl. (1974) The meaning of drills and exercises. *Language Learning,* 24:1-22.

Stevick, Earl. (1976a) *Memory, Meaning and Method*. Rowley, Mass.: Newbury House Publishers.

Stevick, Earl. (1976b) English as an alien language. In John F. Fanselow and Ruth H. Crymes (editors), *On TESOL 76*. Washington, D. C.: TESOL.

Stockwell, Robert, Bowen, J. Donald, and Martin, John W. (1965) *The Grammatical Structures of English and Spanish*. Chicago: University of Chicago Press.

Strevens, Peter. (1977) Causes of failure and conditions for success in the learning and teaching of foreign languages. In H. Douglas Brown, Carlos Alfredo Yorio, and Ruth H. Crymes (editors), *On TESOL 77: Teaching and Learning English as a Second Language—Trends in Research and Practice*. Washingon, D. C.: TESOL.

Sullivan, Edmund V. (1967) *Piaget and the School Curriculum: A Critical Appraisal*. Toronto: Ontario Institute for Studies in Education.

Swain, Merrill. (1977) Future directions in second language research. In Henning.

Tarone, Elaine. (1979) Interlanguage as chamelon. *Language Learning*, 29:181-191.

Taylor, Barry P. (1974) Toward a theory of language acquisition. *Language Learning*, 24:23-35.

Taylor, Barry P. (1975) The use of overgeneralization and transfer learning strategies by elementary and intermediate students in ESL. *Language Learning*, 25:73-107.

Twaddell, Freeman. (1935) *On Defining the Phoneme*. Language Monograph Number 166.

Twain, Mark. (1880) *A Tramp Abroad*. Hartford, Conn.: American Publishing Co.

Twain, Mark. (1869) *The Innocents Abroad*, Vol. 1. New York: Harper & Brothers.

Uhlman, F. W., and Saltz, E. (1965) Retention of anxiety material as a function of cognitive differentiation. *Journal of Personal and Social Psychology*, 1:55-62.

Upshur, John A. (1976) Discussion of "A program for language testing research." *Language Learning*, Special Issue No. 4:167-174.

Vallette, Rebecca M. (1967) *Modern Language Testing: A Handbook*. New York: Harcourt, Brace & World.

Vigil, Neddy A., and Oller, John W. (1976) Rule fossilization: A tentative model. *Language Learning*, 26:281-295.

Wagner-Gough, Judy. (1975) Comparative studies in second language learning. *CAL-ERIC/CLL Series on Languages and Linguistics*, 26.

Wardhaugh, Ronald. (1970) The contrastive analysis hypothesis. *TESOL Quarterly*, 4:123-130.

Wardhaugh, Ronald. (1971) Theories of language acquisition in relation to beginning reading instruction. *Language Learning*, 21:1-26.

Wardhaugh, Ronald. (1972) *Introduction to Linguistics*. New York: McGraw-Hill Book Co.

Wardhaugh, Ronald. (1974) *Topics in Applied Linguistics.* Rowley, Mass.: Newbury House Publishers.

Wardhaugh, Ronald. (1976) *The Contexts of Language.* Rowley, Mass.: Newbury House Publishers.

Wardhaugh Ronald. (1977) *Introduction to Linguistics.* 2nd ed. Rowley, Mass.: Newbury House Publishers.

Wardhaugh, Ronald, and Brown, H. Douglas (editors). (1976) *A Survey of Applied Linguistics.* Ann Arbor: University of Michigan Press.

Watson, John B. (1913) Psychology as the behaviorist views it. *Psychological Review,* 20:158-177.

Webster's New International Dictionary of the English Language. (1934) ed. W. A. Neilson. Springfield, Mass.: G. and C. Merriam Co.

Webster's Third New International Dictionary of the English Language. (1961) G. and C. Merriam Co.

Weir, Ruth H. (1962) *Language in the Crib.* The Hague: Mouton Publishers.

Whitman, Randal. (1970) Contrastive analysis: Problems and procedures. *Language Learning,* 20:191-197

Whitman, Randal L., and Jackson, Kenneth L. (1972) The unpredictability of contrastive analysis. *Language Learning,* 22:29-41.

Whorf, Benjamin. (1956) Science and linguistics. In John B. Carroll (editor), *Language, Thought and Reality: Selected Writings of Benjamin Lee Whorf.* Cambridge, Mass.: M.I.T. Press.

Widdowson, Henry. (1978) Notional-functional syllabuses 1978: Part IV. In Blatchford and Schachter.

Witkin, Herman A., Oltman, Philip K., Raskin, Evelyn, and Karp, Stephen. (1971) *Embedded Figures Test Manual.* Palo Alto: Consulting Psychologists Press, Inc.

Yorio, Carlos. (1976) Discussion of "Explaining sequences and variation in second language acquisition." *Language Learning,* Special Issue No. 4:59-63.

Zangwill, Oliver. (1971) The neurology of language. In Noel Minnis (editor), *Linguistics at Large.* New York: The Viking Press.

Index

INDEX OF SUBJECTS